鼓 舞

gǔ wǔ

for secondary Mandarin Chinese

Kwun Shun Shih   Yan Wang

OXFORD
UNIVERSITY PRESS

OXFORD
UNIVERSITY PRESS

Great Clarendon Street, Oxford, OX2 6DP, United Kingdom

Oxford University Press is a department of the University of Oxford.
It furthers the University's objective of excellence in research, scholarship,
and education by publishing worldwide. Oxford is a registered trade mark of
Oxford University Press in the UK and in certain other countries

British Library Cataloguing in Publication Data
Data available

978 0 19 840832 1

1 3 5 7 9 10 8 6 4 2

Paper used in the production of this book is a natural, recyclable product
made from wood grown in sustainable forests. The manufacturing process
conforms to the environmental regulations of the country of origin.

Printed in Great Britain by Bell and Bain Ltd., Glasgow

Acknowledgements

The publishers would like to thank the following for permissions to use their
photographs:

Cover image: Tony Leung/Getty Images; p5: Hello Lovely/Corbis/Getty Images;
p6: Imaginechina/Rex Shutterstock; p8(L): Kae Ch/ Shutterstock; p8(CL):
PeopleImages/iStockphoto; p8(C): Preto Perola/ Shutterstock; p8(CR): Daniel
Heighton/Shutterstock; p8(R): Ljupco Smokovski/Shutterstock; p10(a): Tony
Campbell/Shutterstock; p10(b): Rita Kochmarjova/Shutterstock; p10(c):
Ladtanan Santanakanit/EyeEm/Getty Images; p10(d): Pavla/Shutterstock;
p10(e): Nikolai Tsvetkov; p10(f): Imagenavi; p10(g): Jagodka/Shutterstock;
p11: Blue Jean Images/Getty Images; p12(a): XiXinXing/Shutterstock; p12(b):
Alexander Lukatskiy/Shutterstock; p12(c): Wichansumalee/iStockphoto;
p12(d): Hangingpixels/Shutterstock; p12(e): Tinxi/Shutterstock; p12(f): Image
Source/Rex Shutterstock; p12(g): Kiselev Andrey Valerevich/Shutterstock;
p12(h): Paul Bradbury; p13(b): Yitewang/Shutterstock; p13(c): Yulia Lavrova/
Shutterstock; p13(e): Alla_s/Shutterstock; p14(a): Jacek Chabraszewski/
Shutterstock; p14(b): Nestor Rizhniak/Shutterstock; p14(c): Africa Studio/
Shutterstock; p14(d): Anton Gvozdikov/Shutterstock; p14(e): Pikul Noorod/
Shutterstock; p14(f): Imtmphoto/Shutterstock; p14(g): Jack.Q/Shutterstock;
p16(a): Vnlit/Shutterstock; p16(b): Snvv/Shutterstock; p16(c): Graphic
Compressor/Shutterstock; p16(d): Andy Dean Photography/Shutterstock;
p16(e): Photodisc; p16(f): Rogkov Oleg/Shutterstock; p16(g): Alexander Raths/
Shutterstock; p16(h): Lenkadan/Shutterstock; p17: Antonio Guillem/
Shutterstock; p19: Zkruger/Shutterstock; p20(3a): Cool Stuff/Shutterstock;
p20(3b): Irina Adamovich/Shutterstock; p20(3c): Browndogstudios/
Shutterstock; p20(3d): Ganibal/Shutterstock; p20(3e): Den2/Shutterstock;
p20(3f): Ganibal/Shutterstock; p20(4b): OUP; p20(4c): Valeriya_sh/
Shutterstock; p20(4e): 4zevar/Shutterstock; p22(TL): Billion Photos/
Shutterstock; p22(TR): India Picture/Shutterstock; p22(B): Susan Law Cain/
Shutterstock; p24(b): Maxx-Studio/Shutterstock; p26(a): Hxdbzxy/
Shutterstock; p26(b): Leungchopan/Shutterstock; p26(c): Vereshchagin
Dmitry/Shutterstock; p26(d): Christian Mueller/Shutterstock; p26(e):
Volodymyr Kyrylyuk/Shutterstock; p26(f): Urbancow/iStockphoto; p26(g):
Robert Nicholas/Getty Images; p26(h): Andrey_Kuzmin/Shutterstock; p29:
Leungchopan/Shutterstock; p34(a): Denis Rozhnovsky/Shutterstock; p34(b):
Urbanbuzz/Shutterstock; p34(c): Dima Moroz/Shutterstock; p34(d): Cobalt88/
Shutterstock; p34(e): Sergey Rusakov/Shutterstock; p34(f): KariDesign/
Shutterstock; p34(g): Ingram/Alamy; p34(h): Happyland/Shutterstock; p34(i):
Pbombaert/Shutterstock; p34(j): Radius Images; p36(a): OUP; p36(b): Nikshor;
p36(c): Mark Mason; p36(d): Spaxiax/Shutterstock; p36(e): Graja/Shutterstock;
p36(f): ArtWell/Shutterstock; p36(g): Soulart/Shutterstock; p36(h): Joy Tasa/
Shutterstock; p36(i): StockPhotosArt/Shutterstock; p36(j): Jose Ignacio Soto/
Shutterstock; p38(TL): Chris Dorney/Alamy Stock Photo; p38(TR): Monkey

Business Images/Shutterstock; p38(BL): NetPhotos/Alamy Stock Photo;
p38(BR): NetPhotos/Alamy Stock Photo; p39: Monkey Business Images/
Shutterstock; p40(d): Hxdbzxy/Shutterstock; p40(e): Ingram/Alamy; p40(f):
Siobj/Comstock/Getty Images; p40(g): Protasov AN/Shutterstock; p40(h):
Pbombaert/Shutterstock; p40(i): Nicholas Kamm/AFP/Getty Images; p40(j):
Chris Dorney/Alamy Stock Photo; p40(k): NetPhotos/Alamy Stock Photo;
p40(l): Maxx-Studio/Shutterstock; p41(a): David Pino Photography/
Shutterstock; p41(b): Science Photo Library; p41(c): Dr. Heinz Linke/Getty
Images; p41(d): Nikkytok/Shutterstock; p41(e): Resul Muslu/Shutterstock;
p41(f): Maremagnum/Photolibrary/Getty Images; p41(g): Chris King; p41(h):
Chris Hill/Shutterstock; p41(i): ChrisAt/iStockphoto; p42(a): OUP; p42(b):
Valentyn Volkov/Shutterstock; p42(c): Svariophoto/Shutterstock; p42(d):
Bildagentur Zoonar GmbH/Shutterstock; p42(e): Hannamariah/Shutterstock;
p42(f): Billion Photos/Shutterstock; p42(g): Mayneemore/Shutterstock; p42(h):
AntoinetteW/Shutterstock; p46(TL): Turtix/Shutterstock; p40(e): Bonchan/
Shutterstock; p46(BL): dennis Kitchen Studio, Inc; p46(BR): Photodisc; p47:
Silberkorn/Shutterstock; p49(a): CarmanPetite/Getty Images; p49(b):
Cbenjasuwan/Shutterstock; p49(c): Lewis Tse Pui Lung/Shutterstock; p49(d):
Billion Photos/Shutterstock; p49(e): Valentyn Volkov/Shutterstock; p49(f):
Bonchan/Shutterstock; p49(g): Billion Photos/Shutterstock; p49(h): MeBream/
Shutterstock; p49(i): Tatiana Belova/Shutterstock; p49(j): Milan Gonda/
Shutterstock; p49(k): CarmanPetite/Getty Images; p49(l): Ian Woolcock/
Shutterstock; p49(B): Lou-Foto/Alamy Stock Photo; p51: Samuel Borges
Photography/Shutterstock; p51: Samuel Borges Photography/Shutterstock;
p56(TL): Marlee/Shutterstock; p56(TC): Vereshchagin Dmitry/Shutterstock;
p56(TR): Dudarev Mikhail/Shutterstock; p56(BL): Alex Mares-Manton/Getty
Images; p56(BR): Jacf5244/Fotolia; p57: VCG/Getty Images; p58(TL): Zhu
Difeng/Shutterstock; p58(TC): Zhu Difeng/Shutterstock; p58(TR): Cozyta/
Fotolia; p58(BL): Andrey Popov/Shutterstock; p58(BR): Beijing Eastphoto
stockimages Co.Ltd/Alamy Stock Photo; p59: Bo1982/iStockphoto; p60(L):
Photopixel/Shutterstock; p60(CL): Baona/iStockphoto; p60(C): Izusek/
iStockphoto; p60(CR): Leungchopan/Shutterstock; p60(R): Stefano Cavoretto/
Shutterstock; p62(TL): Wong Yu Liang/Shutterstock; p62(TR): UpperCut;
p62(BL): Photobank gallery/Shutterstock; p62(BR): Wong Yu Liang/
Shutterstock; p63: Donnay Style/Shutterstock; p67: Lane Oatey/Blue Jean
Images/Getty Images; p68: Monkey Business Images/Shutterstock; p69: Peter
Titmuss/Alamy Stock Photo; p71: Jutta Klee/Getty Images; p72(a): Shariff
Che'Lah/Fotolia; p72(b): BeeBright/Shutterstock; p72(c): Steve Vidler/Alamy
Stock Photo; p72(d): John Henshall/Alamy Stock Photo; p72(f): Olga
Danylenko/Shutterstock; p72(f): Iryna Rasko/Shutterstock; p72(g): Jph9362/
iStockphoto; p72(h): Sean Pavone/Shutterstock; p72(B): Yitewang/
Shutterstock; p74(b): Tmicons/Shutterstock; p79: Richard Hutchings/Getty
Images; p82(a): Grigvovan/Shutterstock; p82(b): Juhku/Shutterstock; p82(c):
AsiaTravel/Shutterstock; p82(d): Chuyuss/Shutterstock; p82(e): Zhao Jian
Kang/Shutterstock; p84(a): Hxdyl/Shutterstock; p84(b): Xbrchx/Shutterstock;
p84(c): Swen Stroop/Shutterstock; p84(d): Catalin Lazar/Shutterstock; p84(e):
Sean Pavone/Shutterstock; p84(R): Bertl123/Shutterstock; p86(a): Stewart
Smith Photography/Shutterstock; p86(b): Stockphoto Mania/Shutterstock;
p86(c): Mexrix/Shutterstock; p86(d): Matthewshutter/Shutterstock; p86(e):
Wong Sze Fei/Fotolia; p88(T): Canghai76/Shutterstock; p88(B): Dailin/
Shutterstock; p89: Anton Gvozdikov/Shutterstock; p90(TL): Photodisc;
p90(TR): NorGal/Shutterstock; p90(BL): DWD-Media/Alamy Stock Photo;
p90(BR): Guo Zhong Hua/Shutterstock; p91: Kalapangha/Shutterstock; p93:
Pashamba/Shutterstock; p94: Testing/Shutterstock; p95: Paul Brown/Rex
Shutterstock; p96(a): Africa Studio/Shutterstock; p96(b): Testing/Shutterstock;
p96(c): Wavebreakmedia/Shutterstock; p96(d): Dailin/Shutterstock; p96(e):
Brian Kinney/Shutterstock; p96(f): Joinmepic/Shutterstock; p96(g): Testing/
Shutterstock; p96(h): Box of pic/Shutterstock; p97: Bertl123/Shutterstock;
p99: Monkey Business Images/Shutterstock; p100: Brian Kinney/Shutterstock;
p101: Jonathan Hordle/Rex Shutterstock; p102(a): Chokchai Poomichaiya/
Shutterstock; p102(b): Supertrooper/Shutterstock; p102(c): Doug Baines/
Shutterstock; p102(d): Sunny studio/Shutterstock; p102(e): TTphoto/
Shutterstock; p102(f): Alessia Giangrande/Shutterstock; p102(g): Joyce
Vincent/Shutterstock; p104(a): I'm Puripat/Shutterstock; p104(b): I'm Puripat/
Shutterstock; p105: Alberto Loyo/Shutterstock; p107: 24Novembers/
Shutterstock; p108(a): Karkas; p108(b): Evikka/Shutterstock; p108(c):
Gnilenkov Aleksey/Shutterstock; p108(d): Anton Burakov/Shutterstock;
p108(e): Nadia Cruzova/Shutterstock; p108(f): TValencia/Shutterstock;
p108(g): Adisa/Shutterstock; p108(h): Sagir/Shutterstock; p109: Iamtui7/
Shutterstock; p115: TTphoto/Shutterstock; p116(a): Frances A. Miller/
Shutterstock; p116(b): Xinhua News Agency/REX/Shutterstock; p116(c): Mary
Terriberry/Shutterstock; p116(d): Hung Chung Chih/Shutterstock; p116(e):
FloridaStock/Shutterstock; p121: Thomas Barrat/Shutterstock; p122(a): Lukasz
Stefanski/Shuttp123: Chantal de Bruijne/Shutterstock; p124: Ababsolutum/
Getty Images; p126(a): Graphi-Ogre; p126(b): Ocean; p126(c): Graphi-Ogre;

Continued on last page

CONTENTS

CONTENTS

ABOUT THIS BOOK

Gǔ Wǔ for Secondary Mandarin Chinese is a thematic course which will build students' confidence and ability in all of the key language skills – reading, writing, speaking, and listening. In-built support for grammar and vocabulary ensure that Mandarin acquisition is grounded in the fundamentals of the language, whilst relevant and contemporary themes engage students in their learning. Revision and assessment spreads in each unit allow progress to be tracked, for a confident transition to the next stage of education.

Written by an international team of expert teachers and examiners, the thematic and skills-based approach is suitable for a range of international curricula, including Cambridge IGCSE®, IB Ab Initio, and MYP Language Acquisition (Phases 1–3). Each of the content units (1-11) begins with a revision spread and ends with a progress check, testing the four key skills.

The Student Book is accompanied by a CD-ROM containing all listening activity recordings. A Teacher Pack is also available, containing answers, lesson ideas, worksheets, and syllabus and differentiation support.

Each double page spread has been designed to cover one 45-60 minute lesson.

Lesson objective

Objectives given in English to set the context for learning.

Essential vocabulary

Spotlight on terms from the vocabulary lists for Cambridge IGCSE® and IB Ab Initio.

Language skills

Icons denote coverage of the four key skills - reading, writing, speaking, and listening. Listening activities are supported by recordings on the CD-ROM.

Glossary

Extra vocabulary support to aid understanding and build confidence.

Cultural spotlight

Extend learning with stretching activities and features based on Chinese culture.

Grammar focus

Fundamentals of grammar are clearly highlighted in context, with additional support in a dedicated grammar unit.

Writing workshop

Step-by-step guidance for writing complex Chinese characters.

5.10 复习
PROGRESS CHECK

 1. 写以下词组的英文意思。

> a. 环境 b. 空气 c. 风景 d. 森林 e. 树林 f. 大河 g. 小湖 h. 海边 i. 山区

2. 和你的同学谈谈你们家乡的环境，轮流提出和回答下面的问题。

a. 你住在山区、郊区还是市区？　　b. 家乡有没有森林、大河或湖？

c. 你的家乡在不在海边？　　d. 你觉得家乡的风景怎么样？

e. 你觉得你的家乡的环境好不好？为什么？

3. 先读问题，再听录音，然后写下答案。

a. 米娜今天去了哪儿？　　b. 杰克的家乡最有名的是什么？

c. 小文在百货商场买了什么礼物？花了多少钱？

d. 日晴住的小区这个周末将组织什么活动？

e. 本杰明觉得他现在住的小镇怎么样？

4. 尼克和朋友在电话里谈谈住在上海的感觉。阅读他们的对话，然后选择唯一正确的答案来完成句子。

> 朋友：尼克，你喜欢上海吗？
> 尼克：喜欢，因为上海非常现代，有很多有意思的地方。我最爱去的地方就是新天地娱乐中心，常常去那里逛街，那里有很多有特色的餐馆、咖啡馆、时装店、商店和书店。
> 朋友：尼克。你现在住在哪里？
> 尼克：我现在住在上海中山路上的一个小区里。
> 朋友：小区的设施怎么样？
> 尼克：小区的设施很棒，游泳池，网球场都有。附近还有一条大河。我常常去河边跑步。
> 朋友：小区的人怎么样？
> 尼克：邻居们都很友好，看到我都会跟我招呼。
> 朋友：住在那里方便吗？
> 尼克：很方便，因为附近有超市和购物中心，而且交通也方便，附近就有地铁站。
> 朋友：那我下次去上海可以住在你家吗？
> 尼克：可以，没问题。欢迎来我家。

a. 尼克觉得上海很……。
　　i. 安静　　ii. 无聊　　iii. 现代

b. 尼克常常去新天地娱乐中心……。
　　i. 跑步　　ii. 逛街　　iii. 打保龄球

c. 尼克现在住的地方附近有……。
　　i. 一座小山　　ii. 一条大河　　iii. 一个公园

d. 尼克常常去小区附近的河边……。
　　i. 跑步　　ii. 打太极　　iii. 跳舞

e. 他觉得小区的人很……。
　　i. 友好　　ii. 吵闹　　iii. 不亲切

f. 那个小区的交通很方便，因为附近……。
　　i. 有火车站　　ii. 有地铁站　　iii. 可以坐船

5. 写一篇电邮给你在国外的朋友，介绍你的家乡。写60-80个字。其中应该包括：

a. 家乡的基本信息

b. 名胜古迹和其他好玩的地方

c. 家乡的一些好吃的餐馆

6. 你的朋友来到你住的城市，你带他/她参观你住的城市的旅游咨询中心。和你的同学角色扮演你们之间的对话，轮流提出和回答下面的问题。

a. 旅游咨询中心在哪儿？

b. 旅游咨询中心有什么设施和服务？

c. 旅游咨询中心里可不可以换钱？

d. 那儿有没有卖纪念品的商店？可以买到什么有特色的纪念品？

Tourist Information Centre

Each unit ends with a Progress Check to consolidate learning and test key skills.

A dedicated Grammar Focus unit expands all of the key grammar points from units 1–12, with additional examples and exercises to check understanding.

Complete these sentences by choosing the correct verbs and using them in the context of the above grammatical structure.

> 滑　去　看　收

a. 生日那天 / 他 / 很多礼物。

b. 他们 / 今年秋天 / 中国的北京。

c. 去年冬天 / 我和同学们 / 在日本 / 雪。

d. 上个周末 / 我和好朋友 / 一起 / 电影。

Grammar focus 1.6　p.13

2. 最: most
★ subject + 最 + stative verb
在他们班上他最聪明。
上海的冬天冷，北京的冬天更冷，哈尔冰的冬天最冷。
★ subject + 最 + verb + action
我最讨厌唱歌，因为我唱得很难听。
我喜欢跑步，更喜欢打羽毛球，最喜欢爬山。

Answer these questions following the grammatical structure above.

a. 周末你最喜欢做什么事情？

b. 你觉得哪一种运动最好玩？

c. 在你们家谁长得最高？

Grammar focus 1.6　p.13

3. 不: not (to express a negative action or statement)
★ subject + 不 + verb
我不打网球。
她不会说中文。
★ subject + 不 + stative verb
那个地方不远。
他不高。

Following the grammatical structure above, reorder the words to make proper sentences. Translate these sentences into English.

a. 不去 / 这个周末 / 爸爸 / 郊外 / 了 / 拍照 / 。

b. 有很多 / 所以 / 作业 / 他 / 不看电视 / 今天 / 了 / 。

c. 唱得不好听 / 因为 / 所以 / 她 / 不唱歌了 / 。

Grammar focus 1.7　p.14

完: to complete or finish
★ activity A + 完 (以后)，subject + activity B
骑完自行车以后，他们去了一家咖啡馆喝茶聊天。
吃完饭以后，他们就走路回家了。

Identify the grammatical error in each sentence, then write the sentence out correctly.

a. 她看了一会儿电视，做完作业以后。

b. 他想画完画以后去钓鱼河边。

c. 去音乐厅看了一场音乐会，米娜退完街以后。

Grammar focus 1.8　pp.16–17

1. 要: be going to; be planning to
★ subject + 要 + verb
这个周末我们要去森林公园骑自行车。
今年冬天心美要去日本滑雪。

Write out these sentences in Chinese following the grammatical structure above.

a. We are going to Hong Kong to visit my grandparents next summer.

b. She is going to watch a concert this weekend with her family.

Mandarin Chinese (中文 ^{zhōng wén}) is the standard form of Chinese which is used in Mainland China and other areas including Taiwan, Singapore, Malaysia, and Indonesia. It is also called 汉语 ^{hàn yǔ} (the language of Han people) and 普通话 ^{pǔ tōng huà} (common speech) in Mainland China, 国语 ^{guó yǔ} (national language) in Taiwan, and 华语 ^{huá yǔ} (Chinese language) in Singapore, Malaysia, Indonesia, and in other Southeast Asian countries.

Pinyin 拼音

Pinyin, literally meaning 'matched sounds', is the official romanisation system for Mandarin Chinese, and is often used when learning Standard Chinese.

Pinyin can be used to show the phonetic pronunciation of words, with or without the use of Chinese characters. The tables below give examples of initials and finals used in the pinyin system.

Initial	Similar to...	Initial	Similar to...
b	bike	q	cheese
p	play	x	shout
m	mum	zh	junk
f	feed	ch	church
d	day	sh	sure
t	take	r	garage
n	not	z	birds
l	like	c	cats
g	girl	s	sit
k	kill	w	water
h	horse	y	yes
j	Jay		

Final	Similar to...	Final	Similar to...
a	father	iao	yao
e	brother	ian	yan
i	bee	in	yin
o	look	iang	yang
u	woo	ing	ying

Final	Similar to...	Final	Similar to...
ü	über (German) or lune (French)	iong	yong
ai	eye	ou	low
an	ran	ong	Hong Kong
ang	angst	ua	wa
ao	ouch	uai	wai
ei	hey	uan	wan
en	token	uang	wang
eng	length	ui	wei
er	word	un	weren't
ia	ya	uo, o	wo
ie	ye	ue, üe	yue
iu	you	uan	yuan
		un	yun

Tones

The pinyin system contains 4 audible tones and 1 neutral tone. These are placed on the vowels of the pinyin.

- The 1st tone (**flat or high-level**) is marked by a macron (¯) on the vowel of the pinyin: ā, ō, ē, ī, ū, ǖ.

  Example: 妈 ^{mā}, meaning 'mum'

- The 2nd tone (**rising**) is denoted by an accent (´): á, ó, é, í, ú, ǘ.

  Example: 麻 ^{má}, meaning 'numb'

- The 3rd tone (**falling-rising**) is marked by an accent (ˇ): ǎ, ǒ, ě, ǐ, ǔ, ǚ.

  Example: 马 ^{mǎ}, meaning 'horse'

- The 4th tone (**falling**) is represented by an accent (`): à, ò, è, ì, ù, ǜ.

  Example: 骂 ^{mà}, meaning 'to scold (someone)'

- The 5th tone (**neutral**) is represented without accent: a, o, e, i, u, ü.

  Example: 吗 ^{ma}, which is the question particle added to the end of a sentence or a statement to form a yes/no question

Chinese characters 汉字

Pen strokes

Chinese characters have evolved from pictograms to the system we have today. This system is based on 8 basic pen strokes, all of which can be found in the character 永 (yǒng) (forever).

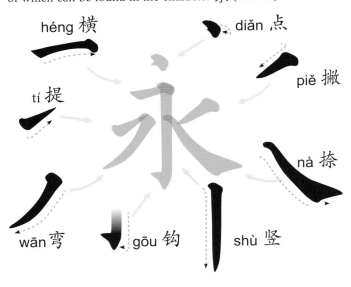

héng 横
diǎn 点
tí 提
piě 撇
nà 捺
wān 弯
gōu 钩
shù 竖

The pen-stroke order for writing this character is described below.

1. 点 (diǎn) (dot), written from the top to the bottom.
2. 横 (héng) (horizontal line), written from left to right.
3. 竖 (shù) (vertical line), starting from the top and falling downwards.
4. 钩 (gōu) (hook), either a sharp change of direction down after a 'héng' or left after a 'shù'.
5. 提 (tí) (flick), an upward stroke to the right.
6. 弯 (wān) (curve), follows a concave path to the left or the right.
7. 撇 (piě), a downward, diagonal stroke to the left, with a slight curve.
8. 捺 (nà), a downward, diagonal stroke to the right.

Radicals

Radicals (部首) (bù shǒu) are parts of Chinese characters that often signify the meaning of the characters themselves. Radicals can be used to organise characters into groups in dictionaries. Identifying radicals in different words will allow these words to be located easily in a dictionary.

Some common radicals which you will meet in this course are listed below.

Radical	Related to...	Examples used within this book
讠	speech 言	说, 话, 讲, 谈, 词, 语, 计, 识
亻	person 人	你, 他, 作, 做, 化, 休, 伤, 住
又	also 又	对, 欢, 难, 友, 双, 圣, 发, 戏
匕	spoon 匕	北, 此, 比, 能, 些
力	strength 力	动, 努, 力, 历, 男, 加, 助, 功
厂	cliff/shelter 厂	历, 厅, 厉, 厌, 厕, 厨, 压
二	two 二	云, 些, 元
十	ten 十	博, 古, 考, 毕, 卖, 南, 真, 华
勹	to wrap 包	句, 包, 够
彳	to move slowly 双	行, 往, 律, 很, 徒, 得, 德
囗	enclosure 方框	国, 四, 因, 园, 圆, 回, 图
艹	grass 草	药, 菜, 蓝, 草, 花, 茶, 艺
纟	silk 丝	红, 级, 纸, 经, 给, 绿, 系
扌	hand 提手	打, 扔, 找, 护, 把, 报, 拍
辶	to go 走	还, 这, 过, 远, 运, 遛, 进
宀	roof 宝盖	家, 安, 字, 完, 宫, 客, 室
氵	water 三点水	汉, 污, 河, 湖, 汤, 洗, 流
忄	heart 竖心	快, 忙, 性, 懒, 慢, 惯, 恼
饣	to eat 食	饮, 饼, 饿, 饭, 饺, 馆, 饱
犭	dog 犬	猫, 狗, 猴, 狼
女	women 女	如, 妻, 婚, 她, 好, 姐, 妈

Radical	Related to...	Examples used within this book
土	earth 土	在，坏，地，寺，城，坐，境
门	gate 门	问，间，闹，阅，闲
灬	heat (four dots) 四点	热，煎，煮，点，然，熊
月	flesh 月	朋，脑，胖，胃
礻	spirit 示	祝，礼，视
攵	tap 反	故，教，收，放，数，散
木	wood 木	来，林，机，极，村，架
心	heart 心	感，意，思，想，忘，总
火	fire 火	灰，烟，炒，烤，灯，炎
方	square 方	旁，放，旅
贝	treasure 贝	贵，赚
日	Day or sun 日	星，早，易，春，时，明，昨
钅	metal 金	钓，银，镇，钱，铁
疒	illness 病	病，瘦，痛，疼
衤	clothing 衣	衬
田	field 田	界，男，累
竹／⺮	bamboo 竹	筷，简，笑，篮，第，筑，算
雨	rain 雨	雨，雪，雾，需

General rules for writing Chinese characters

1. Left to right, top to bottom
   As a general rule, pen strokes are written from left to right, top to bottom.

   Examples: 你，三

2. Horizontal before vertical
   When horizontal and vertical strokes cross, horizontal strokes are usually written before vertical strokes.

   Example: 十

3. Character-spanning strokes last
   Horizontal and vertical strokes that pass through many other strokes are written after the strokes through which they pass.

   Examples: 母 (horizontal), 事 (vertical)

4. Right-to-left diagonals before left-to-right diagonals
   Right-to-left diagonals (丿) are written before left-to-right diagonals (乀).

   Examples: 文，交

5. Central strokes before the sides
   In vertically symmetrical characters, central strokes are written before strokes on the left or the right. Strokes on the left are written before strokes on the right.

   Example: 永，水

6. Outside before inside
   Enclosing strokes on the outside are written before the inside strokes, with the left-vertical stroke written first. The bottom enclosing stroke is written at the end, if present.

   Examples: 日，国，月

7. Bottom strokes last
   Where the character is not enclosed by a box, bottom strokes are still written last.

   Example: 边

   The exception is when characters are finished with a dot.

   Examples: 我，龙

UNIT OBJECTIVES

- Share information about yourself and your family for a range of purposes.
- Discuss why people keep pets.
- Share your views on a range of hobbies and interests.
- Discuss what you do in your leisure time.
- Discuss how people celebrate special occasions.

1. 看看下面的国旗，把它们和正确的国家名称搭配起来。

Look at the flags below. Match them with the correct country names.

i. 中国　**ii.** 印度　**iii.** 澳大利亚　**iv.** 法国　**v.** 美国　**vi.** 英国

zhōng guó
中国 China

yìn dù
印度 India

ào dà lì yà
澳大利亚 Australia

fǎ guó
法国 France

měi guó
美国 United States of America

yīng guó
英国 United Kingdom

Grammar focus p.258

正在: used before verbs to express that an action is *ongoing* or *in progress*.

★ subject + 正在 + action

最近爸爸正在写一本新书。

2. 小华正在谈论自己的家人。先读问题，再听录音，然后写下答案。

Xiaohua is talking about his family. Read the questions before you listen to the recording, then write your answers.

a. 小华家有几口人？

b. 他的哥哥多大了？

c. 他的妈妈个子高吗？

jiā
家 family

gē ge
哥哥 older brother

mā ma
妈妈 mother

gāo
高 tall

bà ba
爸爸 father

suì
岁 years old

mǐ
米 metre (in height)

3. 阅读下面的短文，然后选择跟小明相关的三幅图片。

Read the paragraph below. Then, look at the pictures and choose three that match the description of Xiaoming.

> 这是我的好朋友。他叫小明。他是中国人。今年他上十年级。小明他人很好，所以大家都喜欢他。小明喜欢玩电子游戏。他也很喜欢动物，但是他家里没有宠物。

| péng you 朋友 friend |
| xǐ huān 喜欢 to like |
| wán 玩 to play |
| chǒng wù 宠物 pet |

a.

b.

c.

d.

e.

f.

4. 练习描述自己。

Practise describing yourself.

a. 完成以下句子，并用中文写下来。

Complete the following sentences, then write them out in Chinese.

> Hello. I am called . . . . I am . . . .
>
> There are . . . people in my family.
>
> We have . . . pets.

b. 现在把以上句子用中文读出来。

Now read out the sentences you have written in Chinese to a partner.

1.2 我自己
ABOUT MYSELF

LESSON OBJECTIVE
- Describe a person's appearance and personality.

1. 看看下面的词语，把它们和正确的图片搭配起来。
   Look at the expressions below. Match them to the correct picture.

a.

b.

i. 漂亮
ii. 帅气
iii. 黑黑的长头发
iv. 金色的短发
v. 棕色的大眼睛
vi. 蓝色的眼睛
vii. 小小的鼻子
viii. 高高的鼻子
ix. 洁白的牙齿
x. 长得高高大大

---

piào liàng
漂亮 pretty

shuài qì
帅(气) handsome

hēi jīn zōng lán
黑 / 金 / 棕 / 蓝 black / blond(e)
(golden) / brown / blue

cháng duǎn
长 / 短 long / short (describing length)

tóu fà
头发 hair

yǎn jīng
眼睛 eye

bí zi
鼻子 nose

jié bái de yá chǐ
洁白的牙齿 white teeth

---

2. 志军正在向他的同学们做自我介绍。先读问题，再听录音，然后写下答案。

Zhijun is introducing himself to his classmates. Read the questions before you listen to the recording, then write your answers.

a. 志军今年多大？　　b. 他来自哪个国家？

c. 他为什么会搬来英国？　　d. 他的性格怎么样？

---

huì
会 will

xìng gé
性格 personality

---

3. 形容自己的性格。

Practise describing your personality.

a. 写下你在下面找到的形容词。

Find and write all the words describing people's personalities in this word search.
(Hint: Use the Essential Vocabulary feature on the side to help you.)

懒	害	认	友	善	活	帅	羞	真	内
向	泼	漂	开	朗	有	聪	努	聪	明
助	热	礼	力	马	马	虎	虎	情	貌

---

rè qíng
热情 friendly; enthusiastic

nèi xiàng
内向 introverted

yǒu lǐ mào
有礼貌 polite; to have good manners

cōng míng
聪明 clever

rèn zhēn
认真 serious

b. 现在运用相关形容词写下一句话形容你自己的性格。写10–20个字。

Now choose a word that describes your personality and make a sentence with it. Write 10–20 words.

4. 阅读段落一和段落二，然后回答问题。

Read passages 1 and 2 below, and answer the questions.

（一）我的好朋友来自法国，他有一张小小的但是十分帅气的脸，大大的蓝色眼睛，短短的头发。他经常笑，笑的时候露出洁白的牙齿，很好看。他身高有一米八。他除了人长得帅以外，还很有礼貌。

a. 我的好朋友有……。
   i. 一张大大的脸
   ii. 一张帅气的脸

b. 他是一个……。
   i. 有礼貌的人
   ii. 没有礼貌的人

（二）我的好朋友叫玛莉，她现在住在英国。她有黑黑的短发，绿绿的眼睛，长得比较矮。玛莉是一个热情的人，对家人朋友都很好。

c. 玛莉的眼睛是什么颜色？
   i. 绿色
   ii. 棕色

d. 玛莉是不是一个热情的人？
   i. 是
   ii. 不是

jīng cháng
经常 often

xiàn zài
现在 present; now

lǜ
绿 green

ǎi
矮 short (when describing height)

Grammar focus p.258

除了……以外，还: apart from ... also; in addition; as well as

★ subject + 除了 + A + 以外，还 + B
他除了人长得特别帅以外，还特别有礼貌。
我除了学汉语以外，还学西班牙语。

5. 和你的同学轮流提出和回答下面的问题。

With a partner, take turns to ask and answer the following questions.

a. 你有很多朋友吗？

b. 你最好的朋友是谁？

c. 他/她多大了？

d. 他/她长什么样？

e. 他/她的性格是什么样的？

LESSON OBJECTIVE

● Give personal information for a range of purposes.

1. 海伦正在自我介绍。先读问题，再听录音，然后写下答案。

   Helen is introducing herself. Look at the questions before you listen to the recording, then write your answers.

   a. 海伦几岁了？

   b. 她在哪儿出生？

   c. 她和家人搬到了哪个城市居住？

   d. 他们是什么时候搬家的？

   e. 她家里有哪些人？

> chéng shì
> 城市 town; city

> jū zhù
> 居住 to live in
>
> bān jiā
> 搬家 to move house

2. 阅读短文，然后复制及填写下面的表格。

   Read the passage, then copy and fill in the table below.

> 林书豪，身高1.91米，1988年8月23日生于美国加州。因为父亲喜欢篮球，所以林书豪小时候就特别爱打篮球，在读高中的时候就是学校篮球队的队长。大学以后他成为了一名美国职业篮球联赛（NBA）球员。

> guó jí
> 国籍 nationality
>
> chū shēng rì qī
> 出生日期 date of birth
>
> chū shēng dì
> 出生地 place of birth
>
> tè bié
> 特别 particularly; especially
>
> lán qiú
> 篮球 basketball
>
> dú
> 读 to read; study
>
> míng
> 名 measure word (for a person)
>
> zhí yè
> 职业 professional

> jiā zhōu
> 加州 California
>
> qiú yuán
> 球员 basketball player

姓名	
国籍	
出生日期	
出生地	
身高	

3. 练习写汉字。
Practise writing Chinese.

a. 按照笔画顺序写下面的字。
Write the characters by following the stroke order.

guó
国 | 国 | 玉 | 玉 | 三 | 干 | 玉 | 玉 | 玉
1 | 2 | 3 | 4 | 5 | 6 | 7 | 8

jí
籍 | 籍 | 籍 | 籍 | 籍 | 籍 | 籍 | 籍 | 籍 | 籍 | 籍 | 籍 | 籍 | 籍 | 籍 | 籍 | 籍
1 | 2 | 3 | 4 | 5 | 6 | 7 | 8 | 9 | 10 | 11 | 12 | 13 | 14 | 15 | 16 | 17

籍 | 籍 | 籍
18 | 19 | 20

b. 写部首，数笔画。
Write the radical and count the number of strokes for each character.

4. 阅读简历，然后回答问题。
Read the CV below, then answer the questions.

姓名	李日晴
性别	女
年龄	十八岁
身高	一米八十
国籍	中国
出生地	中国广州市
住址	上海市大学路560号
电子邮件	liriqing@example.com
电话	00-86-555555
爱好	唱歌，跳舞
特长	说唱R&B

a. 日晴长得高不高?

b. 日晴是在哪儿出生的?

c. 她的爱好有哪些?

nián líng
年龄 age

zhù zhǐ
住址 address

diàn zǐ yóu jiàn
电子邮件(电邮) email

ài hào
爱好 hobby

chàng gē
唱歌 to sing

tiào wǔ
跳舞 to dance

Grammar focus p.258

是……的: is (used to emphasise a detail from an event)

★ subject + 是 + description + 的
陈丽是在巴西出生的。

5. 和你的同学轮流提出和回答下面的问题，然后写出自己的简历。写100–120个字。

With a partner, take turns to ask and answer the following questions. Then write your own CV answering these questions. Write 100–120 characters.

a. 你的生日是什么时候?

b. 你是在哪里出生的?

c. 你以前在哪里居住过?

d. 现在住在哪儿?

e. 你有什么爱好?

LESSON OBJECTIVE
● Identify, recall, and share information about your family members.

1. 复制下面的图，然后用下列词组填空。

Make a copy of the family tree. Complete it by filling in the missing words.

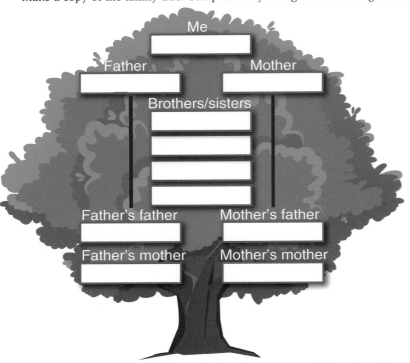

Me

Father   Mother

Brothers/sisters

Father's father   Mother's father

Father's mother   Mother's mother

爷爷，奶奶，外公，外婆，爸爸，妈妈，哥哥，姐姐，弟弟，妹妹，我

2. 安娜正在介绍她的家人。先看看下面的图片，再听录音，然后把家庭成员和正确的图片搭配起来。

Anna is introducing the members of her family. Look at the pictures before you listen to the recording, then match each one with the correct family member.

ān jìng
安静 quiet

a. 安娜 **b.** 爸爸 **c.** 妈妈 **d.** 爷爷 **e.** 哥哥

| i | ii | iii | iv | v |

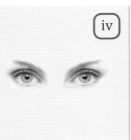

3. 练习写汉字。

Practise writing Chinese.

a. 按照笔画顺序写下面的字。

Write the characters by following the stroke order.

máng

忙 忙 忙 忙 忙 忙 忙
　　1　2　3　4　5　6

jīng

经 经 经 经 经 经 经 经
　　1　2　3　4　5　6　7　8

cháng

常 常 常 常 常 常 常 常 常 常 常
　　1　2　3　4　5　6　7　8　9　10　11

jué de
觉得 to feel
kuài lè
快乐 happy
bù cuò
不错 not bad; pretty good
máng
忙 busy
chéng jì
成绩 exam result; grade

yán lì

严厉 strict

b. 用 "忙" 和 "经常" 造句。用 10–20 个字。

Now make two sentences using these characters. Write in 10–20 characters.

4. 阅读下面这篇关于玛莉家庭的短文。

Read the passage below about Mary's family.

> 我的家里有三个人，爸爸、妈妈和我。我的爸爸爱说笑话，有他在，你会觉得快乐。我的妈妈工作很努力，而且还很会做饭，大家都说她做的饭菜很好吃。但是我觉得妈妈有时候对我太严厉。还有我的爷爷，虽然他不和我们住在一起，但是住得很近。有时候爷爷会来我家给我们做晚饭。我在学校里学习不错，还会唱歌跳舞，每天都很快乐。这就是我的家。我们是快乐的一家人。

从下面的叙述中选择四个正确的。

Choose four statements that are true about the paragraph.

i. 玛莉和她的父母一起住。

ii. 玛莉和她的爸爸、妈妈和爷爷一起住。

iii. 玛莉妈妈会做美味可口的饭菜。

iv. 玛莉妈妈不会做饭。

v. 玛莉的爷爷有时候会去她家给她们做晚饭。

vi. 玛莉爷爷工作很忙。

vii. 玛莉的学习成绩不太好。

viii. 玛莉会跳舞。

5. 和你的同学轮流提出和回答下面的问题。

With a partner, take turns to ask and answer the following questions.

gèng

更 more

a. 你的家里有几个人？

b. 你觉得他们的性格怎么样？

c. 你觉得爸爸妈妈谁更严厉？

d. 你们跟你的爷爷和奶奶一起住吗？

1.5 我家的宠物
PETS IN MY FAMILY

LESSON OBJECTIVES
- Describe a variety of common animals people keep as pets.
- Discuss why some people like to keep pets.

1. 看看下面的图片。
   Look at the pictures below.

   a. 把它们和正确的宠物名称搭配起来。
   Match them with the correct names of pets.

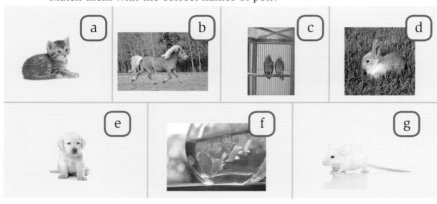

   i. 一只狗 ii. 一只猫 iii. 一只小兔子 iv. 一只小老鼠
   v. 一匹马 vi. 两只鸟 vii. 两条金鱼

   b. 回答下面的问题。
   Now answer these questions.

   i. 哪一种宠物被称为人类的好朋友？
   ii. 哪一种宠物喜欢抓老鼠？
   iii. 哪一种宠物又小又毛茸茸的？
   iv. 哪一种宠物又高大又跑得快？
   v. 哪一种宠物的叫声很好听，有时候像唱歌一样？
   vi. 哪一种宠物喜欢生活在水里，看上去非常漂亮？

2. 五个人正在谈论家里的宠物。先读问题，再听录音，然后写下答案。

   Five people are talking about their pets. Read the questions before you listen to the recording, then write your answers.

   a. 小明为什么没有养宠物？   **b.** 丽青的爷爷养了什么样的鸟？
   c. 约翰住在什么样的地方？ 他养了什么动物？
   d. 海伦家里有什么宠物？
   e. 阿里以前养的猫怎么了？ 他想以后养什么宠物？

---

gǒu
狗 dog

māo
猫 cat

tù zi
兔子 rabbit

lǎo shǔ
老鼠 mouse

mǎ
马 horse

niǎo
鸟 bird

jīn yú
金鱼 goldfish

chēng
称 to be called

zhuā
抓 to catch

máo róng róng
毛茸茸 fluffy

Grammar focus p.258

1. 量词: Measure words
   ★ number + measure word + noun
   一只: 狗、猫、兔、
         小老鼠
   一条: 鱼、蛇、龙
   一匹: 马

2. 看上去 : looks as if
   ★ subject + 看上去 + stative verb
   这只兔子看上去十分可爱。

yǎng
养 to keep or raise

dì fang
地方 place

3. 日晴和姐姐讨论送爷爷什么生日礼物。阅读她们的对话，然后回答问题。

Riqing and her sister are discussing choosing a birthday present for their grandfather. Read their conversation, then answer the questions.

姐姐：爷爷的生日快到了。我们送他什么礼物好呢？

日晴：我觉得我们可以给爷爷买一部新的智能手机，可以上网的。

姐姐：我觉得爷爷不会喜欢的。你还记得上个月家庭聚餐时，大家都在玩手机，爷爷非常生气的事情吗？

日晴：哦，对哦。还是不要送手机。那送什么好呢？

姐姐：我想到一个好主意。我们给爷爷买一对鹦鹉吧，会学说话的那种鸟，特别好玩。我想爷爷肯定会喜欢的。

日晴：这真是一个好主意。每天早上爷爷可以提着鸟笼子去公园玩儿，既锻炼了身体，还会觉得心情好。

a. 一开始日晴想给爷爷什么礼物？

b. 在上个月的家庭聚餐上爷爷为什么生气？

c. 为什么日晴和她的姐姐都认为送鸟给爷爷是一个好主意？你们都同意吗？

4. 和你的同学聊宠物，轮流提出和回答下面的问题。

With a partner, have a conversation about pets. Take turns to ask and answer the following questions.

a. 你和家人住在什么样的地方？

b. 你觉得为什么会有那么多人喜欢养狗或养猫？

c. 如果是你，你会养宠物吗？会养什么宠物？为什么？

Grammar focus   p.258

给 : for

★ subject + 给 + recipient + verb + object

妈妈给我买了一双运动鞋。

---

kuài dào le
快到了 will arrive soon; almost here

lǐ wù
礼物 gift

shǒu jī
手机 mobile phone

shàng wǎng
上网 to surf the internet

shàng gè
上个 last; previous

shēng qì
生气 angry

shì qíng
事情 thing; matter

zǎo shang
早上 morning

gōng yuán
公园 park

kāi shǐ
开始 to begin

tóng yì
同意 to agree

---

zhì néng
智能 smart (technology)

hǎo zhǔ yi
好主意 good idea

yīng wǔ
鹦鹉 parrot

kěn dìng
肯定 surely

tí zhe
提着 to carry

lóng zi
笼子 bird cage

我的兴趣和爱好
MY INTERESTS AND HOBBIES

LESSON OBJECTIVES
- Identify a variety of common hobbies and interests.
- Share your views on different hobbies and interests.

1. 看看下面的图片，把它们和正确的词语搭配起来。

   Look at the pictures below. Match them with the correct expressions.

i. 跳舞   ii. 运动   iii. 摄影/拍照   iv. 听音乐   v. 看书
vi. 画画   vii. 唱歌   viii. 看电视

_{yùn dòng}
运动 to exercise

_{shè yǐng pāi zhào}
摄影/拍照 to take photographs

_{tīng yīn yuè}
听音乐 to listen to music

_{kàn shū}
看书 to read

_{huà huà}
画画 to draw

_{kàn diàn shì}
看电视 to watch TV

2. 组词成句，然后把句子读出来。

   Re-arrange the words below to make proper sentences. Then read them out loud to your partner.

   a. 的 / 爱好 / 他 / 看 / 是 / 电视 / 。

   b. 很多 / 她 / 兴趣 / 有 / 。

   c. 除了 / 我 / 喜欢 / 写作 / 还 / 喜欢 / 摄影 / 。

_{xìng qù}
兴趣 interest

_{xiě zuò}
写作 to write (a book)

3. 阅读下面这篇关于小寒兴趣爱好的短文，然后回答问题。

   Read the following passage about Xiaohan's interests and hobbies, then answer the questions.

_{lǚ yóu}
旅游 to travel

_{huá xuě}
滑雪 to ski

_{nán}
难 difficult

_{kù}
酷 cool; trendy

我叫黄小寒，今年上中学九年级。我有很多兴趣爱好，现在我最喜欢旅游和滑雪。小学的时候，因为看到姐姐学跳舞，所以我也学，但是后来觉得太难了，慢慢地就没有兴趣了。中学一年级的时候因为看了《中国好声音》，我喜欢上了唱歌，希望以后成为一名歌手，但是有同学说我唱得不好听，我就很少唱歌了。去年冬天，我们一家人去了日本旅游，在那里我学会了滑雪，我觉得滑雪好玩极了，而且很酷。

a. 小学的时候小寒跟着姐姐一起学了什么？

b. 小寒什么时候开始喜欢上了唱歌？

c. 后来为什么不唱歌了？

d. 去年冬天她学会了什么？

 4. 写出你的五个兴趣爱好。

Make a list of five hobbies and interests you have.

5. 丽青正在谈论家人的兴趣。先看图，再听录音，然后把图和正确的人物搭配起来。

Liqing is talking about her family and their interests. Look at the pictures before you listen to the recording, then match each picture with the right person.

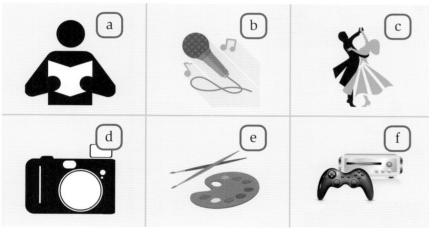

i. 丽青　　**ii.** 爷爷　　**iii.** 奶奶　　**iv.** 爸爸
v. 妈妈　　**vi.** 弟弟

zhōng guó hǎo shēng yīn
中国好声音 *Voice of China*, a singing talent TV show popular across all Chinese-speaking regions in Asia

yóu xì jī
游戏机 game console

měi lì de
美丽的 beautiful

Grammar focus p.258-9

1. 了: indicates an action is completed, or has already happened
   ★ subject + verb + 了 + action
   （郊游那天）小文拍了很多照片。

2. 最: most
   ★ subject + 最喜欢 + verb + action
   我最喜欢游泳。
   ★ subject + 最 + stative verb
   我最有礼貌。

3. 不: not
   ★ subject + 不 + verb
   他们不来。
   我不喜欢唱歌。

Cultural spotlight

zhōng guó rén de xìng shì
中国人的姓氏 Chinese family names

　　跟西方人的姓名不同的是中国人的姓是用在名字前面的，而且用全名称呼中国人很常见。中华姓氏有成千上万个，但是最常见的只有大约一百个，而且大部分是以一个汉字作为姓的单姓，包括 王、李、张、刘、陈、林、杨、何、赵、吴、周等。在一百个常见的姓氏中也包括一些以两个汉字作为姓氏的复姓，最常见的就是司马、诸葛和欧阳。

a. 你知道你自己的姓氏是从哪里来的吗？

b. 在你居住的地方，哪些姓氏最常见？

LESSON OBJECTIVE

● Discuss past and future leisure activities.

1. 看看下面的词语，把它们和正确的图片搭配起来。

   Look at the words below. Match them with the correct pictures.

   a. 钓鱼　**b.** 看电影　**c.** 看戏剧　**d.** 玩电脑游戏
   e. 逛街　**f.** 骑自行车　**g.** 爬山

i ii iii

iv v

vi vii

diào yú
钓鱼 to go fishing

kàn diàn yǐng
看电影 to watch a film

kàn xì jù
看戏剧 to watch a play

wán diàn nǎo yóu xì
玩电脑游戏 to play computer games

guàng jiē
逛街 to do (window) shopping; to take a
stroll down the high street

qí zì xíng chē
骑自行车 to ride a bicycle

pá shān
爬(山) to hike or climb (up a hill or
mountain)

Grammar focus　p.259

完: to complete, finish

★ activity A + 完 (之后),
subject + activity B

看完电影(之后)，我们
去了河边散步。
吃完饭，我们去打保龄
球吧！

2. 五个人正在谈他们的周末计划，先看下面的时间图表，再
听录音，然后写下计划的时间与活动。

   Five people are talking about their weekend plans. Study the table below
   before you listen to the recording, then write down the time and activity each
   person has planned.

人物	时间	活动
1		
2		

zhè gè zhōu mò
这个周末 this weekend

yī qǐ
一起 together

dǎ suàn
打算 to plan

chǎng
场 measure word (for a film or a play)

jiāo yóu
郊游 to go to the countryside

3. 练习写汉字。

Practise writing Chinese.

a. 按照笔画顺序写下面的字。

Write the characters by following the stroke order.

dǎ
打 打 打 打 打 打
1 2 3 4 5

suàn
算 算 算 算 算 算 算 算 算 算 算 算 算 算 算
1 2 3 4 5 6 7 8 9 10 11 12 13 14

b. 写三件你打算这个周末做的事情。

Make a list of three things you plan to do this weekend.

4. 阅读短文，然后回答问题。

Read the passage, then answer the questions.

心美的周末

我喜欢周末，因为周末我不用上学，所以不用早起，可以多睡一会儿。周末我可以做自己喜欢做的事情。我最近在学跳舞，因为我觉得会跳舞的男孩儿又帅又酷，会跳舞的女孩子很漂亮。周末吃完早饭以后，我会在房间里先跟着音乐练一会儿舞，然后出去玩。如果周末天气好，我会约朋友一起去郊游，我们有时候去爬山，有时候去划船；但是如果是雨天，我会和朋友一起去城里的图书馆看书和上网或去朋友家里打游戏机。你周末的时候一般做什么？

a. 心美为什么那么喜欢周末？

b. 最近心美在学什么？

c. 如果周末的时候天气好，心美通常会做什么？

d. 如果下雨，心美会去什么地方？做什么？

5. 和你的同学角色扮演两个朋友在网上聊周末的活动，轮流提出和回答下面的问题。

With a partner, role-play a conversation between two friends chatting about their weekend activities. Take turns to ask and answer the following questions.

a. 周末你常常做什么？   **b.** 上个周末你做了什么？

c. 你是和谁一起做的？   **d.** 下个周末你打算做什么？

LESSON OBJECTIVES
- Identify verbs that are used to form activity words.
- Describe your plans for the weekend.

1. 看看A组的动词，把它们和B组适当的名词搭配起来，组成词语。

   Look at the verbs in group A. Match each one with the appropriate noun in group B to form verb–noun compounds.

   Group A: 听　看　写　玩　唱　跳　画　骑　爬
   Group B: 作　歌　画　山　书　马　音乐　游戏　舞

2. 练习造句。

   Practise making sentences.

   a. 用每一个组好的词语造句，并写下来。

      Write a sentence using each of the word pairs from Activity 1.

   b. 给五个A组的动词搭上新的名词，然后组成新词语。

      Make five more verb–noun compounds by combining verbs in group A with some nouns of your own.

3. 先看图片，然后和你的同学轮流提出和回答表内的问题。

   Look at the pictures. With a partner, take turns to ask and answer the questions in the table.

名字	上个周末他/她做了什么？	这个周末他/她要做什么？
马克		
小文		
日晴		
阿里		

chàng
唱 to sing

xiě
写 to write

tiào
跳 to jump

qí
骑 to ride

pá
爬 to climb

tīng
听 to listen

kàn
看 to see; watch

huà
画 to draw; paint

wán
玩 to play

Grammar focus p.259-260

1. 要: be going to; be planning to
   ★ subject + 要 + verb
   （这个周末）妹妹要去朋友家玩。

2. verb–noun compounds
   ★ verb + noun
   爬 (to climb) + 山 (mountain)
   滑 (to slide, to skid) + 雪 (snow)

4. 玛莉正在谈她的周末计划。先读问题，再听录音。

Mary is talking about her weekend plans. Read the tasks before you listen to the conversation.

a. 写下所有玛莉提到的活动。

Make a list of all of the activities Mary mentions.

b. 回答以下问题。

Answer the following questions.

i. 玛莉通常周末都会做什么？

ii. 上个周末玛莉做了什么？

iii. 这个周末玛莉要做什么？

yǒu kòng 有空 free	
jié hūn 结婚 to marry	
cān jiā 参加 to take part in	
hūn lǐ 婚礼 wedding	

5. 马克跟小文在打电话。阅读他们的对话，然后回答问题。

Mark and Xiaowen are talking on the phone. Read their conversation, then answer the questions.

> 马克： 小文，是我，马克。我想问你这个周末你有什么打算？
>
> 小文： 没什么好的计划。你想做什么？
>
> 马克： 我上网看了看，星期六天气不错，要不要和我的哥哥一起开车去山里玩儿？
>
> 小文： 好啊。我喜欢爬山。我们去爬哪座山？
>
> 马克： 大青山吧，因为去那儿方便。
>
> 小文： 好的。我们几点去？
>
> 马克： 八点半吧，早一点路上车少，可以快点到。
>
> 小文： 那好，我八点先到你家，然后一起出发，可以吗？
>
> 马克： 可以。我们要不要带吃的东西？
>
> 小文： 带上吧，我们可以带水果，三明治和水。
>
> 马克： 好主意。那好，我们星期六早上见！
>
> 小文： 星期六见！

a. 马克和小文周末要做什么？

b. 他们想去哪儿？怎么去？

c. 他们几点出发？为什么要那个时候出发？

d. 他们需要带什么食物？

xiǎng 想 want to; to think	
jì huà 计划 plan	
kāi chē 开车 to drive	
zuò 座 measure word (for a large and heavy object, like a building or a mountain)	
fāng biàn 方便 convenient	
chū fā 出发 to set off	
dài 带 to bring; carry; wear	
xū yào 需要 to need to	

Grammar focus p.260

吧 (ba): used at the end of a sentence to make a suggestion; it is used in a similar context as 'Let's…'

★ command + 吧

我们去参观城市广场吧！

LESSON OBJECTIVES

● Describe and discuss a variety of special occasions.　● Write and respond to invitations.

1. 小文在谈自己的生日。先读问题，再听录音，然后选择唯一正确的答案。

Xiaowen is talking about his birthday. Read the questions before you listen to the recording, then choose the correct answer for each question.

a. 小文的生日是什么时候?
　i. 上个星期五
　ii. 上个月的十五号
　iii. 这个月的五号

b. 他邀请了几个同学去他的生日会?
　i. 三个
　ii. 四个
　iii. 六个

c. 吃完了生日蛋糕，他们去了哪儿吃饭?
　i. 中餐馆
　ii. 西班牙餐馆
　iii. 法国餐馆

d. 吃完了饭，他们还做了什么?
　i. 散步
　ii. 唱歌
　iii. 玩游戏机

e. 什么让小文最高兴?
　i. 因为生日蛋糕很好吃。
　ii. 因为收到了很多生日礼物。
　iii. 因为爸爸妈妈给了他很多钱。

---

qìng zhù
庆祝 to celebrate

yāo qǐng
邀请 to invite

gāo xìng
高兴 happy

shōu dào
收到 (to have) received

---

kǎ lā　 tīng
卡拉OK厅 karaoke bar

---

2. 阅读丽青给海伦的信，然后回答问题。

Read Liqing's letter to Helen, then answer the questions.

海伦:

　你好!

　　中秋节快到了。通常我们家在中秋节这一天都会有家庭聚会，有好多好吃的菜。今年的中秋节是九月二十二日。我想请你来我的家里过中秋节。希望那一天天气好，我们就可以在花园里一边赏月、聊天，一边吃月饼和烤肉。还有我有一个要去英国读大学的表姐也会来我家，她特别希望能见到你，问你一些关于英国的事情。希望你能来。

丽青
九月十五日

---

zhōng qiū jié
中秋节 Mid-Autumn Festival

jù huì
聚会 gathering

jiàn dào
见到 to meet

guān yú
关于 about

---

shǎng yuè
赏月 moon gazing

---

a. 今年的中秋节是什么时候?

b. 中秋节那天丽青家里通常会做什么?

c. 如果天气好的话，丽青和海伦会在花园里做什么?

d. 丽青的哪一个亲戚特别想认识海伦? 为什么?

3. 你去了朋友家里过中秋节，写一封简短的邮件感谢她/他。写80-100个字。其中应该包括：

You have just celebrated Mid-Autumn Festival at a friend's home. Write a thank-you email to them. Write 80–100 characters. Include the following:

a. 对你的朋友和她/他的家人表示感谢；

b. 你喜欢哪些活动/食物？为什么？

c. 下个周末自己有什么计划？会不会请朋友一起？

4. 你有两张音乐节门票，你请朋友在你生日那天和你一起去。和你的同学角色扮演朋友之间的对话，轮流提出和回答下面的问题。

With a partner, role-play a conversation between two friends, in which one person is inviting the other to a music festival on their birthday. Take turns to ask and answer the following questions.

a. 你有没有兴趣跟我去音乐节？

b. 星期六早上几点出发？

c. 音乐节在哪里？要怎么去？

d. 谁会在音乐节上表演？

biǎo shì
表示 to represent

Grammar focus p.260

了: indicates something is about to happen

★ 快/快要/要 + action / description + 了
快到了 be here soon
快要做完了 will be finished soon
要下雨了 will rain soon

biǎo yǎn
表演 to perform

Cultural spotlight

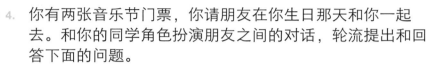

shēng rì chī hóng dàn
生日吃红蛋 A red egg for your birthday

　　生日，就是出生的日子。对一些人来说，这是人生中最最重要的有纪念意义的日子，是个特别的日子，所以一般过生日的人都会受到朋友和家人的特别待遇。在中国南方，小朋友过生日，父母多数会煮一只染成红色的鸡蛋，并给小孩红包。给红色的东西那是因为红色是中国的幸运色。过生日吃红蛋有一种说法，是剥蛋壳代表我们剥开过去，意味新的开始。中国人在生日那天还会吃面条，因为长长的面线有希望长寿的意思。

a. 你通常是怎样庆祝生日的？

b. 按照文化习俗，你们生日的时候需要吃什么特别的食物？为什么？

1. 写下五个宠物的名称。

2. 和你的同学角色扮演两个网友的对话，轮流提出和回答下面的问题。

a. 你叫什么？　　b. 你今年多大了？　　c. 你来自哪个国家？

d. 你现在住在哪里？　　e. 你和谁一起住？

3. 先看下面的图片，再读问题，然后选择唯一正确的图片。

i. 这个周末我打算和朋友一起去看电影。我和朋友打算做什么？

ii. 看完电影以后，我们还要去冬季运动中心溜冰。看完电影以后，我们还要做什么？

iii. 以前周末我经常呆在家里玩电脑游戏，觉得那样很不好。以前周末我经常做什么？

iv. 现在周末我经常做一些户外活动或运动，比如爬山。现在周末我会做什么？

4. 听录音，把图片和正确的人搭配起来，并写下他们是哪一天做这些活动的。

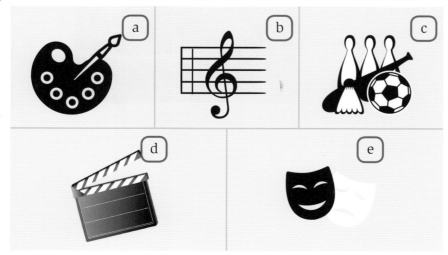

i. 小文　ii. 马克　iii. 米娜
iv. 丽青　v. 海伦

5. 阿里正在谈他的周末生活。阅读短文，然后判断下面哪四个句子是对的。

> 星期六不用上学，所以我常常睡到上午十一点。然后早饭午饭一起吃，吃完饭以后我常常去好朋友杰克家里。我的朋友杰克是一个音乐迷，有时候如果外面天气不好我们会在他的房间里听一个下午的音乐，因为都会吉他，有时候也会一起练一练弹吉他。但是如果天气好，我们通常都会到公园活动。
>
> 放假的时候我和杰克约好一起去风景美丽的地方露营，有时候去山上，有时候去海边。以后如果有机会我想和好朋友一起去中国旅游。

a. 阿里星期六上午常常睡懒觉。

b. 他星期天在家里上汉语课。

c. 阿里的朋友杰克特别爱音乐。

d. 杰克会吉他，但是阿里不会。

e. 天气好的时候他们常常在杰克家的花园里玩。

f. 放假的时候他们去美丽的地方露营。

g. 阿里希望以后去中国旅游。

h. 阿里想一个人去中国看一看。

6. 和你的同学角色扮演两个朋友的电话对话，请对方参加生日聚会，轮流提出和回答下面的问题。

a. 是谁的生日；

b. 在哪一天举行；

c. 在哪儿举行；

d. 什么时候开始；

e. 到时会有什么活动。

7. 写一封信给你的兄弟或姐妹，介绍你的好朋友。写40–50个字。其中应该包括:

a. 你朋友的名字；

b. 你朋友的样子；

c. 你朋友的性格；

d. 你最喜欢他/她什么。

UNIT OBJECTIVES
● Describe and discuss different aspects of your school life.
● Share information about your home.
● Discuss the role digital technology plays in your daily life.

1. 看看下面的图片，把它们和正确的中文词语搭配起来。
Look at the pictures. Match them with the correct vocabulary.

i. 学生   **ii.** 学校   **iii.** 老师

xué shēng
学生 student

xué xiào
学校 school

lǎo shī
老师 teacher

2. 小明将会向他的同学介绍自己，仔细听并选择唯一正确的答案。

Xiaoming is introducing himself to his new classmates. Read the questions before you listen to the recording, then choose the correct answer for each question.

a. 小明读哪一个年级？
   i. 八年级
   ii. 九年级
   iii. 十年级

b. 小明读哪一班？
   i. A班
   ii. B班
   iii. C班

c. 谁是小明的班主任？
   i. 李老师
   ii. 陈老师
   iii. 王老师

d. 小明家有几口人？
   i. 三口人
   ii. 四口人
   iii. 五口人

nián jí
年级 year; grade

bān
班 class

bān zhǔ rèn
班主任 form tutor

shàng kè
上课 attending class; to start a class

3. 阅读志军发给心美的短信，然后回答问题。
Read the text message from Zhijun to Sammy, then answer the questions.

_{jiā jù}
家具 furniture

> 心美，今天我去了小明家。他家的房间真多，一共有五个，每个房间里都有不同的家具。我家的房间没那么多，只有三个，也没有那么多家具。我要睡了，明天再给你发短信！

a. 小明家有多少个房间？

b. 小明家每个房间有什么？

c. 志军什么时候再发短信给心美？

4. 和你的同学轮流练习介绍自己。
With a partner, practise saying the following:

> 亲爱的 …… 老师、同学们，大家好！
> 我叫 …。
> 我很高兴来到 …… 年级 …… 班和大家一起上课。
> 我的爱好是……。
> 我家有 …… 口人。有 ……、……、…… 和我。
> 我住在 ……，我家有 …… 个房间。

5. 练习写汉字。
Practise writing Chinese.

a. 按照笔画顺序写下面的字。
Write the characters by following the stroke order.

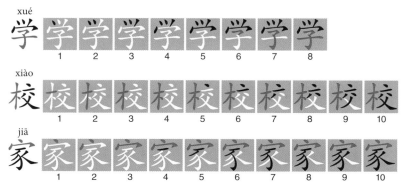

b. 写出十个跟学校和家庭有关的词语。
Make a list of 10 words related to your school and your home.

LESSON OBJECTIVE

● Share your views on the subjects you study at school.

1. 看看下面的图标。

Look at the icons below.

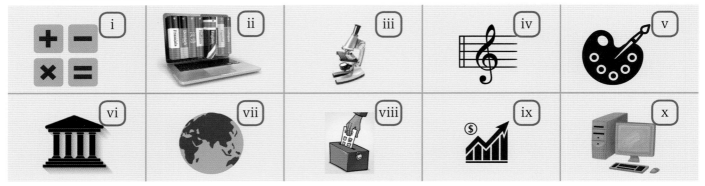

i	ii	iii	iv	v
vi	vii	viii	ix	x

a. 用中文写出这些图标代表的学科。

In Chinese, write out the subject names represented by the icons.

b. 回答下面的问题。

Answer these questions.
(Hint: Use the Essential Vocabulary box on the next page to help you find the words)

i. 你的学校有哪些学科？　　**ii.** 你现在读哪些学科？

2. 阅读下面的对话，然后回答问题。

Xiaoming and Sammy are having a conversation about their school subjects. Read it, then answer the questions.

心美：小明，你今年学哪些学科？

小明：我今年学习中文、德语、数学、生物、化学、物理、音乐和经济。你呢？

心美：我今年读英语、数学、中文、历史、化学、体育、美术、信息技术、经济和政治。小明，你最喜欢哪些学科？

小明：我最喜欢中文和音乐。你呢？

心美：我也喜欢中文。我觉得中文作业很容易。我不喜欢化学，作业太多了。你呢？

小明：我觉得化学还可以。我不喜欢地理，作业很难。

---

xué kē 学科	subject
shù xué 数学	maths
wài yǔ 外语	foreign language
kē xué 科学	science
yīn yuè 音乐	music
měi shù 美术	art
lì shǐ 历史	history
dì lǐ 地理	geography
zhèng zhì 政治	politics
jīng jì 经济	economics
xìn xī jì shù 信息技术	information technology

zhōng wén 中文	Chinese
dé yǔ 德语	German
shēng wù 生物	biology
huà xué 化学	chemistry

a. 小明喜欢中文吗？

    i. 喜欢   **ii.** 不喜欢

b. 心美喜欢哪一门学科？

    i. 中文   **ii.** 科学   **iii.** 美术

c. 为什么心美不喜欢学化学？

    i. 作业太多   **ii.** 作业太难

d. 为什么小明不喜欢学地理？

    i. 作业太多   **ii.** 作业太难

3. 你将听到几个中文句子。先读下面的短文，再听录音，然后选择唯一正确的答案。

Three people are talking about their exams. Read the text before you listen to the recording, then choose the correct answers for each person.

a. 苏菲昨天考了 **(i)** 中文 **(ii)** 地理 **(iii)** 德语，她说考得 **(iv)** 还可以 **(v)** 不好 **(vi)** 很好。她喜欢中文，也喜欢 **(vii)** 英语 **(viii)** 地理 **(ix)** 德语。她觉得中文作业很 **(x)** 难 **(xi)** 容易。

b. 莉莉昨天考了 **(i)** 化学 **(ii)** 英语 **(iii)** 美术。她说考得 **(iv)** 还可以 **(v)** 不好 **(vi)** 很好。她不喜欢中文，也不喜欢 **(vii)** 化学 **(viii)** 英语 **(ix)** 美术。她觉得 **(x)** 化学 **(xi)** 英语 **(xii)** 美术作业很 **(xiii)** 难 **(xiv)** 容易。

c. 志军昨天考了 **(i)** 政治 **(ii)** 历史 **(iii)** 科学，他说考得 **(iv)** 还可以 **(v)** 不好 **(vi)** 很好。他喜欢中文，也喜欢 **(vii)** 政治 **(viii)** 历史 **(ix)** 科学。他觉得 **(x)** 政治 **(xi)** 历史 **(xii)** 科学作业很 **(xiii)** 难 **(xiv)** 容易。

4. 和你的同学轮流提出和回答下面的问题，并用中文写下来。

With a partner, take turns to ask and answer these questions. Then write out your answers in Chinese.

a. 你喜欢读哪些学科？

b. 你觉得中文作业怎么样？

物理 wù lǐ physics

英语 yīng yǔ English

体育 tǐ yù PE

作业 zuò yè homework

容易 róng yì easy

(困)难 kùn nán difficult

一门 yī mén measure word for subjects

法语 fǎ yǔ French

日语 rì yǔ Japanese

考 kǎo to take an exam

还可以 hái kě yǐ acceptable

Grammar focus p.260-1

1. 也: also

★ subject A + verb, subject B + 也 + verb

心美去游泳，小明也去。

2. 很: very

★ subject + 很 + stative verb

作业很容易。

LESSON OBJECTIVES

● Describe your school environment and facilities.
● Share your views on your school facilities and the activities you can do there.

1. 看下面的图片，把它们和正确的名称搭配起来。
   Look at the pictures. Match them with the correct names.

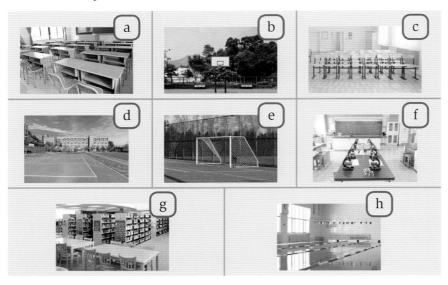

i. 实验室　　ii. 游泳池　　iii. 篮球场　　iv. 图书馆　　v. 操场
vi. 礼堂　　vii. 教室　　viii. 足球场

2. 王老师在介绍学校的设施。阅读下面的这段文字，然后指出这些设施的位置。
   Miss Wang is introducing the facilities in your school. Read her speech below, then copy and complete the table by filling in the missing content.

同学们，早上好！

　　我是你们的班主任王老师。现在让我来介绍我们学校的教学楼。

　　我们的教学楼有五层高。一楼是礼堂。礼堂的右边是食堂，同学们可以在这儿吃午餐。二楼除了教室外，还有一个实验室，让大家上课时做有趣的实验。三楼是学校办公室，你们可以在那儿找校长和老师。喜欢看书的同学可以去四楼的图书馆。你们对中文书感兴趣吗？那儿有很多中文书，是提高中文水平的好

huán jìng
环境 environment

shí yàn shì
实验室 laboratory

yóu yǒng chí
游泳池 swimming pool

lán qiú chǎng
篮球场 basketball court

tú shū guǎn
图书馆 library

cāo chǎng
操场 sports ground

lǐ táng
礼堂 (assembly) hall

jiào shì
教室 classroom

zú qiú chǎng
足球场 football (soccer) pitch

jiào xué lóu
教学楼 teaching building

shí táng
食堂 canteen

yǒu qù
有趣 interesting

bàn gōng shì
办公室 office

tí gāo
提高 to improve or raise

shuǐ píng
水平 level

yǒu yì si
有意思 interesting

xià tiān
夏天 summer

shè shī
设施 facility

jiè shào
介绍 to introduce

céng lóu
层/楼 floor

yī lóu
一楼 ground floor

地方。五楼是体育馆。里面有游泳池和篮球场。到了夏天，同学们可以来这儿游泳。

听完老师的介绍，同学们喜欢我们的教学楼吗？

我们还有一个足球场，在操场旁边。喜欢踢足球的同学一定觉得很有意思。

楼层	教学楼设施
五楼	体育馆：游泳池，**(a)**
四楼	**(b)**
三楼	**(c)**
二楼	实验室，**(d)**
一楼	礼堂，**(e)**

3. 小明和心美正在谈话。先读问题，再听录音，然后回答问题。

Xiaoming and Sammy are talking about their school. Read the questions before you listen to the recording, then answer them.

a. 小明喜欢看书吗？
   i. 喜欢   **ii.** 不喜欢

b. 心美喜欢什么运动？
   i. 游泳和踢足球   **ii.** 游泳和打篮球

c. 为什么小明不去体育馆？

4. 和你的同学轮流提出和回答下面的问题，并用中文写下来。

With a partner, take turns to ask and answer these questions. Then write out your answers in Chinese.

a. 你喜欢学校的哪些设施？

b. 你喜欢学校的哪些活动？

c. 你不喜欢学校的哪些活动？

Grammar focus　**p.261**

1. ……先……，然后……：
… first, then …
★ subject + 先 + verb
+ noun，然后 + verb
+ noun

我们先去图书馆，然后去体育馆。

2. 因为: because
★ situation B, + 因为
+ situation A

我不喜欢游泳，因为游泳很难。

LESSON OBJECTIVE

● Share your views on your school subjects and exams.

1. 先读下面的短文,再听录音,然后用下列词组填空。

   Read the text below before you listen to the recording, then fill in the blanks using the words in the box below.

中文	法语	练习	复习	成绩	考试

   米娜今年要读八个学科,包括 **(a)**、英文、**(b)**、经济、物理、音乐、美术和信息技术。

   米娜最喜欢学 **(c)**。她在考试一星期前开始 **(d)**。

   这次 **(e)** 她取得了好成绩,她觉得很高兴。

   因为她常常 **(f)** 写汉字,所以她的中文考试成绩比上次更好。

2. 以下是米娜的日记。阅读后判断下面的句子对或错。

   Below is Mina's diary entry. Read it and decide if the statements are true or false.

十月五日	星期三	天气:晴

   今天我很高兴!因为在这次中文考试中,我得了九十分,成绩比上次好。老师也说我有进步。

   我的同学有的考得好,有的考得不好。汤姆在考试一个星期前开始复习,所以他的成绩也不错,得了八十分。苏菲很有语言天分,而且她喜欢学习中文词语,她考得最好,得了九十八分。本杰明学习不用功。他不练习写汉字,因为他觉得笔画和笔顺很难。这次考试他成绩最差,不及格,只有三十分。本杰明最不喜欢中文考试,他觉得压力太大。

   a. 本杰明最不喜欢中文考试。

   b. 米娜的成绩比苏菲更好。

   c. 汤姆的成绩比米娜差。

   d. 苏菲的成绩最好。

   e. 本杰明比汤姆学习更用功。

lián xí
练习 (to) exercise

fù xí
复习 to revise

kǎo shì
考试 exam

bāo kuò
包括 to include

qǔ dé le
(取)得(了) to obtain

gèng
更 even (for comparing things)

zhè cì
这次 this time

xiě hàn zì
写汉字 to write Chinese characters

shàng cì
上次 last time

jìn bù
进步 improved

yǔ yán
语言 language

bǐ huà
笔画 number of strokes (in Chinese characters)

bǐ shùn
笔顺 order of strokes (in Chinese characters)

chà
差 bad

jí gé
及格 pass

yā lì
压力 pressure

yòng gōng
用功 hardworking

Grammar focus p.261

1. 比 …… 更: even ... than
- ★ noun A + 比 + noun B + (更) + stative verb

  (心美这次的考试分数很高)，日晴的
  分数比心美的分数(更)高。

2. 最: the most
- ★ subject + particle + object + 最 + stative verb

  日晴的成绩最好。

3. 做一个课堂调查。问以下问题:

Carry out a class survey by asking the following questions:

a. 这次的......考试难不难?

b. 这次考试你得了多少分?

c. 你觉得自己的成绩好不好?

d. 你觉得考试压力大不大?

e. 你觉得这次考试比上次难吗?

f. 你觉得哪位同学读书最用功?

4. 用上面的答案写一份报告。

Now use the answers you have prepared in Activity 3 to write a report.

5. 练习写汉字。

Practise writing Chinese.

a. 按照笔画顺序写下面的字。

Write the characters by following the stroke order.

bǐ
笔 笔 笔 笔 笔 笔 笔 笔 笔 笔 笔
  1 2 3 4 5 6 7 8 9 10

huà
画 画 画 画 画 画 画 画 画
  1 2 3 4 5 6 7 8

b. 用以上的词语造句。写10-20个字。

Write a sentence of your own using the above vocabulary. Write 10–20 characters.

我的一天
MY DAY AT SCHOOL

LESSON OBJECTIVE
- Describe what goes on during a typical school day.

1. 先看课程表，再听录音，然后用下面的词语填空。

   Look at this timetable before you listen to the recording, then fill in the missing information using the words provided.

玛莉的课程表

星期一	节	课程
8:20–8:40	(a)	
8:40–9:30	第一节	英文
9:30–10:20	第二节	(b)
10:20–10:30	休息	
10:30–11:20	第三节	数学
11:20–12:10	第四节	历史
12:10–12:50	午休	
12:50–13:40	第五节	(c)
13:40–14:30	第六节	美术
14:30–15:20	第七节	美术
15:20	(d)	

经济　　放学　　中文　　点名

2. 先读问题，再听录音，然后写下答案。

   Read the questions before you listen to the recording again. Then write the answers.

   a. 九月一号是什么日子？

   b. 什么时候放暑假？

   c. 下午几点放学？

---

xué qī
学期 school term; semester

kè chéng biǎo
课程表 timetable

jié
节 period

kè chéng
课程 course

xiū xi
休息 rest; break

wǔ xiū
午休 lunch break

fàng xué
放学 to finish school

diǎn míng
点名 to take the register

shí / diǎn
时 / 点 hour

fēn
分 minute

xià kè
下课 to finish a class

shǔ jià
暑假 summer holiday

---

kāi xué
开学 start of term

qī mò
期末 end of term

Grammar focus　p.261

1. 之前: before
   - ★ time + 之前 + action
     十年之前我去了中国。

2. 之后: after
   - ★ time + 之后 + action
     午休之后我要上数学课。

---

xià wǔ
下午 afternoon

3. 先阅读玛莉写的电邮，然后回答问题。

Read the email by Mary, then answer the questions.

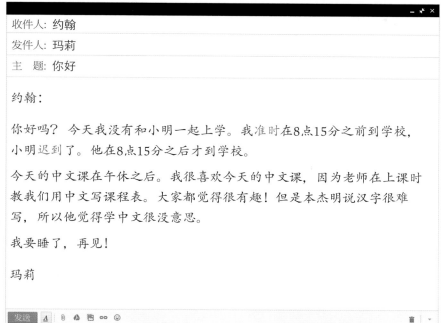

收件人: 约翰
发件人: 玛莉
主　题: 你好

约翰：

你好吗？ 今天我没有和小明一起上学。我准时在8点15分之前到学校，小明迟到了。他在8点15分之后才到学校。

今天的中文课在午休之后。我很喜欢今天的中文课，因为老师在上课时教我们用中文写课程表。大家都觉得很有趣！但是本杰明说汉字很难写，所以他觉得学中文很没意思。

我要睡了，再见！

玛莉

a. 今天谁迟到了？

b. 午休之后，玛莉上了什么课？

c. 为什么本杰明觉得中文课很没意思？

4. 和你的同学谈谈你们的课程表，轮流提出和回答下面的问题。

With a partner, talk about your timetables. Take turns to ask and answer the following questions.

a. 早上点名之后上什么课？　　**b.** 放学之前上什么课？

 5. 练习写汉字。

Practise writing Chinese.

a. 按照笔画顺序写下面的字。

Write the characters by following the stroke order.

kè
课 课 课 课 课 课 课 课 课 课 课
1　2　3　4　5　6　7　8　9　10

chéng
程 程 程 程 程 程 程 程 程 程 程 程
1　2　3　4　5　6　7　8　9　10　11　12

biǎo
表 表 表 表 表 表 表 表 表
1　2　3　4　5　6　7　8

b. 用中文写出你自己的课程表。

Write out your own timetable in Chinese.

2.6 我的家
MY HOME

LESSON OBJECTIVE

● Describe your home in detail, including what it looks like and what furniture you have in it.

1. 看看下面的图。用中文写出以下地方的名称。

Look at the plan of this house. Write out the names of the areas (labelled a to j) in Chinese.

wò shì 卧室 bedroom	yáng tái 阳台 balcony
cè suǒ 厕所 toilet (WC)	huā yuán 花园 garden
shū fáng 书房 study	fàn tīng 饭厅 dining room
kè tīng 客厅 living room	yù shì 浴室 bathroom
chú fáng 厨房 kitchen	chē kù 车库 garage

2. 小明正在介绍自己的家。先读问题，再听录音，然后回答问题。

Xiaoming is introducing his home. Look at the questions before you listen to the recording, then answer the questions.

a. 小明的家有三个……。

　　i. 客厅　　　**ii.** 房间　　　**iii.** 厨房

b. 小明的家有……。

　　i. 三房两厅　　**ii.** 两房三厅　　**iii.** 三房一厅

c. 小明的爸爸在……。

　　i. 厨房里边煮饭　　　**ii.** 书房里边看书　　　**iii.** 客厅里边看电视

sān fáng liǎng tīng
三房两厅 expression to describe a standard-sized home, literally meaning 'three bedrooms, two living rooms'

fáng zi
房子 house

zhù zài
住在 to live in / at

shā fā
沙发 sofa

wèi (xīng diàn) shì
卫(星电)视 satellite (cable) TV

Grammar focus p.262

1. ……在哪儿？ : Where is...?
★ place + 在哪儿?
书房在哪儿？

2. ……在…… : ... is located at ...
★ place + 在 + adverb
书房在（洗手间）
左边。

3. 用 40–50个字写一篇短文来介绍你的家，然后读给你的同学听。

Write a paragraph of 40–50 characters about your home, then read it out loud to your partner.

a. 你的家在哪儿？

b. 你的家有几个房间？

c. 你的家有什么家具？

4. 练习写汉字。

Practise writing Chinese.

a. 按照笔画顺序写下面的字。

Write the characters by following the stroke order.

shuì
睡 | 睡 | 睡 | 睡 | 睡 | 睡 | 睡 | 手 | 手 | 手 | 垂 | 垂 | 睡
1 | 2 | 3 | 4 | 5 | 6 | 7 | 8 | 9 | 10 | 11 | 12 | 13

jiào
觉 | 觉 | 觉 | 觉 | 觉 | 觉 | 觉 | 觉 | 觉 | 觉
1 | 2 | 3 | 4 | 5 | 6 | 7 | 8 | 9

b. 用10–20字写一个句子，说说你什么时候睡觉。

Using 10–20 characters, write a sentence to say what time you normally go to bed.

LESSON OBJECTIVE

● Describe the objects in your room, as well as what you like about your room.

1. 看下面的图片，把它们和正确的中文名称搭配起来。
Look at the photos below. Match them with the correct names.

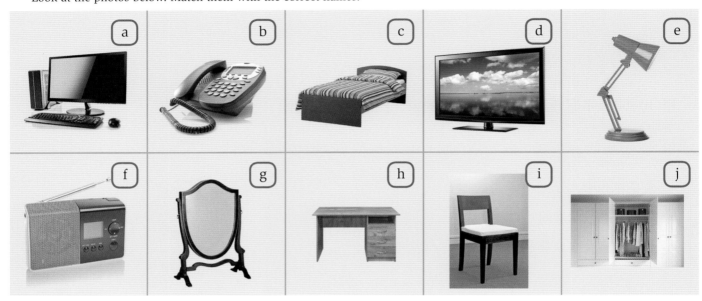

i. 床   ii. 电话   iii. 电脑   iv. 电视机   v. 收音机
vi. 台灯   vii. 衣柜   viii. 椅子   ix. 镜子   x. 书桌

2. 练习写汉字。
Practise writing Chinese.

a. 按照笔画顺序写下面的字。
Write the characters by following the stroke order.

kōng
空 空 空 空 空 空 空 空 空
  1 2 3 4 5 6 7 8

tiáo
调 调 调 调 调 调 调 调 调 调
  1 2 3 4 5 6 7 8 9 10

b. 在你住的国家，在天气热或天气冷的时候，人们常常开空调吗？
In your country, do people often turn on their air-conditioner when the weather gets very warm or cold?

---

chuáng
床 bed

diàn huà
电话 telephone

diàn nǎo
电脑 computer

diàn shì jī
电视机 TV

yǐ zi
椅子 chair

shū zhuō
书桌 desk

---

shōu yīn jī
收音机 radio

tái dēng
台灯 table lamp

chuāng hu
窗户 window

yī guì
衣柜 wardrobe

jìng zi
镜子 mirror

3. 阅读小明的博客，然后回答问题。
Read Xiaoming's blog post, then answer the questions.

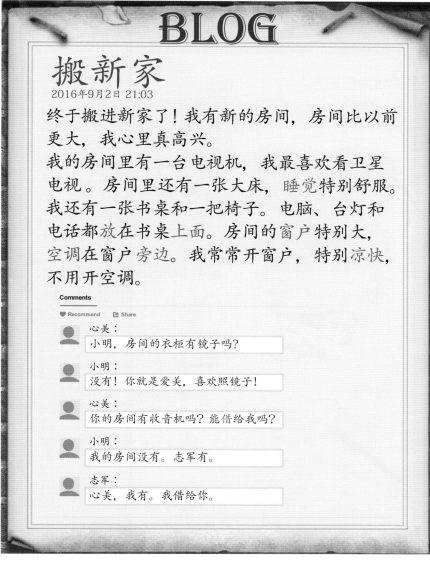

shuì jiào 睡觉	to sleep; go to bed
fàng 放	to place
páng biān 旁边	next to
liáng kuai 凉快	cool

shàng miàn 上面	above
chuāng hu 窗户	window
kōng tiáo 空调	air conditioner
jiè 借	to lend

Grammar focus p.262

1. 的: to indicate possession
 ★ subject + 的 + object
 我的电脑(在书桌上边)。

2. 有: to have
 ★ subject + 有 + object
 小明有三本书。

3. 没有: to not have
 ★ subject + 没有 + object
 房间里没有电视机。

a. 小明的房间有多少台电视机？

b. 小明的书桌上边有什么？

c. 为什么小明不用开空调？

4. 用 40–50个字写一篇短文来描述你的房间和你最喜欢你的
房间的什么东西。然后读给你的同学听。
Write 40–50 characters to describe what you have in your room, and what you like best about it. Then read it out loud to a partner.

LESSON OBJECTIVES
- Describe objects you use for school and home life.
- Describe your basic daily routine.

1. **a.** 看看下面的图片，把它们和正确的词语搭配起来。
Look at the pictures below. Match them with the correct Chinese vocabulary.

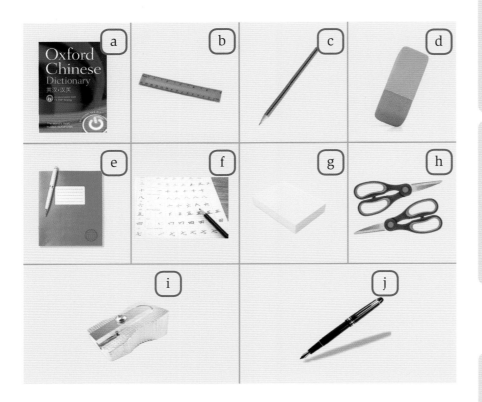

gāng bǐ
钢笔 fountain pen

jiǎn dāo
剪刀 scissors

liàn xí běn
练习本 exercise book

kè běn
课本 textbook

qiān bǐ
铅笔 pencil

xiàng pí
橡皮 rubber; eraser

chǐ zi
尺子 ruler

zhǐ
纸 paper

juǎn bǐ dāo
卷笔刀 pencil sharpener

cí diǎn
词典 dictionary

i. 钢笔　　**ii.** 橡皮　　**iii.** 剪刀　　**iv.** 尺子　　**v.** 纸
vi. 练习本　　**vii.** 课本　　**viii.** 铅笔　　**ix.** 卷笔刀　　**x.** 词典

b. 为上面的文具配上恰当的量词。
Choose the correct measure word for each item above.

本　　把　　支　　块　　张　　个

běn
本 measure word (for a book)

bǎ
把 measure word (for a ruler, a pair of scissors)

zhī
支 measure word (for a pencil, a pen)

kuài
块 measure word (for an eraser, a coin)

zhāng
张 measure word (for a piece of paper)

gè
个 measure word (for a sharpener, a ball)

2. 先阅读志军的日记，再听录音，然后填空。

Read Zhijun's diary entry. then listen to the recording between Zhijun and his mother to work out the missing words.

八月十五日 　　　　星期五 　　　　天气：晴

今天是暑假的最后一天。我早上七点半起床，然后刷牙和洗脸。**(a)** 的时候，妈妈问我什么时候去买文具。我告诉妈妈我的房间里还有 **(b)** 支铅笔、**(c)** 把尺子、**(d)** 块橡皮、**(e)** 个卷笔刀、**(f)** 本练习本。我没有和妈妈外出买文具，因为家里的文具太多了。

明天就开学了，我要十点钟之前 **(g)**。我现在要先去洗澡了。

同学们，明天见！

---

3. 练习描述开学时你要准备的东西。

Practise describing the things you need for school.

a. 明天就开学了。说出五种你要买的文具或和学习有关的东西，并把它们写下来。

School starts tomorrow. Name five stationery or learning items you need to buy, and write them down in Chinese.

b. 和你的同学轮流说一说新学年你要买的文具或和学习有关的东西。

With a partner, take turns to talk about the things you need to buy for the new school term.

---

qǐ chuáng
起床 to wake up; get out of bed

shuā yá
刷牙 to brush one's teeth

xǐ liǎn
洗脸 to wash one's face

wén jù
文具 stationery

xǐ zǎo
洗澡 to have a shower

chī fàn
吃饭 to eat; have a meal

---

mǎi
买 to buy

Grammar focus 　 p.262

1. 多少: how many
　★ subject + verb + 多少 + object?
　你有多少(本)书？

2. 什么时候: when
　★ subject + 什么时候 + action?
　你什么时候上学？

LESSON OBJECTIVE

● Describe and discuss the role digital technology plays in your daily life.

1. 小明和心美正在谈话。先读以下句子，再听他们的对话，然后判断下面的叙述对或错。

   Xiaoming is talking to Sammy. Read the statements before you listen to the recording, then decide if they are true or false.

   a. 小明昨天给北京的朋友发了电邮。

   b. 小明觉得写信比发电邮有意思多了。

   c. 心美常常写信给外国的朋友。

   d. 心美觉得发电邮比写信方便多了。

   > běi jīng
   > 北京 Beijing

2. 看下面的图片，把它们和正确的词语搭配起来。

   Look at the pictures below. Match them with the correct vocabulary.

   > wǎng luò yóu xì
   > 网络游戏 online game
   >
   > fā duǎn xìn
   > 发短信 to send an SMS
   >
   > wǎngshàng gòu wù
   > 网上购物 online shopping
   >
   > wǎngshàng yín háng yè wù
   > 网上银行业务 internet banking

i. 网络游戏   **ii.** 发短信   **iii.** 网上银行业务   **iv.** 网上购物

3. 阅读下面的短文，然后回答问题。
Read the article, then answer the questions below.

智能生活

互联网给我们的生活带来了很多变化。以前，如果想联系在国外的朋友，我们只能写信。有了互联网以后，我们可以用电脑收发电子邮件，和国外的朋友联系变得很容易。

有了能连上网络的手机，我们可以随时上社交网络，给朋友发短信，不用打电话。如果想听音乐或者看电影，我们可以在网上购买后下载到自己的手机或电脑上。想买东西的时候，我们可以在网上购物。我们还可以玩网络游戏和使用网上银行业务。很多事情都可以在网上做，真方便！

a. 以前我们怎样联络在国外的朋友？

b. 现在我们怎样联络在国外的朋友？

c. 连上网络的手机可以做什么？

d. 哪些事情可以在网络上做？

4. 给你在中国的朋友写一封信，用 60–80 个字。其中应该包括：
Write a letter to your friend in China. Write 60–80 characters. Include the following:

a. 你和你的家人从什么时候开始上网的？

b. 你和你的家人上网做什么？

c. 为什么你和你的家人喜欢上网？

---

hù lián wǎng 互联网 the internet
shēng huó 生活 life
biàn huà 变化 change
suí shí 随时 anytime
dǎ diàn huà 打电话 to make a phone call
xià zài 下载 to download

lián xì 联系 contact
wǎng luò 网络 internet network
shè jiāo 社交 social interaction
fāng biàn 方便 convenient
lián luò 联络 to connect

Grammar focus   p.262

1. 给: to / for
★ person A + 给 + person B + action
爷爷给小明写信。

2. ……的时候: when
★ person A + time + 的时候 + action
她五岁的时候离开了（中国）。

Cultural spotlight

fēi gē chuán shū
飞鸽传书 **The use of messenger pigeons**

飞鸽传书是古人之间联系的一种方法。在古代中国，在南方等地区，人们已开始用鸽子传递书信。古代通信不方便，所以聪明的人利用鸽子会飞且飞得比较快、会辨认方向等多方面优点，驯化了鸽子，用以提高送信的速度。飞鸽传书这种通信的方式在古埃及和欧洲部分国家也十分常见。

a. 在你的国家，人们以前是怎样通信的？

b. 相比现在的互联网通信，以前的通信有什么好处和坏处？

1. 看看下面的图片，把它们和正确的词语搭配起来。

i. 网上购物　　ii. 地理　　iii. 网上银行业务　　iv. 厕所　　v. 镜子　　vi. 音乐
vii. 数学　　viii. 手机　　ix. 卧室　　x. 电子邮件　　xi. 椅子　　xii. 教室

2. 用下列词组填空。有些词组可以使用多于一次。

| 的 | 之后 | 多少 | 有 | 沒有 | 台 | 最 | 在 | 在哪儿 | 什么时候 | 比 |

小明：心美，我搬新家了，我 (a) 房子 (b) 以前大。

心美：小明，你住 (c)？

小明：我住在长青街一号。

心美：你的新房子有 (d) 个房间？

小明：我 (e) 家 (f) 三房两厅。

心美：哇！你的家真的很大！你家有卫星电视吗？

小明：我家 (g) 卫星电视。我的房间还有一(h)电脑，可以上网。你喜欢用电脑玩网络游戏吗？你可以来我家玩！

心美：太好了。我 (i) 喜欢玩网络游戏！你的家人 (j)？他们不在家吗？

小明：爸爸 (k) 书房里边看书。妈妈 (l) 厨房做饭。我们可以到我的房间里玩电脑。

心美：好呀！我们可以找志军一起来！我们 (m) 来你家？

小明：你们可以放学 (n) 来我家。

心美：好呀！放学见！

3. 小明第一次去他的新学校。老师正向他介绍学校的设施。

先看下面的图片，再听对话，然后选择五个正确的答案。

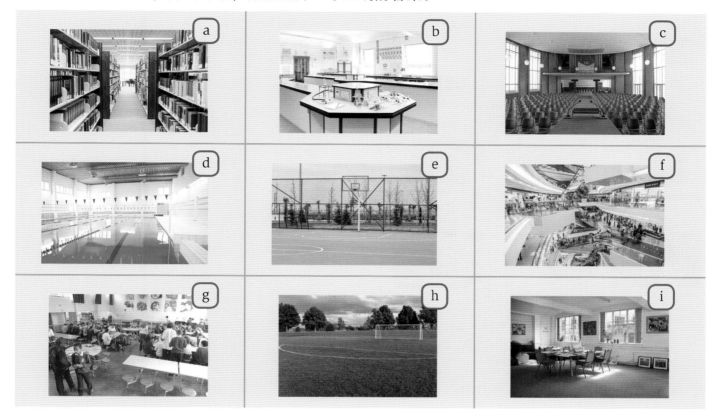

4. 先读问题，再听录音，然后写下答案。

a. 心美第一节和第二节要上什么课　　　　**b.** 第三节和第四节心美要上什么课？

c. 心美什么时候放学？　　　　　　　　　**d.** 为什么本杰明最不喜欢中文课？

e. 为什么本杰明不能和心美一起放学回家？

5. 你和你的朋友在网吧，你们在谈话，轮流提出和回答下面的问题。

a. 你喜欢上网吗？　　　　　　　　　　　**b.** 你是什么时候开始上网的？

c. 你上网做什么？　　　　　　　　　　　**d.** 你最喜欢上网做什么？

e. 为什么？

6. 今天是开学的第一天。用120-150个字写一篇日记。其中应该包括：

a. 你早上起床以后做了些什么？　　　　　**b.** 你的课程表是怎样的？

c. 午休的时候你做了些什么？　　　　　　**d.** 你喜欢今天的哪一门课？为什么？

e. 你放学以后做了些什么？

UNIT OBJECTIVES

- Describe and discuss different types of food and drink.
- Discuss your experiences of dining out.
- Describe the state of your physical health.
- Describe the state of your mental wellbeing.
- Discuss ways to live a healthy life.

1. 看看下面的图片，把它们和正确的词语搭配起来。

Look at the pictures below. Match each one with the correct term.

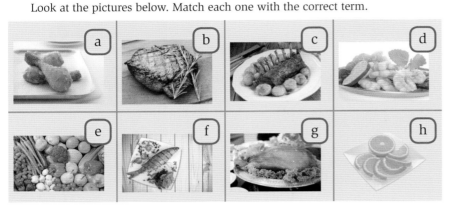

i. 虾 ii. 蔬菜 iii. 鸭肉 iv. 鸡肉 v. 牛肉

vi. 羊肉 vii. 水果 viii. 鱼肉

xiā
虾 prawn

shū cài
蔬菜 vegetable

yā
鸭 duck

ròu
肉 meat

jī
鸡 chicken

niú
牛 beef

yáng
羊 lamb; mutton

shuǐ guǒ
水果 fruit

yú
鱼 fish

2. 阅读下面的对话，然后在表上填入正确的名字。

Read the conversation below, then copy and complete the table by filling in the names.

小文：我们家里常常吃面条，很少吃米饭。

马克：我爱吃土豆。我们家天天吃土豆。

大海：我喜欢喝咖啡，特别是黑咖啡，我每天都喝三杯左右的咖啡。

丽青：我爱吃鱼，我们家每个星期都吃鱼，但是我一点都不喜欢羊肉，因为我觉得羊肉很不好闻。

阿里：我不吃猪肉也不吃牛肉，我喜欢吃蔬菜和水果。我最喜欢吃的蔬菜是西兰花，最喜欢的水果是西瓜。我每天早上都要吃一个香蕉。

miàn tiáo
面条 noodles

mǐ fàn
米饭 rice

tǔ dòu
土豆 potato

kā fēi
咖啡 coffee

zhū
猪 pork

xī lán huā
西兰花 broccoli

wén
闻 to smell

名字	他们说 ……
	我不吃猪肉也不吃牛肉。我吃很多蔬菜水果。
	我特别爱喝咖啡。
	我们家里不常吃米饭，但是经常吃面条。
	我们家吃很多鱼。

3. 写部首，数笔画。

Write down the radicals of the characters listed and note down the number of stokes for each character.

鸡，海，鲜，虾，菜，茶，病，疼，运，动

4. 和你的同学轮流读句子，回答问题。

With a partner, take turns to read the sentences and answer the questions.

a. 昨天哥哥因为吃了太多的海鲜，觉得不舒服。哥哥什么东西吃太多了？

b. 美美不爱吃蔬菜，也不喜欢运动，所以她常常生病。美美为什么常生病？

c. 爸爸晚上喝了三杯咖啡，所以没有睡好。为什么爸爸睡觉睡得不好？

d. 弟弟牙疼，今天一点儿东西都没吃。弟弟怎么了？

e. 妈妈这个月的工作太多了，她常常觉得很累，今天我给妈妈做了鸡汤。我给妈妈做了什么？

hǎi xiān
海鲜 seafood

bù shū fu
不舒服 to feel unwell

shēng bìng
生病 to fall ill

wǎn shàng
晚上 night

yá téng
牙疼 toothache

tāng
汤 soup

5. 先读问题，再听录音，然后回答问题。

Read the questions before you listen to the recording, then answer the questions.

a. 大海喜欢什么运动？

b. 米娜星期几去游泳？

c. 心美常常和谁一起去公园跑步？

d. 除了足球，马克还喜欢什么？

6. 把以下这段话翻译成中文，并写下来。

Translate the passage below into Chinese, then write it out.

Mum doesn't like to eat meat, so we don't eat meat often. She drinks flower tea every day, because she thinks flower tea is very nice. Every Thursday, Mum goes to the sports centre to play tennis. On Saturday mornings, she goes running in the park before having dim sum. She eats lots of vegetables, does plenty of sports, and she is a happy person, so she rarely gets ill.

diǎn xīn
点心 dim sum; light refreshment

LESSON OBJECTIVES

● Identify and discuss different types of food and drink.

● Describe your mealtime routine.

1. 看看下面的图片，然后写出它们的中文名称。

   Look at the picture below. Write out the Chinese names of the food items.

   (Hint: Use the Essential Vocabulary box to help you find the answers.)

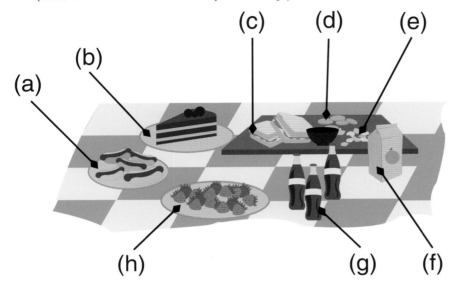

(a) (b) (c) (d) (e) (f) (g) (h)

草莓 cǎo méi strawberry

可乐 kě lè cola

果汁 guǒ zhī juice

热狗 rè gǒu hot dog

饼干 bǐng gān biscuit

三明治 sān míng zhì sandwich

薯片 shǔ piàn potato chips

蛋糕 dàn gāo cake

2. 看看下面的早餐食物与饮料的词语。

   Look at the food and drink terms below.

   牛奶　面包　黄油面包　蛋糕　咖啡
   鸡蛋　面条　麦片　粥　水果　鸡蛋饼　包子
   果汁　热巧克力　奶茶

麦片 mài piàn oatmeal; porridge

粥 zhōu porridge

包子 bāo zi steamed stuffed bun

中式 /西式 / 日式 zhōng shì / xī shì / rì shì Chinese /
Western / Japanese style

   a. 写出它们的拼音和英文名称。

      Write out their pinyin and English names.

   b. 将这些食物与饮料分成三组。

      Organise them into three groups according to the following headings.

      • 第一组: 中式早餐

      • 第二组: 西式早餐

      • 第三组: 饮料

3. 五个人正在谈论他们的早餐习惯。先读问题，再听录音，
然后写下答案。

Five people are talking about their breakfast habits. Read the questions
before you listen to the recording, then write your answers.

a. 小文早餐通常吃什么？

b. 日晴今天吃了面包还是面条？她喝了什么？

c. 海伦早餐除了喝一杯咖啡，还会吃什么？

d. 汤姆在日本吃的早餐食物有什么？饮料有什么？

e. 今天马克在酒店里尝了大米粥还是菜包子？他觉得怎么样？

 4. 翻译下面的句子，并用中文写下来。

Translate these sentences into Chinese and write them out.

a. I often ate an English breakfast when I lived in the UK.

b. I often have bread and a glass of juice for breakfast.

 5. 小文和马克正在谈论他们的一日三餐。阅读他们的对话，
然后判断下面的叙述是对或错。

Xiaowen and Mark are talking about their meals. Read their conversation,
then decide if the following statements are true or false.

> 小文：我喜欢睡懒觉，早上起床比较晚，所以我没时
> 间吃早餐。午饭我在学校的食堂里买，我最爱
> 吃的是蛋炒饭。我们家的晚餐通常是中餐，因
> 为家里只有三口人，所以一般都是三菜一汤。
> 今天我想吃烤鸭。
>
> 马克：对我来说，一日三餐里的早餐很重要，所以我
> 每天都吃早饭，我爱吃烤面包。中午我通常吃
> 自己带的三明治，我的爸爸妈妈下班都很晚，
> 没有太多时间做饭，所以我家的晚餐十分简
> 单。今天我好想吃烤牛肉。

a. 小文常常很晚起床，没有时间吃早饭。　　**b.** 小文中午吃的饭是自己带的。

c. 小文家晚饭爱吃西餐。　　**d.** 今天小文想吃烤鸭。

e. 马克觉得早餐要吃得好。　　**f.** 马克中午常常买学校食堂的三明治。

g. 马克今天想吃烤羊肉。　　**h.** 马克的父母因为工作很忙，所以没时间做饭。

---

shēng yú piàn
生鱼片 Japanese sashimi

Grammar focus　p.263

1. 经常/常常: often
★ subject + 经常/常常 + action
(verb)
我经常（晚上十点左
右）睡觉，（早上六
点）起床。

2. 通常: usually
★ subject + 通常 + action
（中午）我通常吃
三明治。

chǎo
炒 to fry

zhǐ yǒu
只有 only

kǎo
烤 to roast

zhòng yào
重要 important

zhōng wǔ
中午 noon

jiǎn dān
简单 simple

shuì lǎn jiào
睡懒觉 to sleep late

yī rì sān cān
一日三餐 three meals in a day

LESSON OBJECTIVES
● Order food and drink in a restaurant.
● Share with others your experiences of dining out.

1. 阅读以下四个人的要求。
   Read the four requests below.

> 我是小文。我在一家面馆。
> 我要点一碗牛肉面。

> 我是马克。我在餐馆吃饭，
> 可是食物太清淡了，请给我一点盐。

> 我是丽青。吃中餐我一定要放酱油。
> 我们饭桌上没有酱油，请给我一瓶
> 酱油。谢谢。

> 我是大海，我不太会用刀叉，
> 所以请给我一双筷子吧！谢谢。

qǐng gěi wǒ
请给我 Please give me ...
dāo chā
刀叉 knife and fork
kuài zi
筷子 chopsticks

qīng dàn
清淡 plain

a. 把图片和正确的人名搭配起来，选出他们需要的东西。
Match each picture with the correct name to show what each person asked for.

i. 小文　　ii. 大海　　iii. 丽青　　iv. 马克

b. 再看图片，然后给每样东西选择最适当的量词。

Look at the pictures again. Choose the most suitable measure word for each item.

Grammar focus　　p.263

量词: measure words

wǎn
一碗 (a bowl of);

píng
一瓶 (a bottle of);

sháo
一勺 (a spoonful of);

bēi
一杯 (a cup of);

shuāng
一双 (a pair of);

hú
一壶 (a pot of)

2. 海伦正在餐馆点菜。先读问题，再听录音，然后写下答案。

Helen is ordering some food at a restaurant. Read the questions before you listen to the recording, then write your answers.

a. 她点了什么主食：米饭、面包还是土豆？

b. 她点了哪几盘菜？

c. 她点了什么饮料？

d. 这餐饭一共多少钱？

e. 海伦给了服务员多少小费？

> **Grammar focus** **p.263**
>
> diǎn cài
> 点菜 to order (food)
>
> xiǎo fèi
> 小费 tip
>
> cài dān
> 菜单 menu
>
> sù shí
> 素食 vegetarian food
>
> miǎn fèi de
> 免费的 free of charge
>
> zhàng dān
> 帐单 bill

> **Grammar focus** **p.263**
>
> nín   nǐ
> 您和你: two forms of 'you'
>
> ★ 您: a polite and respectful form of address, reserved for elders, teachers, strangers
>
>   爷爷，您身体好吗？
>
> ★ 你: a form of address for people of your age (or younger) and friends
>
>   海伦，你想一起去意大利餐厅吃饭吗？

xiāng là dòu fu
香辣豆腐 fragrant and spicy tofu

suān là tāng
酸辣汤 sour and spicy soup

shāo děng
稍等 to wait a little while

3. 和你的同学角色扮演一个服务员和在餐厅吃饭的客人之间的对话，轮流提出和回答下面的问题。

With a partner, role-play a conversation between a waiter and a diner in a restaurant. Take turns to ask and answer these questions.

a. 请问有几位客人？

b. 你们要来一壶花茶还是绿茶？

c. 你们要点什么菜？

d. 除了茶，你们还需要什么饮料？

e. 今天是星期六，有点忙。上菜需要等二十分钟，可以吗？

4. 写一篇餐馆评论。写80–100个字。其中应该包括：

Write a restaurant review. Write 80–100 characters. Include the following:

a. 这是一家什么样的餐馆？

b. 他们有哪些特色菜？

c. 价钱怎么样？贵不贵？

d. 服务员友好吗？

e. 你会跟朋友推荐这家餐馆吗？

jià qian
价钱 cost; price

yǒu hǎo
友好 friendly

tuī jiàn
推荐 to recommend

LESSON OBJECTIVE
- Describe and express your opinions on cuisines from around the world.

1. 翻译以下词语，并用中文写下来。
Translate these terms into Chinese and write them out.

cài
菜 cuisine; vegetable

a. cuisine
b. tasty cuisine
c. Chinese cuisine
d. Japanese cuisine
e. French cuisine

2. 先读问题，再听录音。 选择唯一正确的答案。
Read the questions before you listen to the recording. Then choose the correct answer for each question.

jù cān
聚餐 dinner party

yàn huì
宴会 banquet

guǎng dōng
广东 Cantonese

cài guǎn
菜馆 restaurant

kè rén
客人 guest

bīng qí lín
冰淇淋 ice cream

tīng shuō
听说 people say

a. 今天大家为什么聚餐？
i. 生日　　**ii.** 春节　　**iii.** 结婚的宴会

b. 大家在哪里聚餐？
i. 广东菜馆　　**ii.** 新加坡西餐厅　　**iii.** 上海素食堂

c. 那家餐馆一共可以坐多少位客人？
i. 两百人　　**ii.** 五十人　　**iii.** 五百人

d. 爷爷喝了什么汤？
i. 鱼汤　　**ii.** 鸡汤　　**iii.** 菜汤

tián diǎn
甜点 dessert

e. 最后菜馆给每个人一份什么作为饭后甜点？
i. 冰淇淋　　**ii.** 蛋糕　　**iii.** 水果

3. 阅读短文，然后回答问题。
Read this passage, then answer the questions.

fēng jǐng
风景 scenery

　　上个周末我和爸妈去了一座海岛游玩。两晚都住在一家海边的五星酒店。第一天我们在酒店里吃了晚饭。我点的是酒店的名菜——苏格兰牛排，肉很鲜美，太好吃了。爸妈点了海鲜餐。主餐之后，还有各式小甜点。我要了一份巧克力蛋糕，又香又甜又可口。我们吃得津津有味，所以付钱的时候还给了小费。第二天我们去了沙滩，沙滩边儿上有个海鲜餐馆，主要卖新鲜龙虾，我们每人点了一盘龙虾沙拉和英国薯条，一边品尝美食，一边看美丽的海滩风景，心情真好！上个周末我们大家都玩得好开心。我希望爸爸妈妈以后周末能经常带我出去玩。

a. 我们住哪儿?

 i. 　**ii.** 　**iii.**

xiān měi
鲜美 tasty; fresh-tasting

yòu xiāng yòu tián
又香又甜 smells great; tastes sweet

kě kǒu
可口 tasty

jīn jīn yǒu wèi
津津有味 phrase to describe eating something with great enjoyment

b. 第一天晚饭的主餐我点了什么?

 i. 　**ii.** 　**iii.**

c. 第一天晚上我吃了什么甜点?

 i. 　**ii.** 　**iii.**

d. 海鲜餐馆在哪儿?

i. 　**ii.** 　**iii.**

4. 和你的同学轮流提出和回答下面的问题。

With a partner, take turns to ask and answer the following questions.

a. 你们家里经常吃中餐还是西餐,还是其他菜?

b. 中国菜、日本菜、法国菜等等,你最喜欢哪一种? 喜欢其中哪一道菜? 为什么?

c. 上一次去餐馆吃饭,你们吃了什么?

d. 以后你最想学做哪一类菜?

Cultural spotlight

huǒ guō
火锅 Hotpot

　　火锅是以水或汤来煮食物的简单的烹饪方式。 其特色为边煮边吃,吃的时候食物热气腾腾。在东亚国家,例如中国、日本、韩国和蒙古国非常受欢迎。火锅食材包括各种肉片、海鲜、蔬菜、豆制品、蘑菇、丸子等。中国南方的年夜饭通常有火锅。首先是因为火锅热气腾腾,有来年红红火火的意思;还有冬天天气冷,大家一起吃火锅会感到很暖和。

a. 你有没有尝试过吃火锅? 是在什么场合吃的?
b. 你居住的国家有没有火锅? 如果有,是用什么食材?

3.5 健康状况
MY HEALTH

LESSON OBJECTIVE

● Describe parts of the human body and some common health issues.

1. 看看右边的图片，用中文字写出以下八个身体部位。

Look at the picture on the right. Write the names of the body parts labelled a to h in Chinese.

2. 看看下面的中文词语。写下拼音，然后把它们和正确的英文名称搭配起来。

Look at the terms below. Write the pinyin for each one, then match them with the correct English translation.

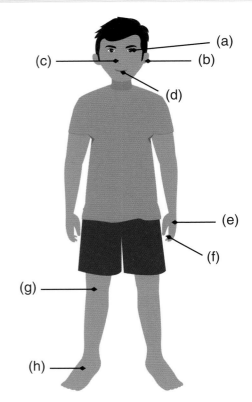

a. 头疼　　**b.** 眼睛红　　**c.** 耳朵发炎　　**d.** 牙痛　　**e.** 嗓子疼

f. 肚子疼　　**g.** 脚受伤　　**h.** 手指受伤　　**i.** 发烧　　**j.** 皮肤痒

i. red eyes　　**ii.** finger injury　　**iii.** fever　　**iv.** itchy skin

v. sore throat　　**vi.** stomach ache　　**vii.** headache　　**viii.** ear infection

ix. toothache　　**x.** foot injury

3. 杰西卡、志军和阿里今天没去上学。阅读他们的对话，然后回答问题。

Jessica, Zhijun, and Ali are not in school today. Read what they are saying, then answer the questions.

杰西卡：老师：您好！我今天要请假一天。我昨天在外面吃饭不小心吃了海鲜，因为我对海鲜过敏，所以今天我觉得很不舒服，肚子很疼。

志　军：我和朋友踢足球的时候，脚受伤了。医生说我这个星期要好好休息，不能跑动。今天上午我得再去一趟医院，所以请假半天。

阿　里：昨天我去了海边，海边风很大，而且很冷，我忘了穿暖和的衣服。今天早上起来的时候头很疼还发烧了。

a. 杰西卡因为吃了什么肚子不舒服？

b. 志军需要请假多久？

c. 阿里在海边的时候忘了什么？

眼睛 yǎn jīng eye
耳朵 ěr duo ear
脚 jiǎo foot
手指 shǒu zhǐ finger
鼻子 bí zi nose
腿 tuǐ leg
嗓子/喉咙 sǎng zi / hóu lóng throat
冷 lěng cold

发炎 fā yán infection; inflammation

4. 杰西卡正在接受一本健康杂志的采访。先读问题，再听录音，然后写下答案。

Jessica is being interviewed by a health magazine. Read the questions before you listen to the recording, then write your answers.

a. 杰西卡几岁开始喜欢跑步？ **b.** 她的饮食是怎么样的？

c. 最近她为什么没有跑步？ **d.** 下次运动会是什么运动会？

e. 她希望自己得什么样的成绩？

5. 练习描述自己哪里不舒服。

Practise describing where you are feeling unwell.

a. 和你的同学角色扮演医生和病人之间的对话，轮流提出和回答下面的问题。

With a partner, role-play a conversation between a doctor and a patient. Take turns to ask and answer the following questions.

i. 你哪里不舒服？ **ii.** 不舒服是什么时候开始的？
iii. 到现在多长时间了？

b. 用中文给你的老师写一张病假条。写25–40个字。其中应该包括:

Write a sick note in Chinese for your teacher. Write 25–40 characters. Include the following:

i. 你为什么请假？ **ii.** 得病的原因是什么？
iii. 需要请多长时间？

---

qǐng jià
请假 to ask for sick leave

duì guò mǐn
(对……)过敏 be allergic to

nuǎn huo
暖和 warm

yī fu
衣服 clothing; garment

yǐn shí
饮食 diet; food and drink

xùn liàn
训练 to train; training

pǎo bù
跑步 to jog

rú yuàn yǐ cháng
如愿以偿 to have one's wish granted

Grammar focus　p.263

地 : particle word used directly after a stative verb to turn it into an adverb, which then appears before a verb to describe an action

★ stative verb + 地 + verb (action)
慢慢地走、快乐地玩

3.6 在医院
AT THE HOSPITAL

LESSON OBJECTIVES
- Identify vocabulary related to health issues.
- Describe your feelings to medical professionals.

1. 看看下面的英文词语。 把它们翻译成中文，组成新词语，并用中文写下来。

Look at the English words below. Translate them into Chinese and form new words, then write them out.

a. medicine + shop = pharmacy

b. west + medicine = Western medicine

c. middle (Chinese) + medicine = Chinese medicine

d. straw (herb) + medicine = herbal medicine

e. sick + bed = hospital bed

f. treatment + yard = hospital

yī yuàn
医院 hospital
yī shēng
医生 doctor
bìng chuáng
病床 hospital bed
yào diàn
药店 pharmacy
xī yào
西药 Western medicine
zhōng yào
中药 Chinese medicine
cǎo yào
草药 herbal medicine

2. 阅读汤姆写给陈大夫的感谢卡，然后回答问题。

Tom has written a thank-you card to Doctor Chen. Read it, then answer the questions.

zhì liáo
治疗 to cure; to treat (a patient)
bāng zhù
帮助 to help

huā fěn
花粉 pollen
fán nǎo
烦恼 trouble; worry

> 敬爱的陈大夫：
>
> 您好!
> 自从尝试了您的传统中医治疗，喝了您开的草药汤
> 药，我对花粉的过敏好了很多。
> 非常感谢您!
>
> 来自英国的汤姆

a. 汤姆是哪国人?

b. 他以前有什么烦恼?

c. 陈大夫怎样帮助了汤姆?

3. 以下是四个小对话。先读问题，再听录音，然后选择唯一正确的答案。

Here are four short conversations. Read the questions before you listen to the recording, then choose the correct answer for each question.

a. 小文怎么了？
- **i.** 脚受伤了
- **ii.** 发烧了
- **iii.** 肚子饿了

b. 马克为什么不吃巧克力？
- **i.** 他不爱甜食
- **ii.** 他生病了，没有胃口
- **iii.** 医生建议他少吃甜食

c. 米娜为什么吃不好东西？
- **i.** 牙痛
- **ii.** 胃痛
- **iii.** 感冒了，没有胃口

d. 心美为什么不想去医院？
- **i.** 害怕打针
- **ii.** 很忙，没有时间
- **iii.** 医院太远了

4. 先阅读下面的对话。

Read the dialogue below.

> 医生：你好。你怎么啦？
> 海伦：大夫，我全身都不舒服，头疼得厉害。
> 医生：我给你量一下体温。有39.5度，发烧了。来，嘴巴张开，我看看。喉咙也有点儿发炎了。我给你开点儿药。等会儿去药房取了药就可以回家了。
> 海伦：多谢大夫。
> 医生：没什么大问题。回去多喝水，好好休息，多喝点儿粥。
> 海伦：谢谢。哦，请问大夫，这药是饭前吃还是饭后吃？
> 医生：记住是饭前吃。
> 海伦：好的，多谢大夫。

a. 判断下面的叙述是对或错。

Decide if the following statements are true or false.

- **i.** 海伦牙疼，她看了牙医。
- **ii.** 海伦感冒了，不仅发烧了，喉咙也发炎了。
- **iii.** 医生给海伦打了针，她感觉好多了。
- **iv.** 医生让海伦多喝水。
- **v.** 医生给海伦开的药是饭前吃的。
- **vi.** 海伦取了药以后还要回医生那里看一看。

b. 和你的同学轮流角色扮演医生和海伦，读出以上的对话。

With a partner, take turns to read out the above conversation as Helen and the doctor.

饿 è hungry

胃口 wèi kǒu appetite

打针 dǎ zhēn to give; have an injection

量 liàng to measure

咳嗽 ké sou to cough

盒 hé box

体重 tǐ zhòng body weight

害怕 hài pà to fear

建议 jiàn yì to advise

体温 tǐ wēn body temperature

Grammar focus p.263

得: used to add descriptive information to a verb, or to indicate the extent of an action

★ action + 得 + adverb

（汤姆）恢复得不错。

恢复 huī fù to recover

度 dù degree

饭前吃 / 饭后吃 fàn qián chī / fàn hòu chī to take before dinner / to take after dinner

记住 jì zhù to remember

不仅 bù jǐn not only

LESSON OBJECTIVE

● Discuss ways of living a healthy lifestyle.

1. 看看下面的图片，然后说出所有你认识的食物名称。

   Look at the picture. Identify and say as many food names in Chinese as you can.

Grammar focus   p.264

应该: should

★ subject + 应该 + action

来英国的朋友们应该去伦敦牛津街逛一逛。

2. 和三位同学分成一组，讨论以下问题，然后做口语演示。

   In groups of four, discuss the following questions on 'healthy diet'. Then, make an oral presentation on the topic.

   a. 你认为你的饮食怎么样？健康吗？为什么？

   b. 你有没有节食过？为什么要节食？

   c. 除了注意饮食，为了健康你认为我们还应该做什么？

3. 请阅读下面的短文，然后回答问题。

   Read the passage, then answer the questions.

   张静是一名女演员，所以她特别注意自己的饮食。她从来都不吃快餐，因为这些食物大多是油炸的，热量很高。她每天吃大量的水果和蔬菜，草莓酸奶也是她最喜欢的。除了注意饮食，张静还每周三都会去她家附近的健身房跑步，每个周五晚上去游泳馆游一个小时泳。周末如果没有工作，她还喜欢和朋友一起去露营和爬山。

---

rèn wéi
认为 to think

jiàn kāng
健康 healthy

jié shí
节食 to go on a diet

yīng gāi
应该 should

---

yǎn yuán
演员 actor

zhù yì
注意 to pay attention to

jiàn shēn fáng
健身房 gym

lù yíng
露营 camping

---

cóng lái dōu bù
从来都不 never

yóu zhá
油炸 deep fried

rè liàng
热量 heat value; calories

a. 张静做什么工作？　　**b.** 她不吃什么样的食物？

c. 她通常做哪些运动健身？　　**d.** 周末张静常常和朋友们一起做什么？

4. 练习写汉字。
Practise writing Chinese.

按照笔画顺序写下面的字。
Write the characters by following the stroke order.

jiàn

健 健 健 健 健 健 健 健 健 健 健
　 1　2　3　4　5　6　7　8　9　10

kāng

康 康 康 康 康 康 康 康 康 康 康
　 1　2　3　4　5　6　7　8　9　10　11

5. 四个人正在谈论自己的健康状况。先看下面的词语，再听录音，然后把词语和正确的名字搭配起来。

Four people are talking about their health. Look at the activity words (i–iv) before you listen to the recording, then match each person (a–d) to the correct activity.

a. 小文　　**b.** 海伦　　**c.** 马克　　**d.** 阿里

i. 少上网　　**ii.** 早点睡觉　　**iii.** 少吃巧克力　　**iv.** 去健身房

Cultural spotlight

sù shí wén huà de xīng qǐ
素食文化的兴起 **The beginnings of vegetarianism**

世界上很多人因为宗教信仰而吃素，比如信佛的人。但是近年来在世界各地，吃素的人越来越多，不仅是信教的人和老年人，而且还有很多年轻人。吃素成为一种时尚，素食餐厅在各个大城市里相当受欢迎。素食之所以越来越受欢迎，简单来说是因为有三大好处：第一就是对自己身体健康的好处，多吃素可以减少肠胃负担，促进消化；第二吃素可以减少对动物的伤害；第三就是吃素有利于保护环境。总之吃素已经成为健康生活的代名词之一，相信以后会有更多的人选择素食。

a. 为什么有些人选择吃素？
b. 你认为你会成为素食者吗？

LESSON OBJECTIVE

● Describe and discuss ways of keeping a healthy mind.

 1. 五个人正在谈他们的减压方式。先看下面的图片，再听录音，然后把图片和正确的名字搭配起来。

Five people are talking about how they deal with pressure. Look at the pictures before you listen to the recording, then match each activity with the correct person.

a. 马克　**b.** 志军　**c.** 心美　**d.** 日晴　**e.** 米娜

　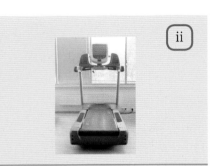

i　ii

iii　iv

v

kāi xīn
开心 happy

hú
湖 lake

jǐn zhāng
紧张 nervous; tense

dà zì rán
大自然 nature

fāng shì
方式 method

fàng sōng
放松 to relax

shén qí
神奇 magical

jiǎn yā
减压 to reduce pressure

Grammar focus p.264

为了: for the purpose of, in order to

★ 为了 + purpose, subject + action.
为了放松自己，我打算下个月去中国旅行。

 2. 用你自己认识的字来完成下面的句子。

Use your own words to complete the following sentence.

为了保持健康，除了需要健康的饮食，还应该……。

3. 阅读下面的短文，然后回答问题。

Read the short passage below, then answer the questions.

> 　　去年过年的时候爸爸妈妈送给我一部智能手机。我除了用它跟朋友打电话，还用它上网和玩游戏。从我有了智能手机以后，我一有空就玩手机，因此我的视力变差了。而且如果手机不在身边，我就会着急。奶奶常常对我说："不要玩手机了。"
>
> 　　我觉得奶奶很健康。她有早睡早起的习惯。她每天都很忙，吃完早饭，她会去公园走路。吃完晚饭，她通常会去我家附近的城市广场和她的朋友们跳广场舞。跳舞既可以健身，还可以一边跳舞一边和朋友聊天，有说有笑，保持心情愉快。走路和跳舞是奶奶最喜欢的健身方式。

a. 日晴过年时收到了什么礼物？

b. 她用它做什么？

c. 奶奶常常跟日晴说什么？

d. 奶奶有哪些好的生活习惯？

e. 为什么奶奶很喜欢跳广场舞？

f. 短文中说到的健康生活方式有哪些？

> zháo jí
> 着急 to become impatient; to panic

> shì lì
> 视力 vision

4. 和你的同学角色扮演两个网友聊生活习惯的对话，轮流提出和回答下面的问题。

With a partner, role-play a conversation between two e-pals talking about their lifestyles. Take turns to ask and answer the following questions.

a. 你一般睡几个小时？

b. 睡前你会看手机还是看书？

c. 有人睡觉前玩手机或看社交网站？你认为这样好吗？

d. 压力大的时候，你怎样减少压力？

Cultural spotlight

guǎngchǎng wǔ
广场舞 Square dancing

　　广场舞是中国老年人为了健身在各个地方的城市广场、公园、小区空地等一起跳的舞。近年来，广场舞因为它简单的舞步越来越受到人们的欢迎，甚至吸引了一些年轻人的加入。老年人们一起跳广场舞不仅可以健身，还给老年人提供了见面和说话聊天的机会，让他们的生活更加丰富多彩。在中国除了广场舞，在公园里练太极拳也是受老年人欢迎的健身方式。

a. 在你住的国家，老年人爱做哪些运动？

b. 你和身边的老人们有没有见面和说话聊天的机会？有空你喜欢和他们一起做什么？

LESSON OBJECTIVE

● Identify and discuss a variety of sports activities.

1. 听人谈家人和运动。先看图，再听录音，然后把图和正确的人物搭配起来。

You will hear someone talking about their family and the sports activities they do. Look at the pictures before you listen to the recording, then match each picture with the correct person.

| a. 爷爷和奶奶 | b. 爸爸 | c. 妈妈 | d. 哥哥 | e. 姐姐 |

bǎo líng qiú
保龄球 ten-pin bowling

jù lè bù
俱乐部 club

bǐ sài
比赛 competition; match

sàn bù
散步 to go for a stroll

zhuō qiú
桌球 pool or snooker

yíng
赢 to win

sāng bā wǔ
桑巴舞 Samba dance

fàng fēng zhēng
放风筝 to fly a kite

pīng pāng qiú
乒乓球 table tennis

2. 看看下面的词语。判断哪一项目与其他的不同，然后说出为什么。

Read the words below. Which is the odd one out? Why?

钓鱼　　放风筝　　乒乓球　　爬山

3. 阅读下面的对话，然后回答问题。

Read the dialogue below, then answer the questions.

> 约翰：老师您好。我是约翰，我想报名参加今年的夏
> 　　　令营。
> 老师：同学你好。欢迎参加我们的夏令营。
> 约翰：老师，请问夏令营有哪些活动？
> 老师：今年夏令营的**主题**是"保持健康，多多运
> 　　　动"，所以有很多不同的体育活动，但是也有
> 　　　几节语言和文化课。
> 约翰：太好了，我很喜欢运动。请问老师夏令营有什
> 　　　么运动？
> 老师：我们的**营地**在海边，早上吃完早餐，我们先跑
> 　　　步去营地附近的沙滩，然后在那儿玩一会儿沙
> 　　　滩**排球**，再回营地上课。午饭后，老师会带同
> 　　　学们去山里爬山或去森林里**徒步**。傍晚吃完饭
> 　　　可以在营地里打乒乓球或**网球**。
> 约翰：夏令营里可以上网吗？
> 老师：不可以，因为没有网络。那里没有电脑、电
> 　　　视，如果不想玩乒乓或网球，大家可以坐在一
> 　　　起聊天。

pái qiú	
排球 volleyball	
wǎng qiú	
网球 tennis	

xià lìng yíng	
夏令营 summer camp	
zhǔ tí	
主题 theme	
yíng dì	
营地 base camp	
tú bù	
徒步 to hike (long distance)	

a. 夏令营有哪些体育活动？

b. 除了体育运动，学生们还需要上什么课？

c. 吃完晚饭，如果不想做运动，大家可以一起做什么？

4. 风筝节即将来临。准备一些资料。

Prepare some information about an upcoming kite festival.

a. 设计一张风筝节海报。写80–100个字。上面需要包括：

Design a poster about a kite festival. Write 80–100 characters. It should include the following:

　　i. 时间是什么时候？地点在哪里？

　　ii. 有哪些活动？

　　iii. 什么人可以参加？

　　iv. 大家为什么参加风筝节？

b. 和你的同学角色扮演参加者与组织者的对话，轮流提出和回答上面的问题。

With a partner, role-play a conversation between a participant and the festival organiser. Take turns to ask and answer the above questions.

1. 阅读以下美食广告，然后完成句子。

如果您喜欢精美的小点心，
如果您对传统的英式下午茶文化感兴趣，
欢迎您来到康德午茶厅。
十月至十一月店内消费满两百元将获免费小礼物一份。
每位一百八十八元，加果汁每位两百五十元。
地址：南洋市平海路一百二十号

a. 这是一家……。
   i. 可以喝茶的地方
   ii. 吃牛排的餐馆

b. 这个地方主要卖……。
   i. 英式下午茶　　ii. 中国绿茶　　iii. 花茶

c. 如果不喝果汁，每人收费是……。
   i. 200 元　　ii. 188元　　iii. 250元

2. 听录音，把人和正确的图片搭配起来。

a. 小文　b. 丽青　c. 马克　d. 汤姆　e. 海伦

3. 阅读下面的对话，然后回答问题 。

> 马　　克：这家餐馆真不错！环境好，服务也周到。
> 丽　　青：是啊，设计简单、干净，服务员有礼貌，而且上菜挺快的，最重要的是这家的
> 　　　　　菜不仅味道好，而且看上去很漂亮。
> 马　　克：说的对。吃完了，我们走吧！我还想去逛一逛商场呢。
> 丽　　青：好啊！我也去看一看。服务员，请给我账单。
> 服务员：一共一百八十元。谢谢。
> 丽　　青：这是两百元。剩下的是小费。谢谢。
> 服务员：谢谢！

a. 为什么丽青和马克觉得这家餐馆好？

b. 吃完了饭，他们打算去哪儿？

c. 他们一共吃了多少钱？ 给了服务员多少小费？

4. 选择正确的词语填空完成句子。
Choose the correct words to complete the sentences.

> 常常　　以后　　聊天　　说一说　　快乐　　公园

> 吃完饭(a)散步是一个非常好的活动。我就经常跟家人一起去(b)、广场或河边散步。我
> 们(c)一边走一边(d)，聊一些有趣的事情，(e)自己的想法。散步聊天让我放松，还让我觉
> 得(f)。

5. 你在中国北京旅行。今天一个朋友的家人带你去了一家餐馆吃饭。回到家以后你给父母写邮件。写
120–150个字。邮件应该写到:

a. 你们去了什么样的饭店吃饭？是四川菜馆、广东菜馆还是杭州菜馆？

b. 觉得餐馆怎么样？

c. 你们都吃了什么菜？

d. 你最喜欢哪一道菜？ 为什么？

e. 吃完饭你们还一起做了什么？

6. 你和同学们聊健康生活，说一说自己对以下问题的看法。

a. 你认为健康生活应该是什么样的？

b. 你自己的生活方式、习惯好不好？

c. 你对很多人不停玩手机怎么看？

UNIT OBJECTIVES

- Plan for your school holidays.
- Learn some facts about Spring Festival and discuss how it is celebrated.
- Discuss how people celebrate Christmas.
- Plan and prepare for a study tour.
- Discuss a range of holiday activities and experiences.

- Discuss your experiences of booking and staying in a hotel.
- Discuss ways of dealing with problems during a holiday.

---

1. 看看下面的图片，把它们和正确的名称搭配起来。

Look at the pictures below. Match each one with its correct name.

chūn jié
春节 Chinese New Year, known also as Spring festival

shèng dàn jié
圣诞节 Christmas

bīn guǎn   jiǔ diàn
宾馆 / 酒店 hotel

xiū xián huó dòng
休闲活动 leisure activity

i. 宾馆 / 酒店   ii. 休闲活动   iii. 春节   iv. 圣诞节

---

2. 阅读下面的句子，用正确的词语填空。

Complete the sentences below by filling in the missing words.

放假	游学	计划	准备	预订	假期

fàng jià
放假 to be on holiday

zhǔn bèi
准备 preparation; to prepare

jià qī
假期 holiday

yóu xué
游学 study tour

yù dìng
预订 to book (a hotel)

心美明天 **(a)**，不用上学。

今年暑假，汤姆 **(b)** 去中国 **(c)**，和中国的学生一起学习中文。

"明天就要坐飞机去中国了，你的行李 **(d)** 好了吗？"

在这个 **(e)**，我们全家一起去旅行，妈妈叫我帮忙 **(f)** 酒店。

3. 你将听到几个中文句子。每个句子听两遍。先读问题，再听录音，然后选择正确的答案。

You will now hear some short phrases. You will hear each phrase twice. Look at the questions before you listen to the recording, then choose the correct answers.

a. 小明明天做什么？

i. ii. iii.

b. 心美最喜欢什么假期？

i. ii. iii.

c. 妈妈什么时候到爷爷、奶奶家去？

i. ii. iii.

d. 哥哥有很多什么？

i. ii. iii.

 4. 练习写汉字。

Practise writing Chinese.

a. 按照笔画顺序写下面的字。

Write the characters by following the stroke order.

jià
假 假 假 假 假 假 假 假 假 假 假
1 2 3 4 5 6 7 8 9 10 11

qī
期 期 期 期 期 期 其 期 其 期 期 期
1 2 3 4 5 6 7 8 9 10 11 12

b. 上一个假期，你做了些什么？用25-40个字写下来。

What did you do on your last holiday? Write your answer using 25–40 characters.

LESSON OBJECTIVES
- Describe when your school holidays are.
- Share your school holiday plans with others.

1. 看看下面的校历，然后回答问题。

Look at the school calendar below, then answer the questions.

2017–18年校历

日期	假期
1月15日到2月10日	寒假
2月3日	春节
4月1日	教师培训日
6月24日到8月10日	暑假
12月25日到12月30日	圣诞节假期

a. 十二月有什么假期?　　**b.** 寒假什么时候开始?

c. 暑假从哪一天到哪一天?

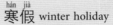

hán jià
寒假 winter holiday

jiào shī péi xùn rì
教师培训日 teacher-training day

Grammar focus p.264

……月……日/号: month / day
★ number + 月 + number
+ 日/号
四月五日/号

2. 日晴和心美正在谈话。先读问题，再听录音，然后写下答案。

Riqing and Sammy are having a conversation. Read the questions before you listen to the recording, then write your answers.

a. 寒假什么时候开始?

b. 日晴和心美三天以后去谁的家?

c. 她们做什么?

3. 和你的同学轮流提出和回答下面的问题。

With a partner, take turns to ask and answer the following questions.

a. 你最喜欢什么假期?　　**b.** 为什么你喜欢这个假期?　　**c.** 假期时你会做什么?

4. 学校假期到了。写三件你会在下面这几个地方做的事。

The school holidays have begun. Write three things you might do if you were at the following places:

a. 在自己家里　　**b.** 在同学/朋友家　　**c.** 在其他地方(例如：公园)

5. 阅读约翰的博客。

Read John's blog post below, then answer the questions on the right.

首页　博文　目录　图片　关于我

放寒假

2016年1月2日 21:03

　　寒假快要到了！我太高兴了！

　　我最喜欢过寒假，因为假期很长。今年的寒假从1月5日到2月1日，差不多有四个星期。

　　妈妈说她会带我去中国旅行，我最喜欢旅行了。我会拍照片给同学们看的。对了，朋友们，你们放假做什么？

转载 ▼

Comments

♥ Recommend　☒ Share

心美：

我寒假不去旅行，我在家休息。

约翰：

可惜！我会多拍一些游览中国的照片给你们看的。

杰西卡：

约翰，爸爸暑假也会带我去中国旅行的。

心美：

我8月生日，为了帮我庆祝生日，妈妈会带我到上海迪斯尼公园游览。

a. 回答下面的问题。

Answer the following questions.

　i. 约翰最喜欢过什么假期？

　ii. 谁会带约翰去中国旅行？

　iii. 约翰在旅行时会做什么？

b. 参考博客中的回复部分，用你自己认识的词语完成下面的填空。

Referring to the comments section, use your own words to fill in the missing words and complete the sentences.

我 **(i)** 不去旅行，我在家休息。

我 **(ii)** 生日，为了帮我庆祝生日，**(iii)** 会带我到 **(iv)** 游览 。

> guò
> 过 to spend, to go on
>
> chà bù duō
> 差不多 almost
>
> xīng qī
> 星期 week
>
> lǚ xíng
> 旅行 travelling
>
> kě xī
> 可惜 a shame; too bad
>
> yóu lǎn
> 游览 to travel around (on a tour)

6. 练习写汉字。

Practise writing Chinese.

a. 按照笔画顺序写下面的字。

Write the characters by following the stroke order.

hán
寒 1 2 3 4 5 6 7 8 9 10 11 12

jià
假 1 2 3 4 5 6 7 8 9 10 11

shǔ
暑 1 2 3 4 5 6 7 8 9 10 11 12

jià
假 1 2 3 4 5 6 7 8 9 10 11

b. 用上面的两个词语造句，写下你在这两个假期里会做的事。写30–40个字。

Write two sentences of your own using these characters to explain what you might do during each of these holidays. Write 30–40 characters.

LESSON OBJECTIVES

- Describe the customs of Spring Festival.
- Describe and discuss different people's plans for Spring Festival.

1. 小华和丽青正在谈论他们春节的计划。先读问题，再听录音，然后写下答案。

Xiaohua and Liqing are talking about their plans for Spring Festival. Read the questions before you listen to the recording, then write your answers.

a. 哪一天是春节？　**b.** 谁喜欢过春节？

c. 小华春节去哪儿？　**d.** 丽青的爷爷、奶奶会给她什么？

2. 志军正阅读一篇关于春节的文章。阅读下面的文章，然后回答问题。

Zhijun is reading an article about Spring Festival. Read it, then answer the questions.

传统中国节日——春节

> 春节是中国新年的第一天，中国人很重视这个节日。在春节前一天的晚上——中国人把这个日子叫做除夕——人们会大扫除。把家里打扫干净后，家人们便一起高兴地吃饭。

> 春节期间，人们会到亲戚朋友们家拜年和聚会。人们见到对方的时候会说"新年快乐"或"新年好"，长辈们会发红包给孩子。

> 过节时，人们常常会吃饺子饺子、年糕、汤圆等食物。

a. 中国人重视过什么节日？

b. 在春节的时候，人们会说什么话？

c. 除了年糕之外，中国人过年时会吃什么食物？

---

hóng bāo
红包 red packet (gift envelope used for giving money)

bài nián
拜年 to pay a New Year call or visit

xīn nián
新年 Chinese New Year

xīn nián kuài lè　xīn nián hǎo
新年快乐 / 新年好 common greeting meaning 'Happy New Year' or 'Best wishes for the New Year'

jiǎo zi
饺子 dumpling

chuán tǒng
传统 tradition

chú xī
除夕 New Year's Eve

dà sǎo chú
大扫除 spring cleaning

qīn qi
亲戚 relative

jù huì
聚会 gathering

zhǎng bèi
长辈 elder family member

guò jié
过节 to celebrate a festival

nián gāo
年糕 New Year cake (a Chinese steamed cake made with glutinous rice flour)

tāng yuán
汤圆 glutinous rice dumplings

zhòng shì
重视 to value, place importance to

Grammar focus p.264

1. 把 : word used to focus on the result or influence of an action

   ★ person + 把 + object + verb + particle

   我把年糕吃了。

2. 们 : to indicate a plural noun

   ★ noun/pronoun + 们

   亲爱的朋友们（，我们一起去打球吧！）

3. 练习描述你春节的计划。

   Practise describing your plans for Spring Festival.

   a. 写一写你会在春节做的事。写 40–50 个字。其中应该包括:

      Write some things you might do during Spring Festival. Write 40–50 characters. Include the following:

      i. 你会吃什么？

      ii. 你会说哪些话？

      iii. 你会去谁的家？

      iv. （去谁的家）做什么？

   b. 和你的同学轮流提出和回答以上问题。

      With a partner, now take turns to ask and answer the above questions.

Cultural spotlight

中国 "红" Chinese "Red"
zhōng guó *hóng*

　　红色是春节的主色调。根据中国传统，长辈会给晚辈红包。红色在中国文化中代表着赶走坏事，带来好运之意；而红包里面的压岁钱必须是双数，以取好事成双之意。

a. 在你的国家，什么东西和好运有关？

b. 在你的国家，哪一种颜色会带来好运？

LESSON OBJECTIVES

● Describe how people prepare for Christmas.

● Share with others your views on Christmas.

1. 威廉和小文正在谈论他们圣诞节的计划。先读问题，再听录音，然后写下答案。

   William and Xiaowen are talking about their plans for Christmas. Read the questions before you listen to the recording, then write your answers.

   a. 圣诞节什么时候到？

   b. 威廉在哪儿过圣诞节？

   c. 威廉圣诞节怎么过？

2. 威廉准备向班里的学介绍美国人怎么过圣诞节。阅读他写的讲稿，然后回答以下问题。

   William is preparing a presentation to his class about how Americans celebrate Christmas. Read his script, then answer the following questions.

   各位同学：

   大家好，今天我会向你们介绍美国人是怎么过圣诞节的。

   每年的十二月二十五日是圣诞节。美国人很早就开始准备过圣诞节了，他们会在家中挂圣诞装饰。圣诞节的前一天晚上是平安夜，有些人会去教堂唱圣诗。孩子们睡了以后，爸爸妈妈会假扮圣诞老人送礼物给他们。

   在圣诞节的早上，孩子们会开开心心地打开礼物。下午会有家庭聚会，家人们会互相送礼物，他们会说"圣诞快乐"。人们也会准备不同的食物，例如火鸡和土豆。到了晚上，人们会一起吃圣诞晚餐，大家都很高兴。

   希望大家喜欢我的介绍！

   a. 圣诞节在哪一天？
   b. 圣诞节的前一天晚上叫什么？
   c. 谁会送孩子礼物？
   d. 人们在圣诞节说什么？
   e. 人们在圣诞节吃什么？

hù xiāng
互相 each other

guà
挂 to hang

kāi kāi xīn xīn
开开心心 happily

zhuāng shì
装饰 decoration

píng ān yè
平安夜 Christmas Eve

jiào táng
教堂 church

shèng shī
圣诗 hymn

jiǎ bàn
假扮 to disguise oneself

shèng dàn lǎo rén
圣诞老人 Santa Claus

shèng dàn kuài lè
圣诞快乐 'Merry Christmas'

huǒ jī
火鸡 turkey

3. 给你的朋友写圣诞卡。写30–50个字。其中应该包括:

Write a Christmas card to a friend using 30–50 characters. Include the following:

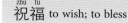
zhù fú
祝福 to wish; to bless

a. 你在哪儿过圣诞?　　**b.** 你怎么过圣诞?

c. 会送什么礼物给他/她?　　**d.** 祝福他/她什么?

 4. 和你的同学轮流提出和回答下面一些关于圣诞节的问题。

With a partner, take turns to ask and answer the following questions about Christmas:

a. 你喜不喜欢过圣诞节?　　**b.** 圣诞节送什么礼物给朋友?

c. 你会在圣诞节吃什么?

Grammar focus　p.265

1. 例如 : such as / for example; used to introduce a list

★ sentence + 例如 + noun 1 + noun 2 + 和 + noun 3

圣诞节时, 妈妈会准备很多食物, 例如火鸡和土豆。

2. 呢/吗 : modal particles used at the end of questions

呢 has a very similar meaning to 'How about you?'

吗 has a very similar meaning to 'Will you ...?'

★ sentence + 呢/吗?

我喜欢圣诞节, 你呢?
你会送礼物给我吗?

---

 5. 练习写汉字。

Practise writing Chinese.

a. 按照笔画顺序写下面的字。

Write the characters by following the stroke order.

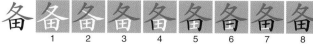

zhǔn
准 | 准 | 准 | 准 | 准 | 准 | 准 | 准 | 准 | 准
1 | 2 | 3 | 4 | 5 | 6 | 7 | 8 | 9 | 10

bèi
备 | 备 | 备 | 备 | 备 | 备 | 备 | 备
1 | 2 | 3 | 4 | 5 | 6 | 7 | 8

b. 写出五种你喜欢或不喜欢的圣诞节习俗。

Make a list of five customs you like or don't like about Christmas.

4.5 假期游学
OVERSEAS STUDY TOURS

LESSON OBJECTIVES

- Identify key vocabulary associated with a typical study tour itinerary.
- Describe how you would plan a study tour.

1. 看看下面的词语，并根据每一个词语的笔划数量，把它们排列次序。先从笔划最少的开始写。

Look at the vocabulary below. Rank them in order of combined number of strokes, starting with the vocabulary with the lowest number.

a. 夏令营　　**b.** 课外活动　　**c.** 行李　　**d.** 飞机　　**e.** 机场

课外活动 kè wài huó dòng extracurricular activity
行李 xíng li luggage
飞机 fēi jī aeroplane
机场 jī chǎng airport

2. 阅读这张关于夏令营的传单，然后回答问题。

Read this flyer about a summer camp, then answer the questions on the right.

船 chuán boat; ship; ferry

行程表 xíng chéng biǎo schedule; itinerary
出发 chū fā departure
课堂活动 kè táng huó dòng classroom activities
短途旅游 duǎn tú lǚ yóu short-distance excursion

台湾

TAIWAN 7.9~13
夏令营：和同学们到台湾一起学中文！

行程表

日期	行程
7月9日	从机场出发到台湾
7月10日	● 开学典礼 ● 课堂活动：写汉字
7月11日	● 课堂活动：看中文电影 ● 课外活动：唱中文歌
7月12日	● 课堂活动：中文朗诵比赛 ● 课外活动：坐船游览日月潭
7月13日	坐飞机 回家

出发啦！

¥ 费用：$10000

联系人：王老师 (jwang@example.com)

注意：

- 行李不用太多，因为这是短途旅游。
- 因为这是学校夏令营，所以同学们在活动的时候要穿校服。

a. 在哪儿出发？

b. 哪一天坐船游览日月潭？

c. 7月11日有什么活动？

d. 为什么行李不用太多？

3. 马克和小华正在谈论关于夏令营的事情。先读问题，再听录音，然后选择唯一正确的答案。

Mark and Xiaohua are talking about the summer camp. Read the questions before you listen to the recording, then choose the correct answers.

a. 小华和马克会一起去台湾夏令营吗？　**i.** 会　**ii.** 不会

b. 参加夏令营有机会坐船去游览日月潭吗？　**i.** 有　**ii.** 没有

c. 电子邮件的地址写在哪儿？　**i.** 邮件里　**ii.** 小册子上

4. 练习描述关于夏令营的计划与行程。

Practise describing the plans and itinerary for a summer camp.

a. 你和同学正在谈论夏令营的计划，轮流提出和回答下面的问题。

You and your partner are talking about an upcoming summer camp. Take turns to ask and answer the following questions:

i. 夏令营在哪儿？　　　**ii.** 从哪儿出发？

iii. 去多少天？　　　　**iv.** 有什么课堂活动？

v. 有什么课外活动？　　**vi.** 你去这个地方需要签证吗？

b. 写一篇日记，说一说上面提到的夏令营计划，以及你觉得这个计划怎么样。写80-100个字。

Write a diary entry about the above plans and your feelings about the camp. Use 80–100 characters.

xiǎo cè zi
小册子 brochure

qiān zhèng
签证 visa

5. 练习写汉字。

Practise writing Chinese.

a. 按照笔画顺序写下面的字。

Write the characters by following the stroke order.

qiān
签 | 签 | 签 | 签 | 签 | 签 | 签 | 签 | 签 | 签 | 签 | 签 | 签 | 签
  | 1 | 2 | 3 | 4 | 5 | 6 | 7 | 8 | 9 | 10 | 11 | 12 | 13

zhèng
证 | 证 | 证 | 证 | 证 | 证 | 证 | 证
  | 1 | 2 | 3 | 4 | 5 | 6 | 7

b. 你去中国要办签证吗？用完整的句子回答问题。写20-30个字。

Do you need a visa to travel to China? Write your answer in full. Write 20–30 characters.

Grammar focus　p.265

1. 和: and
★ noun A + 和 + noun B
约翰和心美

2. 一起: together
★ plural noun + 一起 + action
马克和小华一起去夏令营。

LESSON OBJECTIVE

● Share with others your holiday planning and preparation tips.

1. 看看下面的词语，把它们和正确的图片搭配起来。

Look at the words below. Match them to the correct pictures.

护照　森林　沙滩　来回票　旅行社　海边　郊区　**酒店**

旅行准备

订 (a)　　带 (b)　　去 (c)　　买火车 (d)

计划去哪儿玩?

(e)　　(f)　　(g)　　(h)

2. 志军和马克正在谈论他们的旅行计划。先读问题，再听录音，然后选择正确的答案。

Zhijun and Mark are discussing their holiday plans. Read the questions before you listen to the recording, then choose the correct answers.

a. 马克要准备带什么去台湾?（选出两个正确答案。）

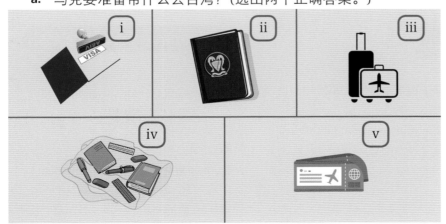

hù zhào 护照 passport	
sēn lín 森林 forest	
shā tān 沙滩 beach	
lái huí piào 来回票 return ticket	
lǚ xíng shè 旅行社 travel agency	
hǎi biān 海边 seaside	
jiāo qū 郊区 countryside; suburb	
lǚ xíng / lǚ yóu 旅行/ 旅游 trip	

b. 酒店在哪儿?（选出一个正确答案。)

| i | ii | iii |

3. 马克会去台湾参加夏令营。写出三样他要准备的东西。

Mark is going to a summer camp in Taiwan soon. Make a list of three things he will need to prepare for his trip.

4. 跟你的同学谈谈你的旅行计划，轮流提出和回答下面的问题。

With a partner, talk about your holiday plans. Take turns to ask and answer the following questions.

a. 暑假要去哪儿? **b.** 计划去那儿(的什么地方)做什么?

c. 住什么酒店? **d.** 要准备什么?

Grammar focus p.265

1. 不用: no need
★ 不用 + verb + noun
不用带护照。

2. 有没有: to have or not have
★ subject +有没有 + object?
志军有没有中国护照?

---

5. 练习写汉字。

Practise writing Chinese.

a. 按照笔画顺序写下面的字。

Write the characters by following the stroke order.

shā
沙 沙 沙 沙 沙 沙 沙 沙
　1　2　3　4　5　6　7

tān
滩 滩 滩 滩 滩 滩 滩 滩 滩 滩 滩 滩 滩
　1　2　3　4　5　6　7　8　9　10　11　12　13

b. 写出三样你会带去沙滩的东西。然后根据这三样东西，用 20–30字造句。

Make a list of three things you might take with you to the beach, then use 20–30 characters to write a sentence about them.

LESSON OBJECTIVES
- Identify a variety of holiday activities.
- Describe and discuss the activities you participate in during your holiday.

1. 四个人正在谈论自己想去的地方。每个句子听两遍。先看下面的图片和问题，再听录音，然后选择正确的图片。

   Four people are talking about where they want to visit. You will hear each sentence twice. Look at the pictures and the questions before you listen to the recording, then choose the correct picture for each person.

a. 小明想去哪儿?
b. 志军想去哪儿?
c. 杰西卡想去哪儿?
d. 阿里想去哪儿?

diàn yǐng yuàn
电影院 cinema

cān guān
参观 to visit

bó wù guǎn
博物馆 museum

dòng wù yuán
动物园 zoo

2. 阅读小明寄来的明信片，然后回答问题。

   Read the postcard from Xiaoming, then answer the following questions.

gāng
刚 just now, a moment ago

měi shù guǎn
美术馆 art gallery

bǎi huò shāng diàn
百货商店 department store

mǎi dōng xi / gòu wù
买东西 / 购物 to go shopping

yóu kè
游客 tourist

jì niàn pǐn
纪念品 souvenir

kè qì
客气 polite

míng xìn piàn
明信片 postcard

lǚ yóu jǐng diǎn
旅游景点 scenic spot

Postcard

杰西卡:
　　我和威廉昨天刚从台湾回来。我们都很累，所以今天才给你写信，不好意思!
　　我们游览了五天，参观了旅游景点，例如公园和动物园。我们也参观了不少博物馆和美术馆。晚上我们去逛街，威廉最喜欢去百货商店买东西，他在那儿买的东西不少。我不喜欢购物，所以买得不多。虽然晚上台湾游客不多，但是百货商店到十点才关门。买完东西后，我们还去了电影院看电影，电影院里的人不少。
　　我们给家人买了很多纪念品。我们很喜欢台湾。虽然我们不太会说中文，但是台湾人都对我们很客气。
　　我觉得台湾是一个很漂亮的地方，人很好，风景很美。我还会再去。
　　你喜欢这张明信片吗?

　　　　　　　　　　　　你的朋友
　　　　　　　　　　　　　小明
　　　　　　　　　　八月十一日

Place Stamp Here

Address:

To: Jessica

25, Evergreen Street,

London, UK

a. 小明跟谁去了台湾？　　**b.** 他们去了多久？

c. 他们参观了哪些旅游景点？　　**d.** 威廉最喜欢去哪儿？

e. 百货商店什么时候关门？

3. 和你的同学谈谈假期的休闲活动，轮流提出和回答下面的问题。

With a partner, talk about your holiday plans. Take turns to ask and answer the following questions.

a. 你假期有什么休闲活动？　　**b.** 你最喜欢哪一个？

c. 为什么？

4. 回复小明的明信片。写80–100个字。其中应该包括：

Write a response to Xiaoming's postcard from Activity 2. Write 80–100 characters. Include the following:

a. 你暑假去了哪儿？　　**b.** 你喜不喜欢去那儿？

c. 你在那儿做什么？　　**d.** 你觉得那地方怎么样？

5. 练习写汉字。

Practise writing Chinese.

a. 按照笔画顺序写下面的字。
Write the characters by following the stroke order.

bó
博 | 博 | 博 | 博 | 博 | 博 | 博 | 博 | 博 | 博 | 博 | 博
1　2　3　4　5　6　7　8　9　10　11　12

wù
物 | 物 | 物 | 物 | 物 | 物 | 物 | 物
1　2　3　4　5　6　7　8

guǎn
馆 | 馆 | 馆 | 馆 | 馆 | 馆 | 馆 | 馆 | 馆 | 馆 | 馆
1　2　3　4　5　6　7　8　9　10　11

b. 你上一次去博物馆是什么时候？用完整的句子回答问题。写30–40个字。

When was the last time you visited a museum? Write out your answer using 30–40 characters.

Grammar focus　p.266

1. 虽然……但是……：
although ... but / yet ...

★ 虽然 + subject + 但是 + contrary reaction

虽然小明不太会说英文，但是美国人都对他很客气。

2. 不多/不少：not much/not less

★ subject + verb + particle + (object) + 不多／不少
他买的东西不少。
我赚的钱不多。

LESSON OBJECTIVES
- Identify the vocabulary of common facilities in a hotel.
- Make a hotel reservation and state your requests.
- Discuss and review your experiences of staying in a hotel.

1. 看看下面的中文词语，把它们和正确的图片搭配起来。
Look at the vocabulary below. Match them with the correct pictures.

> bīng xiāng
> 冰箱 fridge; freezer

a. 游泳池 b. 空调 c. 书桌 d. 健身房 e. 上网 f. 冰箱

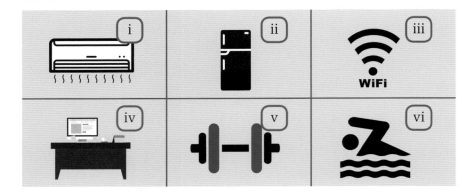

2. 阿里正在和心美谈去上海旅行的事情。先读问题，再听录音，然后写下答案。
Ali and Sammy are chatting about Ali's holiday in Shanghai. Read the questions before you listen to the recording, then write your answers.

a. 阿里喜欢酒店房间有什么？

b. 阿里喜欢住的酒店里有什么？

c. 为什么阿里要房间里有书桌？

d. 为什么心美叫阿里快去订酒店？

3. 和你的同学角色扮演阿里和他家人之间的对话，轮流提出和回答下面的问题。
With a partner, role-play a conversation between Ali and a family member about his holiday. Take turns to ask and answer the following questions:

a. 你要预订几间房？

b. 你要预订什么房间？

c. 你要预订几天？

d. 酒店里要有什么设施？

e. 房间里要有什么设施？

4. 阅读阿里和酒店服务员在电话中的对话，然后回答问题。

Read the conversation between Ali and the hotel staff, then answer the questions.

服务员：您好，这里是假期大饭店。

阿　里：您好，我姓汗，叫阿里。我刚在网上订了一间双人房和一间单人房，想确认一下。

服务员：汗先生您好，您一共订了两间房。从七月三日到七月七日，对吗？

阿　里：对，四个晚上，一共五天四夜。

服务员：因为七月三日到七月七日不是假期，旅客不多，所以我们有很多空房。您想把单人房换成双人房吗？

阿　里：双人房跟单人房的设施和价钱都一样吗？

服务员：都一样，都有空调和书桌，都可以上网。双人房还包括早饭。

阿　里：好的，我换双人房。酒店里有游泳池和健身房吗？

服务员：有。我们酒店不但有游泳池，而且还有一个很大的健身房。游泳池在酒店二楼。健身房在一楼。

阿　里：太好了，谢谢！

服务员：不客气，再见！

阿　里：再见！

a. 阿里预订了哪一间酒店？

b. 阿里预订了多少天晚上的房间？

c. 为什么酒店有很多空房？

d. 双人房包括什么？

5. 根据下面的例子，给一家你以前住过的酒店写一篇网上评论。写50–60个字。

Using the example below, write an online review for a hotel you stayed in recently. Write 50–60 characters.

阿里 假日大饭店　　48人看过
★★★☆☆

上个月从三号到七号，我在假日大饭店住了五天四夜。双人房的床很舒服，但是晚上睡觉的时候空调太热了。

👍 感谢 玩游全球　　　　⚠ 举报

---

fàn diàn
饭店 hotel; restaurant

lǚ kè
旅客 traveller; travel guest

bāo kuò
包括 to include

shuāng rén fáng
双人房 double room

dān rén fáng
单人房 single room

què rèn
确认 to confirm

tiān　　　yè
……天……夜 ... day ... night

kōng fáng
空房 unoccupied room

huàn
换 to exchange; change

Grammar focus　**p.266**

1. 不但……而且/还……:
not only ... but also ...

★ noun + 不但 + description A, 而且(还)/还/也
+ description B

酒店房间里不但有计算机，而且还能免费上网。

2. 都: also, both, all

★ noun A + noun B + 都 + action

陈明和心美都去过中国。

rè
热 hot

LESSON OBJECTIVES
- Identify common signs in public places.
- Report and deal with lost property.
- Describe an incident that happened whilst on holiday.

1. 看看下面的告标牌，把它们和正确的意思搭配起来。

Look at the signs below. Match them with the correct meanings.

zī xún zhōng xīn
咨询中心 information centre

wēi xiǎn
危险 danger; dangerous

jìn zhǐ tíng chē
禁止停车 no parking

qǐng wù zhào xiàng qǐng wù pāi zhào
请勿照相/ 请勿拍照
no photography

jìn zhǐ rù nèi
禁止入内 no entry

i. 禁止停车 **ii.** 请勿拍照 **iii.** 禁止入内 **iv.** 咨询中心 **v.** 危险 **vi.** 注意

2. 阅读以下的故事，然后回答问题。

Read the story below, then answer the questions.

难忘的一天

　　小华和马克一起到动物园参观。因为那天是假期，所以动物园有很多人。小华和马克打算先到森林区去，因为那儿人比较少。

　　在森林区的时候，因为小华没有看清楚警告标牌写着"注意安全"，所以他掉进水里受伤了。马克带他到急诊室看医生。

　　到急诊室以后，小华发觉钱包丢失了。因为马克觉得是小偷偷走钱包的，所以他去了咨询中心，打算请职员帮忙报警。职员说他在取款机旁边找到小华的钱包，他会把它送到急诊室去。小华拿回钱包并向职员道谢，他想：钱包应该是刚才我在换钱时丢失的吧！

　　虽然那一天小华没有看到动物，但是他很高兴，因为他最后还是找回了他的钱包。

dǎ suàn
打算 to plan

jǐng gào biāo pái
警告标牌 warning sign

shòu shāng
受伤 to be injured

jí zhěn shì
急诊室 A & E; emergency room

diū shī
丢失 to lose

xiǎo tōu / pá shǒu
小偷/扒手 thief; pickpocket

zhí yuán
职员 staff

bào jǐng
报警 to call the police

ná
拿 to hold

huàn qián
换钱 to change money

diào jìn
掉进 to fall in

fā jué
发觉 to realise; to find

qǔ kuǎn jī
取款机 ATM

a. 为什么动物园有很多人？　　b. 标牌上写着什么？

c. 为什么马克想报警？　　　　d. 小华的钱包在哪儿找到的？

e. 为什么小华觉得很高兴？

3. 马克正向咨询中心的职员求助。先读问题，再听录音，然后写下答案。

Mark is seeking help from a staff member at the information centre. Read the questions before you listen to the recording, then answer them.

a. 钱包大概在什么时候丢的？　　b. 钱包里大概有多少钱？

c. 钱包是什么颜色？　　　　　　d. 钱包可能是谁的？

4. 和你的同学角色扮演一个警察和旅行时丢了钱包的人之间的对话，轮流提出和回答下面的问题。

With a partner, role-play a conversation between a police officer and a person who's lost their wallet on holiday. Take turns to ask and answer the following questions.

a. 你什么时候丢了钱包？　　b. 你在哪儿丢了钱包？

c. 你的钱包里有多少钱？　　d. 你的钱包是什么颜色的？

5. 写一篇日记谈谈丢失钱包的事。写100–120个字。其中应该包括：

Write a diary entry about losing your wallet. Write 100–120 characters. You should include the following:

a. 什么时候丢失钱包？　　b. 在哪儿丢失钱包？

c. 丢失钱包之前跟谁在一起？　　d. 丢失钱包时在做什么？

e. 钱包最后找到了没有？

Grammar focus　p.266

1. 大概/可能/好像：approximately / probably / likely

★ subject + 大概 / 可能 / 好像 + 是 + situation

小华的钱包不见了，大概是他在兑换外币的时候丢失的吧。

这个钱包可能是小华的。

小华的钱包好像是红色的。

2. 因为……所以……：

Because ... so ...

★ 因为 + complete sentence (cause)，所以 + complete sentence (consequence)

因为今天是假期，所以公园有很多人。

1. 把以下的词语翻译成中文，并写下来。

a. red packet

b. hotel

c. Christmas tree

d. passport

e. beach

f. film or movie

g. air conditioning

h. no photography

i. shopping

j. to celebrate

k. travel agency

2. 阅读下面的广告，然后用右边的词语填空。

北京 BEIJING

活动日期：7 (d) 9 (e) 一7月13日

学校北京夏令营：
(a) 要到暑假了！同学 (b) 准备好了 (c)？

行程表

日期	行程
7月9日以前	同学们要 (f) 行李、护照和机票准备好
7月9日	(g) 上海出发到北京
7月10日	● 开学典礼 ● 课外活动：跟中国的学生一起写汉字
7月11日	● 课堂活动：看中文电影 (h) 四合院
7月12日	● 课堂活动：中文朗诵比赛 ● 游览长城
7月13日	坐飞机 回家

联系人: 陈老师 (kchan@example.com)

注意：
● (i) 北京天气不错，但是同学们要带雨伞。
● 因为这是学校夏令营，
(j) 同学们在活动的时候要穿校服。

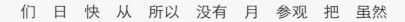
们　日　快　从　所以　没有　月　参观　把　虽然

3. 你将听到几个句子。先读问题，再听录音，然后选择唯一正确的答案。

a. 我们要去哪儿？

i.  ii.  iii.

b. 这间酒店有什么？

i.  ii.  iii.

4. 一位记者正在采访马克。先读问题，再听录音，然后写下答案。

a. 记者为什么选择采访马克？   **b.** 马克是用哪两个方法学会中文的？

c. 马克觉得台湾的故宫博物馆怎么样？   **d.** 马克回家后打算建议他的学校做什么？

5. 你准备去旅行。和你的同学角色扮演与父母之间的对话，轮流提出和回答下面的问题。

a. 你去哪儿旅行？   **b.** 你准备在那儿住几天？   **c.** 你跟谁一起去？

d. 你会带什么东西？   **e.** 你会换多少钱？

6. 上个月，你和朋友一起去了外国旅行。给你爷爷写一封信。写120–150个字。其中应该包括：

a. 你们去了什么地方？   **b.** 怎么去的？   **c.** 在那儿做了什么？

d. 最喜欢做什么？   **e.** 为什么？

UNIT OBJECTIVES

- Describe your home town and the surrounding area.
- Give information about the public facilities in your home town.
- Give information about the local customs and specialities of different places.

- Describe and discuss your shopping experiences.
- Describe a range of banking-related activities.
- Describe and discuss a range of activities and events organised by your local community.

1. 看看下面的中文词语，把它们和正确的英文意思搭配起来。
   Look at the Chinese vocabulary below. Match each one to the correct English meaning.

   a. 博物馆　　**b.** 电影院　　**c.** 动物园　　**d.** 美术馆

   e. 公园　　**f.** 剧场　　**g.** 百货商店

   i. zoo　　**ii.** theatre　　**iii.** park　　**iv.** department store

   v. museum　　**vi.** cinema　　**vii.** art gallery

   jù chǎng
   剧场 theatre

   bǎi huò shāng diàn / gōng sī
   百货商店/公司 department store

2. 看看下面的图片，把它们和正确的词语搭配起来。
   Look at the pictures below and match them to the correct vocabulary.

    a　 b　 c　 d　 e

   i. 城市　　**ii.** 农村　　**iii.** 山区　　**iv.** 海边　　**v.** 郊区

   nóng cūn
   农村 rural area

   shān qū
   山区 hillside

   jiāo qū
   郊区 suburb; countryside

3. 练习写汉字。
   Practise writing Chinese.

   a. 按照笔画顺序写下面的字。
   Write the characters by following the stroke order.

   chéng
   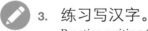
   城 城 城 城 城 城 城 城 城 城
   　　1　2　3　4　5　6　7　8　9

   shì
   市 市 市 市 市 市
   　　1　2　3　4　5

b. 用以上词语造句。写10–20个字。
Write a sentence of your own using the above vocabulary. Write 10–20 characters.

4. 小明正在向他的同学介绍他居住的地方。先读问题，再听录音，然后选择正确的答案。
Xiaoming is introducing himself to his new classmates. Read the questions before you listen to the recording, then choose the correct answers.

a. 小明住在哪个城市？	**b.** 小明家的公寓在几楼？
i. 香港	**i.** 六楼
ii. 伦敦	**ii.** 十一楼
iii. 杭州	**iii.** 十八楼
c. 谁和他一起住？	**d.** 为什么他们喜欢住在那里？
i. 爸爸和妈妈	**i.** 因为楼很古老
ii. 爷爷和奶奶	**ii.** 因为公寓楼是新的
	iii. 因为房子非常大

e. 那栋楼的旁边有一家什么？
   i. 一家超市
   ii. 一所学校
   iii. 一个公园

gōng yù
公寓 apartment

lóu
楼 building or storey; floor

dòng
栋 measure word for a building

xiāng gǎng
香港 Hong Kong

lún dūn
伦敦 London

háng zhōu
杭州 Hangzhou

chāo shì
超市 supermarket

5. 阅读下面的内容，然后回答问题。
Read the passage below and answer the questions.

我叫本杰明，来自苏格兰的爱丁堡。今年夏天我在杭州一所中学参加中文夏令营的时候住在中国学生小平的家里。大多数杭州人都住公寓，小平家也住公寓。他家的公寓在城市的中心，附近有好几家大超市，十分方便。我喜欢他的家，因为他家的公寓很大，而且在高层公寓的十楼，所以从他们家能看到美丽的西湖。

a. 本杰明来自哪一个城市？

b. 本杰明今年夏天在杭州做什么？

c. 小平的家在市中心还是郊区？

d. 为什么本杰明喜欢小平家的公寓？

sū gé lán
苏格兰 Scotland

ài dīng bǎo
爱丁堡 Edinburgh

dà duō shù
大多数 majority

Grammar focus   p.267

的: a particle word that can be used as a possessive indicator

★ pro(noun) A + 的 + noun B
   他的家

6. 和你的同学轮流介绍自己住的地方。
With a partner, talk about where you live.

LESSON OBJECTIVE

● Identify and discuss the features in your home town.

1. 看看下面的图片，把它们和正确的词语搭配起来。
   Look at the pictures below and match them with the correct vocabulary.

guó jì
国际 international

cūn zi
村(子) village

xiǎo zhèn
小镇 small town

hǎi dǎo
海岛 island

i. 国际城市   **ii.** 小城   **iii.** 海边小镇
iv. 小山村   **v.** 海岛

2. 阅读下面的内容，然后判断后面的叙述是对或错。
   Read the passage, then decide if the following statements are true or false.

大家好，我叫本杰明。我来自英国。英国包括英格兰、威尔士、苏格兰和北爱尔兰。我的家乡就是苏格兰的爱丁堡。爱丁堡是一座非常古老的城市，有许许多多的名胜古迹，其中最有名的是爱丁堡城堡。爱丁堡也是英国有名的艺术中心，每年夏天七八月这里有爱丁堡文化艺术节，艺术家们在大街上的免费的精彩表演吸引了来自世界各地的游客。

a. 本杰明来自英国的北爱尔兰。

b. 他的家乡是一座很年轻的城市。

c. 本杰明家乡最有名的古迹是一座城堡。

d. 文化艺术节是在每年的秋季。

e. 文化艺术节期间的活动全都在室内举行。

jiā xiāng
家乡 home town

gǔ lǎo
古老 ancient

míng shèng gǔ jì
名胜古迹 place of interest; historic site

yì shù
艺术 art

miǎn fèi de
免费的 free of charge

chéng bǎo
城堡 castle

jīng cǎi
精彩 splendid

xī yǐn
吸引 to attract

shì jiè gè dì
世界各地 all round the world

shì nèi
室内 indoor

3. 先读下面的短文和词语，再听录音，然后选择正确的答案填空。

Read the paragraph and vocabulary before you listen to the recording. Then choose the correct answers to fill in the gaps.

> 我的名字是海英，来自韩国的 **(a)**。我的家乡是一个 **(b)**，离海很 **(c)**。这个地方因为有 **(d)** 干净的沙滩，所以会有很多 **(e)**，特别是夏天的时候。我爱我的家乡，因为这里不仅风景很美，而且居民也十分 **(f)**。

jū mín
居民 resident

hán guó
韩国 South Korea
shǒu ěr
首尔 Seoul (capital city of South Korea)
fǔ shān
釜山 Busan (a city in South Korea)

a. i. 首尔 　**b. i.** 国际大都市 　**c. i.** 近 　**d. i.** 美丽的 　**e. i.** 游客 　**f. i.** 热情好客

　ii. 釜山 　　**ii.** 旅游名城 　　**ii.** 远 　　**ii.** 安静的 　　**ii.** 买东西的人 　　**ii.** 友好

4. 先读问题，再听录音，然后选择唯一正确的答案。

Read the questions before you listen to the recording. Then choose one correct answer for each question.

a. 大海住在什么样的地方？
- **i.** 农村
- **ii.** 大城市
- **iii.** 小镇

b. 朱莉的家乡什么时候有很多游客？
- **i.** 春天
- **ii.** 夏天
- **iii.** 秋天

c. 为什么小婷喜欢家乡的冬季？
- **i.** 可以吃饺子
- **ii.** 可以在冰上钓鱼
- **iii.** 可以玩滑雪

d. 小宝的家乡是在哪儿？
- **i.** 一座国际城市
- **ii.** 一座海边小镇
- **iii.** 一个美丽的小山村

chūn tiān
春天 spring
qiū tiān
秋天 autumn
mǎ lù
马路 road
dù jià
度假 (to go on) holiday
dōng tiān
冬天 winter

sì miàn
四面 all sides

Grammar focus　p.267

动词的重叠: two-syllable, duplicated verbs

★ verb + verb + noun

（这里有许多）来来往往的人们。

5. 和你的同学轮流提出和回答下面的问题，并写出答案。

With a partner, take turns to ask and answer the following questions. Then write out your answers.

a. 你现在住在哪里？

b. 你的家乡是一个什么样的地方？叫什么？

c. 你的家乡最有名的名胜古迹是什么？

d. 你觉得你的家乡怎么样？

LESSON OBJECTIVE

● Describe and discuss the natural and manmade features in your home town.

1. 看看下面的图片，把它们和正确的词语搭配起来。
   Look at the pictures below and match them with the correct vocabulary.

 a
 b
 c
 d
 e

| **i.** 公园 | **ii.** 树 | **iii.** 花 | **iv.** 绿草地 | **v.** 小山 |

shù
树 tree

cǎo dì
草地 grassland; meadow; lawn

2. 翻译以下词语，并用中文写下来。
   Translate these English terms into Chinese and write them out.

mountain   sea   river   lake   geography   scenery

3. 阅读下面的内容，然后选择正确的词组填空。
   Read the passage, then choose the correct words to fill the blanks.

高高兴兴地   一点儿   因为   美丽的   秋天   一条

我的家乡是一个(a)小山村。村子附近的山上是一片一片的水果园，果园里有很多苹果树。每到(b)，大家就(c)上山采摘水果。村子的后面有(d)长长的小河，河水很干净，可以看到鱼儿们在水里游来游去。这里的夏天(e)都不热，也不常常下雨，是家乡的最好的季节，也是最美的季节，(f)处处都是五颜六色的花。

jì jié
季节 season

cǎi zhāi
采摘 to pick (fruit)

chù chù
处处 everywhere

wǔ yán liù sè
五颜六色 colourful

4. 四个人正在谈论自己的家乡。先读问题，再听录音，然后选择正确的答案。

Four people are talking about their home towns. Read the questions before you listen to the recording, then choose the correct answers.

a. 海岛因为什么吸引了很多游客？
  i. 友好的人
  ii. 高高的大楼
  iii. 迷人的海景

b. 小文的家乡是一个什么样的地方？
  i. 国际化的大城市
  ii. 美丽的海边小城
  iii. 古老的历史名城

c. 保罗家乡的小镇上有什么？
  i. 很多古老的树木
  ii. 很多很老的房子
  iii. 很多汽车

d. 为什么小月不想住在她的家乡？
  i. 有很多工厂，有污染
  ii. 有很多车子
  iii. 有很多狗，晚上不安静

5. 阅读下面艾玛写的短文，然后回答问题。

Read the short passage by Emma, then answer the questions.

> 我叫艾玛，来自温哥华。我觉得温哥华是北美最棒的城市。温哥华在加拿大的西海岸，不仅城市中心有很多公园、绿地，而且周边还有高山、森林和海洋。这里既有北美最好的滑雪场，又有迷人的海滩。也许你会觉得奇怪，但这是真的：如果你夏天来温哥华，在一天的时间里真的既能滑雪，又能冲浪。温哥华是一个多元文化的地方，在这里居住着来自世界各地的人，是一个重要的华人聚居地，这里有北美洲第二大的唐人街。总之温哥华是一个十分有意思的城市，欢迎您来我的家乡！

6. 和你的同学谈谈家乡的环境，轮流提出和回答下面的问题。

With a partner, talk about the environment in your home town. Take turns to ask and answer the following questions.

a. 你的家乡在哪里？

b. 你的家乡的环境好不好？有没有山、河、湖或海？

c. 你的家乡是一个热闹的地方吗？

d. 去你的家乡哪一个季节最好？为什么？

---

dà lóu
大楼 skyscrapers; high rises

gōng chǎng
工厂 factory

wū rǎn
污染 pollution

xīn xiān
新鲜 fresh

kōng qì
空气 air

shāng diàn
商店 shop

jiàn zhù
建筑 architecture; building

---

hǎi àn
海岸 coast

zhōu biān
周边 surroundings

jì　　　yòu
既……又…… both ... and ...

mí rén de
迷人的 charming

chōng làng
冲浪 surfing

duō yuán wén huà
多元文化 multicultural

jù jū dì
聚居地 settlement

táng rén jiē
唐人街 Chinatown

a. 艾玛的家乡是哪一个城市？

b. 这个城市在加拿大的哪个方向？

c. 那个城市的周边有哪三个地理景观？

d. 夏天的时候在那里可以做哪两个很特别的运动？

e. 为什么说那是一个多元文化的地方？

Grammar focus p.267

第: ordinal number

★ 第 + number + stative verb
这里有北美洲第二大的（唐人街）。

rè nao
热闹 lively

LESSON OBJECTIVES
- Identify the leisure facilities in your home town.
- Describe and discuss the leisure activities you can do in your home town.

1. 写下五个休闲设施。
Make a list of five leisure facilities.

2. 先读问题，再听录音，然后选择正确的答案。
Read the questions before you listen to the recording, then choose the correct answers.

a. 马克住的城市的图书馆哪天不开放？
- **i.** 星期一
- **ii.** 星期二
- **iii.** 星期三

b. 小月家附近的休闲中心里除了可以跑步、游泳，还可以做什么？
- **i.** 打篮球
- **ii.** 踢足球
- **iii.** 打羽毛球

c. 本杰明住的小镇上没有什么？
- **i.** 健身中心
- **ii.** 电影院
- **iii.** 剧场

d. 日晴住的小城很方便，因为附近有什么？
- **i.** 网吧
- **ii.** 电影院
- **iii.** 购物的地方

kāi fàng
开放 open

wǎng bā
网吧 internet cafe

lìng yī gè
另 (一个) another

bàng wǎn
傍晚 early evening; dusk

Grammar focus p.267

děi
得 : to have to

★ subject + 得 + action

他（每天）得坐一个小时的火车去上班。

3. 阅读下面内容，判断下面的叙述是对或错。
Read the following passage and decide if the following statements are true or false.

> 　　我住的城市中心有一座非常现代化的图书馆。图书馆是免费的，那里很安静，而且有很多大大的书桌和舒服的椅子，所以很多学生喜欢去那儿看书或做作业。因为我家的公寓楼离图书馆很近，所以每个星期六上午我都会走路到图书馆看书，看累了，就会在图书馆的咖啡厅里买点儿东西吃，然后继续看。夏天图书馆会开放到晚上九点，因为有空调，吸引了很多市民去那里看书。

a. 图书馆在市中心。

b. 图书馆很受学生们的欢迎。

c. 我的家离图书馆很远，所以去那儿要坐公共汽车。

d. 图书馆里有一家小吃店。

e. 夏天图书馆里因为开空调吸引了很多市民去那里看书。

> xiàn dài huà
> 现代化 modern

> jì xù
> 继续 to carry on; to continue

4. 在你住的地方，青少年最喜欢去哪个地方？为什么？写40–50个字。
In your home town, which place is the most popular among teenagers and why? Write your answer in 40–50 characters.

5. 和你的同学谈谈你们居住的城市的休闲娱乐设施，轮流提出和回答下面的问题。
With a partner, talk about the leisure facilities in your home town. Take turns to ask and answer the following questions.

a. 这里最好的游泳馆是哪一家？为什么？

b. 你多久去一次游泳馆？和谁一起？

c. 除了游泳馆，这里还有哪些青少年爱去玩的地方？

d. 这个周末我们可以一起去这个城市的哪个地方玩儿？

LESSON OBJECTIVE
- Talk about the local specialities and customs of different places.

1. 看看下面的价目表。把图片和正确的价钱搭配起来。
   Look at the price list. Then match each picture with the correct price.

chuán tǒng mín zú fú zhuāng
传统民族服装 traditional costume

mín gē
民歌 folk song

茶杯 50元/个　　　传统民族服装 200元/件
民歌CD 65元/张　　　筷子 6元/双

a
b
c
d

i. 六元　**ii.** 五十元　**iii.** 六十五元　**iv.** 两百元

yìn dù ní xī yà / yìn ní
印度尼西亚/印尼 Indonesia

qì hòu
气候 climate

2. 阅读下面三段关于家乡特产的文字，然后回答问题。
   Read the following passages about local specialities, then answer the questions.

马来西亚的一年四季都很热，而且常常下雨。在马来西亚，一年四季都可以吃到各式各样的热带水果。

印度尼西亚有名的手工艺品有很多，最受欢迎的就是皮影木偶。如果你有爱喝咖啡的朋友们，印尼咖啡也是很不错的。

rè dài
热带 tropical

shǒu gōng yì pǐn
手工艺品 artifact; handicraft

pí yǐng mù ǒu
皮影木偶 shadow puppet

chū chǎn
出产 to produce

a. 马来西亚出产的是什么？
   i. 苹果　　**ii.** 茶　　**iii.** 热带水果

b. 马来西亚的气候怎么样？
   i. 一年四季都很热，而且雨水也多。
   ii. 一年四季都很热，但是很少下雨。

c. 印度尼西亚的什么很有名？举两个例子。

Grammar focus　p.267

的: added between a modifier and a noun
★ modifier (stative verb) + 的 + noun
特别的活动

3. 用 "传统" 造一个10–20字的句子，并写下来。
Write a sentence of your own using the vocabulary. Write 10–20 characters.

> huài
> 坏 bad/broken

4. 先读问题，再听录音，然后完成句子。
Read the questions before you listen to the recording, then complete the sentences.

> má pó dòu fu
> 麻婆豆腐 ma po tofu: a spicy Chinese
> dish from Sichuan province

a. 她买的中国传统
服装……。
  i. 太大了
  ii. 太小了
  iii. 颜色不对

b. 他要一份……
麻婆豆腐。
  i. 非常辣的
  ii. 不辣的
  iii. 有一点辣的

c. 她买的民歌
CD……。
  i. 丢了
  ii. 不见了
  iii. 是坏的

d. 他想看……。
  i. 电影
  ii. 民歌表演
  iii. 传统舞蹈表演

5. 和你的同学谈谈家乡的特产，轮流提出和回答下面的问题。
With a partner, talk about the local produce and specialities from your home town. Take turns to ask and answer these questions.

a. 你的家乡在哪里？

b. 你的家乡出产哪些特产，比如水果、酒、茶叶？

c. 如果我去你的家乡玩，你推荐我买什么纪念品？

d. 如果我去你的家乡，你推荐我吃什么特色菜？

Cultural spotlight

> xī shuāng bǎn nà de pō shuǐ jié
> 西双版纳的泼水节 Xishuangbanna's water festival

西双版纳位于中国的云南省西南部。那里气候四季温暖湿润，有中国唯一的热带雨林区。西双版纳除了有美丽的自然景观，还有丰富的人文历史。西双版纳泼水节是傣族人民一年一度的传统节日，是他们的春节。泼水节也被称为宋干节，是云南少数民族中影响最大，参加人数最多的节日。一般在每年的四月中旬举行，为期三至五天。这期间，大家用纯净的清水相互泼洒。节日的活动除了泼水，还包括跳舞、浴佛、赛龙舟。这样盛大的传统节日当然还少不了放烟花和节日美食—糯米饭。

a. 你觉得泼水这动作象征什么？

b. 在你住的国家，哪个民族节日参加的人数最多？为什么那个节日最受欢迎？

5.6 购物
SHOPPING

LESSON OBJECTIVES
- Identify a range of shopping places and what they sell.
- Describe and discuss your shopping experiences.

1. 看看下面的英文词语，把它们和正确的中文名称搭配起来。
Look at the English words. Match them with their correct Chinese names.

a. shopping mall   b. market   c. department store   d. book shop

i. 书店   ii. 购物中心   iii. 市场   iv. 百货公司

rì cháng yòng pǐn
日常用品 everyday item

tíng chē chǎng
停车场 car park

máo jīn
毛巾 towel

2. 阅读下面的百货大楼楼层分布，然后回答问题。
Read the following floor sign of a department store, then answer the questions.

a. 买露营需要的东西要去哪层楼？
b. 买几件男生穿的衬衣去哪层楼？
c. 肚子饿了，可以去哪儿吃东西？
d. 买纪念品去哪层楼？
e. 买日常用品比如毛巾去哪层楼？
f. 百货大楼的停车场在哪儿？

五楼	小吃店/咖啡馆/甜品店
四楼	女装/女鞋/女包
三楼	男装/男鞋/男包
二楼	运动装/运动鞋/户外用品馆
一楼	童装/手机/电脑/相机
地下一层	食品区/纪念品/日常用品
地下二层	停车场

gù kè
顾客 customer

fù qián
付钱 to pay

fú wù yuán
服务员 shop-floor assistant

dǎ zhé
打折 to give a discount

shōu jù
收据 receipt

3. 你将会听到两段录音。先读问题，再听录音，然后完成句子。
You will hear two recordings. Read the questions before you listen to each clip, then complete the sentences.

录音 1
a. 杰西卡在北京……。
  i. 上大学   ii. 工作   iii. 旅游
b. 杰西卡给妈妈买了……。
  i. 绿茶   ii. 红茶   iii. 花茶
c. 她给爸爸买了……。
  i. 一本书   ii. 一部手机
  iii. 一幅山水画

录音 2
d. 顾客买了……。
  i. 一条小号的黑裤子   ii. 一条中号的黑裤子
  iii. 一条大号的黑裤子
e. 那家商店这个周末商品都是……。
  i. 七折   ii. 六折   iii. 半价
f. 顾客用……付钱。
  i. 手机   ii. 现金   iii. 银行卡

4. 和你的同学角色扮演一个服务员和时装店顾客之间的对话，轮流提出和回答下面的问题。

With a partner, role-play a conversation between a shop assistant and a customer in a clothes shop. Take turns to ask and answer the following questions.

a. 您好。您买什么？

b. 您喜欢什么颜色的？

c. 您需要多大号的？

d. 您需要试一试吗？

e. 除了……，您还需要什么？

f. 您是用现金还是信用卡？

5. 一名杂志记者正在访问一位游客。阅读他们的对话，然后回答问题。

A magazine journalist is interviewing a tourist in London. Read their dialogue, then answer the questions.

记者：这是您第一次来伦敦吗？

游客：不是的，这是我第四次来伦敦了。 我特别喜欢这个城市。

记者：您觉得伦敦怎么样？

游客：我觉得伦敦是一个购物天堂。这里很适合购物，特别是这个月很多商场都在大减价。

记者：您在伦敦去了哪些地方购物呢？

游客：伦敦的几家有名的百货公司我都逛过了，这些百货公司卖很多各式各样的品牌，但是有点儿贵。在伦敦一定得逛一逛牛津街，有很多适合我们年轻人的衣服和鞋子的品牌。

记者：您买了一些什么东西？

游客：我买了一个很时尚的蓝色的书包，打算送给我上中学的弟弟。我给自己买了一件深绿色的毛衣。还有伦敦的巧克力又精美又便宜，我买了很多，打算带回去送给朋友们。

记者：如果有朋友来伦敦，你推荐他们去哪里购物？

游客：除了要看一看这些百货公司和牛津街，来英国的朋友们更应该去伦敦各区的二手市场，因为在这些市场的小店里常常能找到独一无二的纪念品。

jiǎn jià
减价 to reduce (in price); reduction or sale

pián yi
便宜 cheap

tiān táng
天堂 heaven

shì hé
适合 be suitable for; suit; fit

pǐn pái
品牌 brand

shí shàng de
时尚的 fashionable

jīng měi de
精美的 fine; exquisite

èr shǒu
二手 second-hand; pre-owned

dú yī wú èr de
独一无二的 unique

a. 游客已经来过伦敦几次了？

b. 游客去了哪些地方购物？

c. 她买了什么东西？ 是给谁买的？

d. 为什么她买了很多巧克力？

e. 最后游客还推荐去哪里逛？ 为什么？

5.7 在银行
AT THE BANK

LESSON OBJECTIVES
- Identify and describe a variety of everyday banking needs.
- Identify a range of currencies from around the world.

1. 你将会听到六个关于银行的词组。每个词组听两遍。
   You will hear six banking-related terms in Chinese. You will hear each term twice.

   a. 把你听到的词组写下来。
   Write them in the order you hear.

   b. 看看以上词语。根据每一个词语的笔划数量，把它们排列次序。先从笔划最少的开始写。
   Look at the terms above. Rank them in order of combined number of strokes, starting with the term with the lowest number.

yín háng	银行 bank
xiàn jīn	现金 cash
xìn yòng kǎ	信用卡 credit card
zhī piào	支票 cheque

2. 阿里今年在北京一所中学做交换生，他和小文谈话。
   阅读下面的对话，然后选择唯一正确的答案回答问题。
   Ali is an exchange student in Beijing. He is talking to his classmate Xiaowen. Read their conversation, then choose the correct answer for each question.

cún qián	存钱 to deposit money
qǔ qián kuǎn	取钱/款 to withdraw money

jiāo huàn shēng 交换生 exchange student

> 阿里：小文，学校附近有没有银行？我需要去一趟银行。
>
> 小文：有，在学校大门对面那条街上就有一家比较大的银行。你想去银行做什么？
>
> 阿里：哦，我想去银行存钱，我身上的现金太多了。
>
> 小文：我和你一起去吧。我正好要去银行取款，我身上没有钱了。

a. 阿里在北京做什么？
   i. 旅游　　ii. 工作　　iii. 做交换生

b. 阿里需要去哪儿?
   i. 学校　　ii. 银行　　iii. 医院

c. 阿里要去那里做什么？
   i. 换钱　　ii. 办银行卡　　iii. 存钱

3. 三个人正在与银行工作人员谈话。先读问题，再听录音，然后选择正确的答案。

Three people are talking to staff members in a bank. Read the questions before you listen to each recording, then choose the correct answers.

a. 第一个人需要换多少美元？
- **i.** 八百美元
- **ii.** 五百美元
- **iii.** 三百美元

b. 第二个人需要什么？
- **i.** 换钱
- **ii.** 办一张银行卡
- **iii.** 开办网上银行

c. 第三个人在银行做什么？
- **i.** 给女儿办银行卡
- **ii.** 给女儿汇款
- **iii.** 给女儿换钱

4. 和你的同学角色扮演一个银行服务员和顾客之间的对话，轮流提出和回答下面的问题.

With a partner, role-play a conversation between a bank clerk and a customer. Take turns to ask and answer these questions.

a. 您好。您需要办什么？取钱还是换钱？

b. 您要换什么钱？　　**c.** 您有多少人民币/美元/英镑？

d. 您的护照带来了吗？　　**e.** 您还需要什么服务？

5. 你在中国旅游，可是钱不够用了。给你的父母发一个50字以内的短信，请他们给你汇钱。

Your travel funds have run out while travelling in China. Send a text of less than 50 characters to ask your parents to send you some money.

---

rén mín bì
人民币 Chinese currency (Renminbi)

bàn lǐ
办(理) to arrange for something to be done

měi yuán
美元 American dollar

huì kuǎn
汇款 to transfer money

yīng bàng
英镑 British Sterling (pound)

fú wù
服务 service

Grammar focus　p.268

1. Money expressions in Chinese
- ★ number + measure word + currency

两千块人民币、五百镑英镑、九十九美元

2. 两 and 二
- ★ Both mean "two" and are used in number expressions.
We say 二十、二十五 (not 两十、两十五), and we can say 二百、二千 but 两百、两千 are more common.

Cultural spotlight

huì fēng yín háng de lì shǐ
汇丰银行的历史 The History of HSBC

汇丰银行的中文名称有汇集财富的意思，英文名HSBC是从香港上海汇丰银行的首字母而来。香港上海汇丰银行有限公司于1865年在香港和上海成立，是汇丰集团的创始成员，并于当年在香港及中国发行货币，为当时亚洲和欧洲之间越来越频繁的商业贸易活动提供了资金。银行至今已有一百五十多年的历史了。现在汇丰银行的业务网络遍及欧洲、亚太区、中东及北非、北美和拉丁美洲的七十多个国家和地区，是世界上最大的银行之一。

a. 列出银行账户的三个功能。

b. 你认为未来所有的银行都会变成网上银行吗？

LESSON OBJECTIVES
- Describe the local amenities and public facilities in your community.
- Share with others your views on your community.

1. 看看下面的图片，把它们和正确的词语搭配起来。
   Look at the pictures below and match them to the correct Chinese words.

i. 地铁   ii. 火车站   iii. 汽车站   iv. 银行   v. 邮局   vi. 药店   vii. 警察局   viii. 停车场

2. 阅读下面广告的内容，然后回答问题。
   Read the advert below and answer the questions.

北京西城区现代化小区，小区里有健身房和游泳池。小公寓在北京西城区，现代化的高楼，两室一厅，不带家具，不带洗衣机和冰箱。周围有购物街、购物中心。离地铁四号线动物园站只有三百米，交通方便。而且邻居是一位非常好的人。

月租：六千人民币

如果你有兴趣，请给李丽发邮件：rental@example.com

a. 小区里面有哪些体育设施?

b. 公寓有几间卧室?

c. 地铁4号线离小区多远?

d. 公寓每个月的租金是多少?

---

dì tiě
地铁 underground train

huǒ chē zhàn
火车站 train station

qì chē zhàn
汽车站 bus terminal

yóu jú
邮局 post office

jǐng chá jú
警察局 police station

dài
带 to include

jiāo tōng
交通 transport

lín jū
邻居 neighbour

zhōu wéi
周围 surroundings

yuè zū
月租 monthly rent

zū jīn
租金 rent

3. 你将会听到两段录音。先读问题，再听录音，然后选择正确的答案完成句子。

You will hear two recordings. Read the questions before you listen to each clip, then choose the correct answer to complete each sentence.

rù zhù	
入住 to move in or check in	
xìng yùn	
幸运 fortunate; lucky	

录音 1

a. 小云家的公寓有……。

　ⅰ. 两间卧室

　ⅱ. 三间卧室

　ⅲ. 四间卧室

b. 小云不喜欢住那里，因为……。

　ⅰ. 是郊区

　ⅱ. 房子太小

　ⅲ. 离学校太远

Grammar focus　p.268

就 : just

★ noun + 就 + verb phrase

公园就在小区旁边。

录音 2

c. 珍妮住的老房子在上海的……。

　ⅰ. 郊区

　ⅱ. 市中心

　ⅲ. 外边

d. 小区的附近有一个……。

　ⅰ. 邮局

　ⅱ. 警察局

　ⅲ. 公园

e. 从珍妮家坐地铁到她的学校需要坐……。

　ⅰ. 十分钟

　ⅱ. 二十分钟

　ⅲ. 半个小时

4. 和你的同学谈谈你们住的小区，轮流提出和回答下面的问题，并写下你的回答。

With a partner, discuss the community you live in. Take turns to ask and answer the following questions, then write out your answers.

a. 你们的小区在市中心还是郊区？

b. 你们的小区里有哪些体育设施？

c. 小区的树多不多？

d. 小区的交通方便吗？为什么？

e. 小区有没有停车场？

5. 写你对小区的一种想法和怎么样让小区更好的建议，写30–50字。

Using 30–50 characters, express one opinion you have about your community, and what can be done to improve the area.

社区活动
COMMUNITY LIFE

LESSON OBJECTIVES
- Identify a range of community activities and events.
- Describe past and future events in your local community.

1. 看看下面关于社区活动的词语，把它们和正确的英文意思搭配起来。

Match these Chinese terms related to community activities with their correct English translations.

a. 春节晚会	**i.** tree-planting day
b. 制作彩灯	**ii.** lantern-making activity
c. 夏季慈善日	**iii.** Chinese New Year gala
d. 小区运动会	**iv.** summer charity event
e. 植树日	**v.** community sports day

> wǎn huì
> 晚会 evening party; gala
> cí shàn rì
> 慈善日 charity day

> zhì zuò
> 制作 to make
> cǎi dēng
> 彩灯 lantern
> zhí shù rì
> 植树日 tree-planting day

2. 先阅读下面的短文和答案选项，再听录音，然后用正确的词组填空。

Read the passage and the answer options below before you listen to the recording. Then choose the correct answer to fill in each gap.

> dǎ zhāo hū
> 打招呼 to greet
> chǎo nào
> 吵闹 noisy, raucous

我和家人都很喜欢我们现在住的小区，因为这里的人都很(a)，看到你都会和你打招呼。小区里有一个(b)社区活动中心，活动中心里有一个小的(c)。那里比较(d)，除了可以在那儿看书，还可以(e)。中心的一楼还有一间(f)，小孩子都喜欢去那里玩。小区活动中心因为有(g)，所以夏天晚上去那里聊天的人比较多。小区每个(h) 都会举行活动。

a. **i.** 快乐 **ii.** 友好		**b.** **i.** 很大的 **ii.** 很小的	
c. **i.** 教室 **ii.** 图书馆		**d.** **i.** 吵闹 **ii.** 安静	
e. **i.** 上网 **ii.** 聊天		**f.** **i.** 乒乓球室 **ii.** 羽毛球馆	
g. **i.** 电风扇 **ii.** 空调		**h.** **i.** 月 **ii.** 季节	

3. 阅读短文，判断下面的叙述是对或错。
Read the short passage and decide if the statements are true or false.

> 我们住的小区每年的九月都会组织一个慈善日。慈善日一般是星期六或星期天，因为是周末，所以有很多人参加。慈善日这天，你可以去老人院帮助老人，跟他们说说话或者唱歌给他们听，或者带他们去看电影，让他们不觉得无聊。你也可以去街上捡垃圾，让我们的城市更干净。

wú liáo	
无聊 bored; boring	
jiē	
街 street	

zǔ zhī	
组织 to organise	
lǎo rén yuàn	
老人院 old people's home	
jiǎn lā jī	
捡垃圾 to pick up litter/rubbish	

a. 小区慈善日是一个在秋天的活动。

b. 慈善日一般是在周末。

c. 慈善日参加的人不是很多。

d. 慈善日那天人们去老人院给老人们做饭。

e. 除了去老人院，你也可以去街上帮助游客。

f. 捡垃圾可以让我们住的地方干净。

4. 翻译下面的句子，并用中文写下来。
Translate the sentences below into Chinese, and write them down.

a. Last year I didn't participate in any charity events.

b. Every year during Spring Festival, our community centre organises many different activities.

5. 设计一张社区活动——植树日的海报。海报可以包括：
Design a poster to advertise a community activity–tree planting day. Include the following information:

a. 活动名称是什么？

b. 活动的目的是什么？

c. 时间是什么时候？地点在哪里？

d. 活动日那天你应该做什么？

6. 和你的同学轮流提出和回答下面一些关于社区活动的问题。
With a partner, take turns to ask and answer the following questions about activities in your community.

a. 你们社区经常有活动吗？

b. 你们小区最近组织了什么活动？

c. 你参加了吗？觉得怎么样？

d. 你希望小区以后组织什么有意思的活动？为什么？

> **Grammar focus** p.268
>
> 希望: to wish/to hope (to indicate future desires)
>
> ★ subject + 希望 + action
> 他希望明年去美国。

1. 写以下词组的英文意思。

a. 环境　b. 空气　c. 风景　d. 森林　e. 树林　f. 大河　g. 小湖　h. 海边　i. 山区

2. 和你的同学谈你们家乡的环境，轮流提出和回答下面的问题。

a. 你住在山区、郊区还是市区？　　　　b. 家乡有没有森林、大河或湖？

c. 你的家乡在不在海边？　　　　　　　d. 你觉得家乡的风景怎么样？

e. 你觉得你的家乡的环境好不好？为什么？

3. 先读问题，再听录音，然后写下答案。

a. 米娜今天去了哪儿？　　　　　　b. 杰克的家乡最有名的是什么？

c. 小文在百货商场买了什么礼物？花了多少钱？

d. 日晴住的小区这个周末将组织什么活动？

e. 本杰明觉得他现在住的小镇怎么样？

4. 尼克和朋友在电话里谈住在上海的感觉。阅读他们的对话，然后选择唯一正确的答案来完成句子。

朋友：尼克，你喜欢上海吗？
尼克：喜欢，因为上海非常现代，有很多有意思的地方。我最爱去的地方就是新天地娱乐中心，常常去那里逛街，那里有很多有特色的餐馆、咖啡馆、时装店、商店和书店。
朋友：尼克。你现在住在哪里？
尼克：我现在住在上海中山路上的一个小区里。
朋友：小区的设施怎么样？
尼克：小区的设施很好，游泳池，网球场都有。附近还有一条大河。我常常去河边跑步。
朋友：小区的人怎么样？
尼克：邻居们都很友好，看到我都会跟我打招呼。
朋友：住在那里方便吗？
尼克：很方便，因为附近有超市和购物中心，而且交通也方便，附近就有地铁站。
朋友：那我下次去上海可以住在你家吗？
尼克：可以，没问题。欢迎来我家。

a. 尼克觉得上海很……。

   i. 安静   **ii.** 无聊   **iii.** 现代

b. 尼克常常去新天地娱乐中心……。

   i. 跑步   **ii.** 逛街   **iii.** 打保龄球

c. 尼克现在住的地方附近有……。

   i. 一座小山   **ii.** 一条大河   **iii.** 一个公园

d. 尼克常常去小区附近的河边……。

   i. 跑步   **ii.** 打太极   **iii.** 跳舞

e. 他觉得小区的人很……。

   i. 友好   **ii.** 吵闹   **iii.** 不亲切

f. 那个小区的交通很方便，因为附近……。

   i. 有火车站   **ii.** 有地铁站   **iii.** 可以坐船

5. 写一篇电邮给你在国外的朋友，介绍你的家乡。写60–80个字。其中应该包括:

a. 家乡的基本信息

b. 名胜古迹和其他好玩的地方

c. 家乡的一些好吃的餐馆

6. 你的朋友来到你住的城市，你带他/她参观你住的城市的旅游咨询中心。和你的同学角色扮演你们之间的对话，轮流提出和回答下面的问题。

a. 旅游咨询中心在哪儿？

b. 旅游咨询中心有什么设施和服务？

c. 旅游咨询中心里可不可以换钱？

d. 那儿有没有卖纪念品的商店？可以买到什么有特色的纪念品？

UNIT OBJECTIVES

- Describe and discuss the weather and climate in different places.
- Discuss what to wear in different weather conditions.
- Share information about your location and give directions.
- Share your views on a range of environmental and conservation issues.
- Discuss your experiences of being around animals.

qíng tiān
晴天 sunny day

yīn tiān
阴天 cloudy day

1. 看看下面的图片，把它们和正确的词语搭配起来。

Look at the pictures below and match them with the correct vocabulary.

i. 晴天   ii. 夏天   iii. 秋天   iv. 下雨   v. 阴天   vi. 冬天   vii. 春天

2. 用正确的词语填空。

Complete the sentences by filling in the missing words.

tiān qì yù bào
天气预报 weather forecast

tài yáng
太阳 sun

cháo shī
潮湿 damp

gān zào
干燥 dry; arid

季节   天气   气候   天气预报

今天(a) 非常好，可以看到太阳。
一年有四个(b)：春、夏、秋、冬。
(c) 说今天天气很好，我们可以去公园玩。
北京春天的(d)和香港的很不一样。香港的春天很暖和和潮湿，
北京的春天很凉快也很干燥。

3. 志军正在跟小明谈话。先读问题，再听录音，然后选择唯一正确的答案。

Zhijun and Xiaoming are talking. Read the questions before you listen to the recording, then choose the correct answer for each question.

dōng jīng 东京 Tokyo	

a. 志军觉得哪儿的气候很不一样？
  i. 北京
  ii. 东京
  iii. 美国

b. 志军说明天的天气怎么样？
  i. 很好
  ii. 很差
  iii. 不知道

c. 志军喜欢什么季节？
  i. 春天
  ii. 天气
  iii. 冬天

d. 小明听天气预报说明天英国的天气怎么样？
  i. 晴天
  ii. 下雨
  iii. 阴天

4. 练习写汉字。

Practise writing Chinese.

a. 按照笔画顺序写下面的字。

Write the characters by following the stroke order.

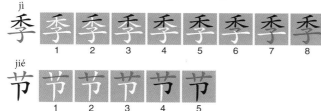

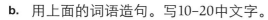

b. 用上面的词语造句。写10–20中文字。

Write a sentence of your own using the above vocabulary. Write 10–20 words in Chinese.

5. 和你的同学轮流提出和回答下面的问题。

With a partner, take turns to ask and answer the following questions.

a. 你最喜欢哪一个季节？

b. 你最喜欢什么天气？

c. 你最不喜欢什么天气？

d. 你最喜欢哪儿的气候？

e. 你最不喜欢哪儿的气候？

6.2 天气与气候
WEATHER AND CLIMATE

LESSON OBJECTIVES
- Describe a range of weather and climate conditions.
- Discuss activities you did and will do in response to changes in the weather.

1. 你将听到几个句子。先看图片，再听录音，然后选择唯一正确的答案。

   You will hear some short phrases. Look at the pictures and questions before you listen to the recording, then choose the correct answer for each question.

a. 昨天早上天气怎么样？

b. 今天中午天气怎么样？

c. 今天晚上天气怎么样？

d. 明天早上天气怎么样？

2. 阅读玛莉寄给汤姆的信，然后回答问题。

   Read this letter from Mary to Tom, then answer the questions.

> 汤姆：
>
> 　　你好吗？
>
> 　　今天是我在东京的第十天。我很喜欢东京，这儿天气很好，差不多每天都有太阳，天很蓝，有很多白云，很美！昨天我参观了不少旅游景点，例如公园、博物馆和动物园，我在这儿玩得很开心！
>
> 　　东京的气温变化很大。虽然早上和中午很凉快，但是下午气温会升高，没有风会有点热。晚上气温下降，气温在十度左右，有点冷。但是没十一月的伦敦那么冷，十一月的伦敦常常下雨，天气最冷的时候，屋顶上还会有一层冰呢！东京十一月的天气比伦敦好多了！
>
> 　　因为东京的气候跟伦敦的不一样，东京人很友好，风景很美，所以我很喜欢这里。听说明天天气暖和，我会和朋友一起去购物。
>
> 　　你在台湾夏令营的学习怎么样？
>
> 玛莉
十一月二十一日

yún 云 cloud	
tí gāo / shēng gāo 提高/升高 to increase	
xià jiàng 下降 to decrease	

qì wēn 气温 temperature	
fēng 风 wind	
wū dǐng 屋顶 roof	
bīng 冰 ice	

a. 东京的天气怎么样？   **b.** 东京早上和中午气温怎么样？

c. 东京下午和晚上的 气温怎么样？   **d.** 伦敦十一月的天气怎么样？

e. 为什么玛莉喜欢东京？

Grammar focus   p.268

1. Using 昨天/今天/明天

in a sentence

★ 昨天/今天/明天

   + description

昨天/今天/明天天气 很好。

2. 在 + location: in/at (a location)

★ subject + 在 + location + action

她在澳大利亚学习 英语。

---

3. 和你的同学谈谈这几天的天气，轮流提出和回答下面的 问题。

With a partner, talk about this week's weather. Take turns to ask and answer the following questions.

a. 昨天天气怎么样？   **b.** 今天早上天气怎么样？

c. 今天下午天气怎么样？   **d.** 明天天气怎么样？

---

4. 练习写汉字。

Practise writing Chinese.

a. 按照笔画顺序写下面的字。

Write the characters by following the stroke order.

nuǎn

暖 暖 暖 暖 暖 暖 暖 暖 暖 暖 暖 暖 暖 暖
   1   2   3   4   5   6   7   8   9   10   11   12   13

huo

和 和 和 和 和 和 和 和
   1   2   3   4   5   6   7   8

b. 请用上面的词语造句。写10–20个字。

Write a sentence of your own using the above vocabulary. Write 10–20 characters.

---

5. 你在加拿大旅行。用60–80个字给朋友写明信片。其中应该 包括：

You are on holiday in Canada. Write a postcard to your friend using 60–80 characters. It should include the following:

a. 那儿的气候怎么样？

b. 昨天天气怎样？你做了什么？

c. 今天天气怎样？你打算做什么？

d. 明天天气怎样？你会做什么？

e. 你觉得这次旅行怎么样？

6.3 天气预报
WEATHER FORECASTS

LESSON OBJECTIVES
- Recognise a range of weather conditions.
- Recall information and advice from weather forecasts and news reports.
- Describe the weather up to a week ahead.

1. 看看下面的词语，把它们和正确的图片搭配起来。

Look at the vocabulary below. Match each one with the correct picture.

a. 刮风　**b.** 晴天　**c.** 下雾　**d.** 下雪　**e.** 下雨　**f.** 阴天／多云　**g.** 打雷

2. 你会听到北京未来五天的天气预报。先看下面的词组，再听录音，然后把左边和右边的词组搭配起来，完成句子。

You will hear a five-day weather forecast for Beijing. Look at the phrases below before you listen to the recording. Match each weekday with the correct weather forecast to make complete sentences.

a. 星期一　　　　　　　**i.** 是晴天。

b. 星期二　　　　　　　**ii.** 下午晚些时候会刮风。

c. 星期三　　　　　　　**iii.** 大雨，会打雷。

d. 星期四　　　　　　　**iv.** 阴天多云。

e. 星期五　　　　　　　**v.** 下雾。

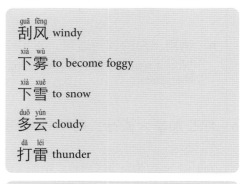

guā fēng
刮风 windy

xià wù
下雾 to become foggy

xià xuě
下雪 to snow

duō yún
多云 cloudy

dǎ léi
打雷 thunder

wèi lái
未来 future

3. 阅读以下的新闻报道，然后判断下面的叙述对或错。

Read the news report below, then decide if the following statements are true or false.

北京周末的第一场雪

昨天是周末，晚上北京下了今年的第一场雪以后，不少游客都忙着照相留念。这一场雪让市民非常高兴，很多人都准备第二天到滑雪场滑雪。

今天是晴天，可以看见太阳。但是根据天气预报，从下个星期一到星期三多云，都是阴天。

根据天气预报，下星期四和星期五会刮大风，气温会下降五度，市民应该注意保暖。

a. 下雨让北京的市民非常高兴。	**b.** 下个星期一到星期三都是阴天。
c. 下星期四会刮大风。	**d.** 下星期五气温会下降十五度。

4. 和你的同学轮流提出和回答下面关于天气的问题。

With a partner, take turns to ask and answer the following questions about this week's weather.

a. 昨天是星期几？天气怎么样？	**b.** 今天是星期几？天气怎么样？
c. 明天是星期几？天气怎么样？	**d.** 下个星期天气怎么样？

5. 翻译以下句子，并用中文写下来。

Translate these sentences into Chinese and write them out.

a. I couldn't see the sun yesterday.

b. The weather tomorrow will be cloudy and windy.

c. The temperature will drop by 5 degrees on Wednesday.

---

gēn jù
根据 according to

liú niàn
留念 to keep (as a souvenir)

bǎo nuǎn
保暖 to keep warm

Grammar focus   p.269

1. 根据 : according to

★ 根据 + noun, + complete sentence

根据天气预报，明天会下雨。

2. 星期/周（一至六）；周末（星期六、星期日）: days of the week

这个周末（我会和爸爸妈妈去公园玩）。星期一到五（我要上学）。

LESSON OBJECTIVES
- Describe items of clothing worn in different seasons and types of weather.
- Use appropriate measure words to describe items of clothing.

---

1. 看看下面的图片，把它们和正确的词语搭配起来。

   Look at the pictures below. Match each one with the correct vocabulary.

i. 帽子　ii. 大衣　iii. 毛衣　iv. 围巾　v. 雨衣
vi. 手套　vii. 雨伞　viii. 短裤

2. 判断下面的叙述是否合理，然后为不合理的叙述提供解释。

   Decide if the following statements make sense or not, and provide explanations for those that don't make sense.

   a. 春天到了，常常会下雨，陈明应该带雨伞。

   b. 夏天到了，心美应该穿一件大衣。

   c. 秋天到了，天气会变冷，志军应该穿短裤上学。

   d. 冬天到了，天气会很冷，日晴应该戴围巾上学。

3. 汤姆要去北京旅行。爸爸正在和他谈话。先读问题，再听录音，然后写下答案。

   Tom is going on a trip to Beijing. His dad is talking to him. Read the questions before you listen to the recording, then write the correct answers.

---

mào zi
帽子 hat

dà yī
大衣 overcoat

máo yī
毛衣 sweater

wéi jīn
围巾 scarf

yǔ yī
雨衣 raincoat or waterproof coat

shǒu tào
手套 glove

yǔ sǎn
雨伞 umbrella

duǎn kù
短裤 shorts

Grammar focus　p.269

1. measure words for items of clothing

   tiáo
   一条：裤子、围巾

   jiàn
   一件：衣服、毛衣、雨衣

   shuāng
   一双：手套

2. 会：will

   ★ subject + 会 + action

   明天会下雪。

---

chuān
穿 to wear

dài
戴 to wear (accessories)

a. 汤姆星期一应该带什么？   **b.** 汤姆星期三应该带什么？

c. 汤姆不用带什么？   **d.** 汤姆爸爸买不到什么？

4. 和你的同学角色扮演百货公司售货员和顾客之间的对话，轮流提出和回答下面的问题。

With a partner, role-play a conversation between a salesperson and a customer in a department store. Take turns to ask and answer the following questions.

a. 你要买几条裤子？   **b.** 你要买几双手套？

c. 你要买几条围巾？   **d.** 你要买几件毛衣和大衣？

e. 你要买几件雨衣？   **f.** 你要买几双鞋子和袜子？

xié zi	
鞋子 shoe	
wà zi	
袜子 sock	

jiàn	
件 measure word for a top (e.g. t-shirt)	
shuāng	
双 measure word for a pair of gloves	

5. 练习写汉字。

Practise writing Chinese.

a. 按照笔画顺序写下面的字。

Write the character by following the stroke order.

dài
戴 戴 戴 戴 戴 戴 戴 戴 戴 戴 戴 戴 戴 戴 戴 戴 戴
   1   2   3   4   5   6   7   8   9   10   11   12   13   14   15   16   17

b. 冬天时你会穿戴什么？用前面学的词语，写一个完整的句子。写20–30个字。

What do you wear in winter? Using the above vocabulary, make a sentence of your own. Write 20–30 characters.

6. 志军将会在八月到香港旅行。发一个短信提醒他带什么衣服。写 25–40个字。其中应该包括：

Zhijun is going to Hong Kong for a holiday in August. Send him a text message to remind him what clothes to pack. Use 20–40 characters. Include the following:

a. 那时是什么季节？   **b.** 天气会怎么样？

c. 要穿什么衣服？   **d.** 下雨要带什么？

6.5 方位
LOCATIONS

LESSON OBJECTIVES
- Describe the positions and locations of different objects and places.
- Give the location of one thing or place in relation to another.

1. 看看下面的图片，然后用下列词语完成句子。

Look at the picture, then complete the sentences using the words in the box.

shàng biān	上边 on top of; above
xià biān	下边 below
zuǒ biān	左边 left
yòu biān	右边 right
qián biān	前边 in front of
hòu biān	后边 at the back

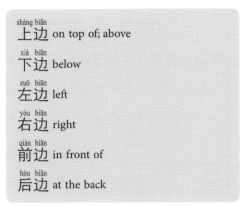

四楼

教室			教室
图书馆			卫生间
(b)			教室

三楼

教室			教室
(c)			卫生间
教室			教室

二楼

教室			教室
教室			卫生间
教室			实验室

一楼

(a)		食堂
正门		

收音机在铅笔的(a)边。　　橡皮在铅笔的(c)边。
镜子在铅笔的(b)边。　　书在铅笔的(d)边。

上　下　左　右　前　后

2. 明天是家长日。阅读小华和他爸爸的对话，认出右边图中A到C的设施。

Tomorrow is Parents' Day. Look at the floor plan on the right before you read the conversation between Xiaohua and his dad, then identify the facilities marked a, b, c on the plan.

爸爸：小华，明天我要去你的学校，请问到礼堂怎么走？

小华：从学校的大门进来，一直往前走就会看到教学楼。走进了教学楼以后，你会看到食堂在一楼，食堂的对面就是礼堂。

爸爸：你的教室在哪儿？我要去教室见你的班主任。

小华：我的教室在四楼。从礼堂向左拐，你会看到楼梯，走到四楼以后，你会看到图书馆在两间教室的中间。

爸爸：我还要去办公室找你的中文老师，请问从图书馆到办公室要怎么走？

小华：办公室在图书馆的楼下。办公室就在楼梯的附近，向右拐就看到了。

qǐng wèn	
请问 May I ask...?	

dào	zěn me zǒu
到……怎么走? How can I get to...?	

yī zhí	
一直 to go straight	

xiàng zuǒ	yòu guǎi zhuǎn
向左/右拐/转 to turn left/right	

zhōng jiān	
中间 in the middle of	

lóu xià	
楼下 downstairs	

fù jìn	
附近 nearby	

shùn zhe	
顺着 along	

3. 小华的爸爸想在学校附近的地方逛逛。先读问题，再听录音，然后选择正确的答案。

Xiaohua's father is exploring the area around the school. Read the questions before you listen to the recording, then choose the correct answer for each question.

a. 公园在学校的哪一边？
   i. 前边
   ii. 后边
   iii. 左边

b. 博物馆在学校的哪边？
   i. 前边
   ii. 左边
   iii. 中间

c. 美术馆的附近有什么？
   i. 酒店
   ii. 百货商店
   iii. 学校

d. 从博物馆到美术馆怎么走？
   i. 顺着博物馆一直走
   ii. 往公园一直走
   iii. 往电影院一直走

4. 和你的同学角色扮演小华爸爸和学校接待员之间的对话，轮流提出和回答下面的问题。使用第二题的图来帮助你回答问题。

With a partner, role-play a conversation between Xiaohua's father and the school receptionist. Take turns to ask and answer the following questions. Use the plan from Activity 2 to help you.

a. 请问从办公室到实验室要怎么走？

b. 请问从办公室到图书馆要怎么走？

c. 从图书馆到食堂要怎么走？

Grammar focus p.269

1. 从: from one place to another
   ★ 从 + location 1 + 到 + location 2
   从酒店到机场(不太远)。

2. 往: to (for direction)
   ★ 往 + direction + verb
   往前走(就到图书馆了)。

LESSON OBJECTIVES
- Describe your location in relation to your surroundings.
- Ask for and give detailed directions to various places.

1. 看看下面的指南针。给它填上正确的方向。

   Look at the compass below. Fill in the missing points.

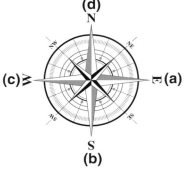

| 东 南 西 北 |

dōng
东 east
nán
南 south
xī
西 west
běi
北 north

2. 看看这幅地图，然后完成右边的句子。

   Look at the map, then complete the sentences on the right.

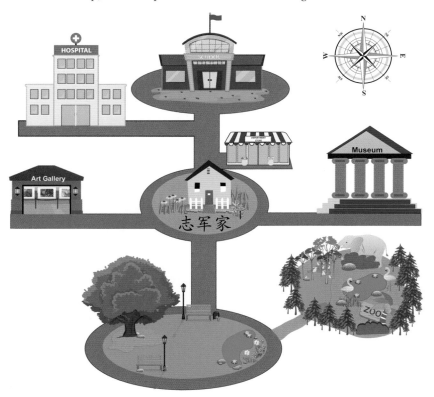

学校在志军家的**(a)**边。
美术馆在志军家的**(b)**边。
博物馆在志军家的**(c)**边。
公园在志军家的**(d)**边。

Grammar focus   p.270

1. 怎么: how to
   ★ subject + 怎么 + verb ?
   百货商店怎么走？

2. 在这儿/那儿: here, there
   ★ place + 在这儿/那儿
   百货商店在这儿，公园
   在那儿。

3. 苏菲迷路了，她正在问路。先读问题，再听录音，然后完成下面的填空。

Sophie is lost. She is asking for help. Read the questions before you listen to the recording, then complete it by filling in the missing information.

a. 百货公司离这儿远吗？怎么走？

百货公司很(i)。从这儿往(ii)走五十(iii)，就看到百货公司了。

b. 公园离这儿有多远？怎么走？

公园离这儿不远。(i)百货公司往(ii)一直走，在路口往(iii)就会看到公园了。

c. 动物园在哪儿？怎么走？

动物园在公园的(i)边。顺着这儿的路口走一百米，往(ii)，到那儿你就会看到动物园了。

d. 医院离这儿远吗？怎么走？

医院离这儿有点儿(i)，它在动物园的(ii)边。顺着动物园(iii)走，你会看到一个(iv)，向(v)走一千米就会看到医院了。

……离这儿远吗/有多远？

Is ... far from here?

yuǎn
远 far away

mǐ
米 metre

jìn
近 nearby

shí zì lù kǒu
十字路口 crossroad

yǒu diǎnr
有点儿 a little; a bit

4. 练习问路及指路。

Practise asking for and giving directions.

a. 和你的同学轮流问路，使用第二题的地图来回答对方的问题。

With a partner, take turns to ask and give directions to the following places. Use the map in Activity 2 to help you answer the questions.

i. 请问百货商店在哪儿？
iii. 请问动物园在哪儿？

ii. 请问公园怎么走？
iv. 请问医院怎么走？

b. 用中文写出你同学给的答案。

Now write out your partner's answers in Chinese.

Cultural spotlight

sì hé yuàn
四合院 **Siheyuan**

四合院是一种中国传统的建筑形式。四是指东、南、西、北四面；合即四面房屋围在一起，包围着中间的庭院，形成一个「口」字形。四合院的装修和布局处处体现着中国的传统文化，表现出人们对幸福、富裕、和谐的追求，例如四合院大门通常坐落在东南边，意指「紫气东来」。

从外面看，四合院四面都是墙，像是警告外人不得随便闯入；四合院内一家人却可以安安静静地生活。院内房子各自独立，又互相连结。其中最大的北房，冬暖夏凉，由家中的长辈居住。就算天气不好，后辈也可以沿着游廊到北房向长辈问安。这种布局正体现了中国传统家庭观念的价值观。

a. 在你的国家，哪些建筑物的风格和四合院相似？

b. 长幼有序、追求和谐这些传统中国思想往往能在生活环境的装修和布局中体现。在你国家的文化中，有没有相似的看法或观念？

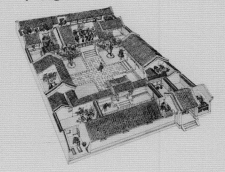

LESSON OBJECTIVES
- Identify and describe common features in a natural environment.
- Discuss what you like or dislike about the natural environment.

1. 你将听到几个关于自然环境的句子。先读下面的叙述，再听录音，然后判断叙述是对还是错。

   You will hear some phrases about the natural environment. Look at the statements below before you listen to the recording, then decide if they are true or false according to the recording.

   a. 森林里有河。河里有很多草。

   b. 沙漠里有湖。湖很大。

   c. 高原上有草、花，还有很多动物。

   d. 平原上有花，有山，也有湖。

shā mò	
沙漠 desert	
hú	
湖 lake	
gāo yuán	
高原 plateau	
píng yuán	
平原 plain	

2. 志军的爸爸是地理学家。他在巴西。阅读他写的信。

   Zhijun's father is a geographer. He is working in Brazil. Read his letter below.

   志军：

   　　你好！

   　　对不起，今天才给你回信。请原谅。

   　　我现在住在巴西的一间酒店里。先说说这儿的环境吧！酒店的附近有一条河，酒店就在河南边的平原上，所以它叫做河南酒店。我在这儿住了一个多月了，常常看到很多野生动物。河的西边是一座山，东边是一个湖，北边就是我要去考察的森林。我的工作是在森林中找一些濒危物种，例如花、草、树等等。我有一位朋友在森林里住了很多年了，我常常找他帮忙。

   　　我很喜欢巴西，这儿风景很美。对了，你去了北京旅行也有十天了，那儿好玩吗？请回信！

   　　祝

   　　身体健康

   爸爸
九月十日

qǐng yuán liàng	
请原谅 please forgive (me)	
yě shēng dòng wù	
野生动物 wild animal	

bā xī	
巴西 Brazil	
kǎo chá	
考察 to investigate (during the field trip)	
bīn wēi wù zhǒng	
濒危物种 endangered species	

a. 找出地图上不同的地方。写上正确的答案。

On the map, locate the different places according to the passage. Write down the correct answers.

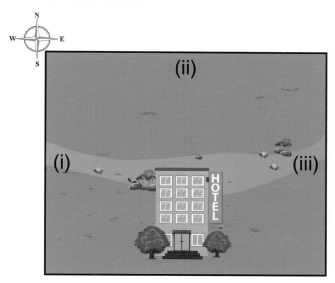

Grammar focus p.270

什么: what

★ subject + verb + 什么 + object

这里有什么东西?

b. 回答下面的问题。

Answer the following questions.

   i. 志军爸爸住在巴西的哪一间酒店?   **ii.** 志军爸爸住的地方附近有什么?

  iii. 志军爸爸要找哪些濒危物种?   **iv.** 志军爸爸的朋友住在哪儿?

3. 志军的妈妈到了巴西探望他爸爸。和你的同学角色扮演志军爸爸妈妈之间的对话,轮流提出和回答下面的问题。

Zhijun's mother is visiting his father in Brazil. With a partner, practise having a conversation as Zhijun's parents. Take turns to ask and answer the following questions.

a. 爸爸,森林在酒店的哪个方向?

b. 妈妈,你想去森林看什么?

c. 妈妈,你想去哪儿参观?

4. 你最喜欢(哪个国家的)哪种自然环境(例如森林、高原、平原等等)? 用 30–45个字写出原因。

What kind of natural environment do you like the most? Write 30–40 characters to explain why.

LESSON OBJECTIVES

● Discuss different types of natural disasters and their causes.
● Share your views on a range of conservation issues and activities.
● Describe the details of a conservation activity.

1. 看看下面的图片，把它们和正确的词语搭配起来。
Look at the pictures below and match them with the correct vocabulary.

hàn zāi 旱灾 draught	
shuǐ zāi 水灾 flooding	
quán qiú nuǎn huà 全球暖化 global warming	
kōng qì wū rǎn 空气污染 air pollution	
suān yǔ 酸雨 acid rain	

i. 旱灾　　**ii.** 水灾　　**iii.** 全球暖化
iv. 空气污染　　**v.** 酸雨

2. 日晴将会在班里演讲。阅读她的演讲稿，然后判断下面的叙述对或错。

Riqing is going to give a speech to her classmates. Read her speech, then decide if the statements on the right are true or false.

各位同学：

　　大家好！我是环保小组的日晴。同学们都应该在上地理课的时候学过水灾、旱灾、空气污染、酸雨、全球暖化这些环境问题吧！因为人类一直在破坏自然环境，所以才会有这些问题。作为人类的一份子，我们每一个人都有责任。

　　为了保护环境，环保小组将会在学校举办一些环保活动，活动将会在下个月开始，有兴趣的同学可以放学后来找我报名。谢谢！

wèn tí 问题 issues	
pò huài 破坏 to destroy; destruction	
bǎo hù 保护 to protect	

huán bǎo 环保 environmental conservation	
rén lèi 人类 humanity; mankind	
jǔ bàn 举办 to host	

a. 日晴参加了环保小组。

b. 同学们在地理课上学过水灾和全球暖化这些环境问题。

c. 人类一直在保护自然环境。

d. 环保小组下一年会在学校举办环保活动。

e. 有兴趣的同学可以找老师报名。

3. 日晴正在和同学们谈话。先读问题，再听录音，然后选择唯一正确的答案。

Riqing is in conversation with her classmates. Read the questions below before you listen to the recording, then choose the correct answer for each question.

a. 环保小组将会举办什么活动？
   i. 森林绿化和植树
   ii. 垃圾回收利用和环境绿化
   iii. 垃圾回收利用和种花

b. 为什么要回收利用垃圾？
   i. 破坏自然资源
   ii. 使用自然资源
   iii. 节约自然资源

c. 绿化环境活动做什么？
   i. 植树
   ii. 种花
   iii. 去森林

d. 环保小组会请地理老师来讲什么？
   i. 回收垃圾
   ii. 节约用水
   iii. 节省能源

huí shōu lì yòng
回收利用 recycle and reuse
lǜ huà
绿化 greening (the process in which someone takes an interest in protecting the environment)
zì rán zī yuán
自然资源 natural resource
jié yuē / jié shěng
节约/节省 to save
néng yuán
能源 energy

zhí
植 to plant (trees)

4. 和你的同学轮流提出和回答下面和环保有关的问题。

With a partner, take turns to ask and answer the following questions on environmental conservation.

a. 你知道有哪些环境问题吗？

b. 为什么会有这些环境问题？

c. 如果你学校的环保小组举办上面提到的一些活动，你打算参加哪一个？

d. 为什么你要参加这一个活动？

5. 环保小组将要举办一个活动。用 80–100个字写一张海报，邀请学校的学生参加。其中应该包括:

The environmental conservation group is organising an activity. Use 80–100 characters to write a poster inviting other students in your school to participate. It should include:

a. 举办什么活动
b. 为了什么
c. 什么时候
d. 在哪儿
e. 做什么
f. 怎么联系。

Grammar focus　　p.270

将/将会/将要: going to
★ subject + 将/将会/将要
　+ imminent event
我将会在暑假参加环保小组的活动。

LESSON OBJECTIVES
- Recognise the names and the characteristics of different animals.
- Describe and discuss your experience of visiting a zoo.

1. 选择正确的动物名称回答问题。
   Choose the correct answer for each question.

   a. 以下哪一种动物沒有脚?
   　　i. 蛇　　**ii.** 大象　　**iii.** 猴子

   b. 以下哪一种动物的身体上大部分颜色是灰色的?
   　　i. 熊猫　　**ii.** 大象　　**iii.** 鱼

   c. 以下哪种动物的性情最温和?
   　　i. 猴子　　**ii.** 老虎　　**iii.** 羊

2. 小明和朋友们今天去了动物园参观。阅读他的日记，然后回答问题。
   Xiaoming and his friends went to the zoo today. Read his diary entry, then answer the questions.

七月十七日	星期三	天气：晴

　　　　　　　　参观动物园
　　今天天气很好。我和心美、米娜一起去了动物园参观。我们先去了森林区，在那儿我们看到了两只老虎。我最喜欢老虎，因为它们长得很好看。我们也看到了很多只猴子。心美很喜欢猴子，她觉得它们很有趣，她想喂它们吃东西。但是动物园的饲养员告诉我们，喂猴子很危险，只有他们才可以喂。 我们还看到了两只大象，它们长得高高的，有大大的耳朵，也有长长的鼻子，可以把树上的香蕉拿下来吃。米娜最喜欢熊猫，我们看到了一只熊猫，它长得胖胖的，很可爱。
　　动物园里的其他地方还有很多动物，例如：牛、羊、蛇、鸭子、猪和鱼。因为时间不够，所以我们打算下次再去看。

Vocabulary (sidebar):

dòng wù 动物 animal
shé 蛇 snake
dà xiàng 大象 elephant
hóu zi 猴子 monkey
xióng māo 熊猫 panda
xìng qíng 性情 temperament; nature
lǎo hǔ 老虎 tiger

wēn hé 温和 mild

yā zi 鸭子 duck
zhū 猪 pig

sì yǎng yuán 饲养员 animal keeper
wèi 喂 to feed
xiāng jiāo 香蕉 banana

a. 什么动物长得很好看？　　**b.** 什么动物长得胖胖的？

c. 什么动物有大大的耳朵　　**d.** 为什么心美不可以喂猴子？
和长长的鼻子？

3. 跟你的同学分享一次你去动物园的经验，轮流提出和回答
下面的问题。

Share your experience of visiting a zoo with a partner. Take turns to ask and
answer the following questions.

a. 你什么时候去过动物园？

b. 你看了什么动物？

c. 你最喜欢什么动物？

d. 为什么你最喜欢（动物的名字）？

4. 看下面的地图，然后用10–20个字写出动物园的方位。

Read the map below. Use 10–20 characters to write down the location of
the zoo.

1. 看看下面的图片，把它们和正确的词语搭配起来。

i. 晴天　ii. 刮风　iii. 多云　iv. 下雨　v. 东　vi. 南　vii. 左　viii. 右
ix. 十字路口　x. 草　xi. 树　xii. 雨伞

2. 阅读下面的内容，然后判断右面的叙述对还是错。

　　今天天气很冷。心美穿了一件大衣，也戴了帽子。
　　心美要去图书馆。图书馆不远，在她家的北边，就在美术馆的附近。汤姆也想去，但是他不知道图书馆怎么走。心美跟他说，只要他顺着学校的方向一直走，就会看到一个十字路口，之后往左拐就到了。
　　心美说她会在图书馆三楼的中文图书区等汤姆，中文图书区就在英文图书区的前面，在厕所的右边。心美等了三十分钟，汤姆还没到。看来他应该迷路了。

a. 心美穿了一件毛衣。

b. 图书馆不远，在汤姆家附近。

c. 汤姆知道图书馆怎么走。

d. 顺着学校方向一直走，在十字路口往左拐就到图书馆了。

e. 心美在图书馆三楼的中文图书区等汤姆。

f. 中文图书区在英文图书区的后面。

g. 汤姆迷路了。

3. 先读短文，再听录音，然后完成下面的填空。

围巾　夏天　冬天　毛衣　秋天　手套　短裤

(a)来了，天气会变热。妈妈叫我把衣柜里(b)穿的衣服都收起来，有一条(c)、一双(d)和一件(e)。
这些衣服都是去年(f)买的。由于天气变热，妈妈说她会带我去百货商店买新的(g)。

4. 阅读以下的信，然后写出答案回答后面的问题。

亲爱的志军：

你好吗？

我去了巴西找你爸爸。我到了巴西三天了，现在住在巴西的一间酒店里。先说说这儿的环境吧！酒店的附近有一条河，酒店就在河南边的平原上。河的西边是一座山，东边是一个湖，北边就是你爸爸要去考察的森林。明天我会和你爸爸一起去森林考察，他会带我去看森林里的一些濒危物种，例如花、草、和野生动物等等。他的朋友也会来。

我很喜欢巴西。虽然这儿天气有点热，但是风景很美，每天都可以看到太阳。听说你刚从北京回到美国，你觉得北京好玩吗？

请给我写信！

祝

身体健康！

妈妈

十月一日

   a. 志军的妈妈住的酒店附近有什么？　　**b.** 志军的妈妈去森林看什么？

   c. 为什么志军的妈妈喜欢巴西？

5. 先读问题，再听录音，然后选择唯一正确的答案。

   a. 妈妈明天要去哪儿？　　**b.** 食堂的左边是什么？

     i. 博物馆　　 **i.** 教室

     ii. 学校　　 **ii.** 礼堂

     iii. 美术馆　　 **iii.** 办公室

   c. 丽青的教室在几楼？　　**d.** 美术室在图书馆的什么位置？

     i. 一楼　　 **i.** 楼上

     ii. 二楼　　 **ii.** 楼下

     iii. 三楼　　 **iii.** 旁边

6. 你和朋友们今天去了动物园参观。用120-150个字写一篇日记。其中应该包括：

   a. 今天的天气怎么样？　　**b.** 看了什么动物？　　**c.** 这些动物长得什么样？

   d. 你和朋友们最喜欢什么动物？　　**e.** 为什么？

7. 和你的同学讨论学校环保小组举行的环保活动，轮流提出和回答下面的问题。

   a. 请问学校环保小组将会举办什么活动？　　**b.** 为什么要回收利用垃圾？

   c. 绿化环境活动做什么？　　**d.** 除了这些活动之外，环保小组以后还会举办其他活动吗？

UNIT OBJECTIVES

- Practise greeting people and holding polite conversations in different situations.
- Share information and your views on a range of cities and countries.
- Learn about some interesting traditions and festivities from around the world.
- Describe and discuss different modes of transport and transport-related issues.
- Share your experiences of dealing with lost property.

1. 看看下面的国旗，把它们和正确的国家名称搭配起来。

Look at the pictures of the flags below. Match them with the correct countries.

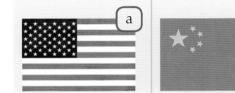   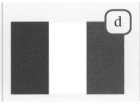 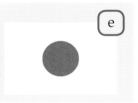

i. 英国   **ii.** 法国   **iii.** 日本   **iv.** 中国   **v.** 美国

2. 写下以下词语的英文意思和拼音。

Write down the English meaning and pinyin of each of the words below.

a. 交通   **b.** 飞机   **c.** 火车   **d.** 地铁   **e.** 汽车   **f.** 自行车

3. 五个人正在谈论他们的旅游体验。先读问题，再听录音，然后选择正确的答案完成句子。

Five people are talking about their travelling experiences. Look at the questions before you listen to the recording, then choose the correct answer to complete each sentence.

> bīng mǎ yǒng
> 兵马俑 Terracotta Army

> wài miàn
> 外面 outside

a. 海伦觉得上海的地铁……。
   i. 十分干净   **ii.** 又快又方便   **iii.** 太忙了，人太多了

b. 上个周末马克带妈妈从北京……去了西安。
   i. 坐飞机   **ii.** 坐很快的火车   **iii.** 坐旅游大巴士

c. 在美国北部旅游的时候，米娜一家人……。
   i. 开车去了各个风景区   **ii.** 在森林里露了营
   iii. 坐了火车旅游

d. 本杰明在新加坡的……买了几件衣服和两本书。

   i. 市中心的百货商场里

   ii. 火车站的纪念品商店里

   iii. 国际机场

e. 明天日晴和同学们将……。

   i. 去山区爬山和徒步

   ii. 去动物园看大熊猫

   iii. 去森林公园骑自行车

4. 填空完成句子。

Complete these sentences by filling in the missing information.

我们是坐……去……的。

在…… 旅游的时候，我们乘坐了……。

我们觉得……。

chéng zuò
乘坐 to ride (in a vehicle)

shài tài yáng
晒太阳 to sunbathe

5. 阅读下面去海边小镇一日游的时间表，然后判断右边的叙述是对或错。

Read the timetable of a day trip to a seaside town below, then decide if the statements on the right are true or false.

海边小镇一日游时间表	
时间	行程 *xíng chéng itinerary*
八点半	在火车站前面的小广场见面。
九点	坐火车前往海边小镇—海蓝多。
十点半	到海蓝多火车站，然后走路去小镇的海边。
十二点	在海滩上吃当地有名的海鲜餐。
下午一点到四点	在沙滩上自由活动，可以晒太阳，也可以去附近的小山上徒步，还可以看看当地有趣的动物和植物。
下午四点半	乘坐火车返回市区

a. 会面的小广场就在火车站的前面。

b. 大家将坐八点半的火车出发。

c. 他们去的是一个有名的动物园。

d. 他们到了小镇以后是走路去海滩的。

e. 中午大家在沙滩上吃自己带的三明治。

f. 吃完饭，可以在沙滩上晒太阳，也可以去附近走走看看。

6. 和同学谈谈你们居住的地方的交通，轮流提出和回答下面的问题。

With a partner, talk about the transport system where you live. Take turns to ask and answer the following questions.

a. 你住哪个地方？那是一个什么样的地方？

b. 你住的城市有没有飞机场？火车站？

c. 城里的交通方便吗？为什么？

d. 你每天是坐什么去上学的？为什么？

LESSON OBJECTIVES

- Identify a range of greeting words and phrases.
- Hold polite conversations in different situations.

1. 写下以下日常用语的英文意思和拼音。

Write down the English meanings and pinyin of these everyday greeting words.

您好吗？

谢谢！

不用谢！

不客气！

对不起！

没关系！

老师好！

早安！

晚安！

再见！

wèn hòu
问候 to send a greeting

2. 先读问题，再听录音，然后选择唯一正确的答案完成句子。

Read each question before you listen to the recording, then choose the correct answer to complete each sentence.

míng bai
明白 to understand

wǎn le
晚(了) running late

a. 他要和陈先生去……。
  i. 茶馆
  ii. 咖啡馆
  iii. 餐馆

b. 为了谢谢小海，她要……。
  i. 请他吃饭
  ii. 请他看电影
  iii. 请他一起玩电子游戏

c. 他请您再说一遍是因为……。
  i. 刚刚很吵，他没有听到
  ii. 他的中文不太好，没有听明白

d. 她……回家。
  i. 走路
  ii. 开车
  iii. 坐公共汽车

e. 他上学迟到了是因为……。
  i. 坐的火车晚了二十分
  ii. 坐的火车晚了半个小时
  iii. 坐爸爸的车上学，但是爸爸的车坏了

3. 阅读下面的对话，选择唯一正确的答案。
Read the dialogue and choose the correct answer for each question below.

小佳： 先生您好。请问您是林文风吗？

文风： 你好。我是。你是麦可的朋友小佳吗？

小佳： 是啊。欢迎来到新加坡。您在新加坡这几天我带你玩。

文风： 小佳你好。我来正式介绍一下，我叫林文风，我跟麦可是在美国一起上中学时认识的。

小佳： 您好。认识您我很高兴。我是小佳，是麦可从小一起长大的朋友。这是您第一次来新加坡吗？

文风： 我也很高兴认识你。是的，这是我第一次来。我以前一直想来新加坡看一看，但是都没有机会。这次因为工作要在新加坡参加一个电子游戏的展览，所以就来了。不好意思这几天要打扰你了。

小佳： 不客气。这是我应该做的。好的。那我先带您坐地铁去你住的酒店，然后带您去吃饭。

nín hǎo 您好 Hello (formal way of greeting)
xīn jiā pō 新加坡 Singapore
wǒ lái jiè shào yī xià 我来介绍一下 Let me introduce ...
hěn gāo xìng rèn shí nǐ 很高兴认识你 Nice to meet you!
dǎ rǎo nǐ 打扰你 Sorry to bother you.

zhèng shì 正式 formally; officially
yī zhí 一直 always
zhǎn lǎn 展览 exhibition

a. 文风现在在哪里？
 i. 美国
 ii. 新加坡
 iii. 酒店

b. 文风和麦可是怎么认识的？
 i. 在美国旅游的时候认识的
 ii. 在美国上中学的时候认识的
 iii. 在美国的一所大学里认识的

c. 小佳是麦可的……。
 i. 好朋友
 ii. 表姐
 iii. 同学

d. 文风为什么来新加坡？
 i. 看他的爷爷奶奶
 ii. 看他的老朋友麦可
 iii. 参加一个电子游戏的展览

e. 这是文风……来新加坡。
 i. 第一次
 ii. 第二次
 iii. 第三次

4. 你去中国西安旅游。导游来机场接你。和你的同学角色扮演导游和游客之间的对话，轮流提出和回答下面的问题。

You are on holiday in Xi'an. You have just been picked up by your tour guide at the airport. With a partner, role-play the conversation between the tour guide and the tourist. Take turns to ask and answer the following questions.

a. 先生/小姐您好。您是……吗？

b. 从……到西安坐飞机要多长时间？

c. 我们先去酒店还是先去餐馆吃饭？

d. 您以前来过西安吗？

e. 这次来西安您最想参观什么名胜古迹？

Grammar focus p.271

是……的: used to emphasise or confirm an action

★ subject + 是 + action + 的
我们是（在伦敦一起）读大学时认识的。

LESSON OBJECTIVES

● Identify the names of different continents, countries, and cities.
● Describe and discuss cities from around the world.

1. 看看下面的地图。写下七大洲的中文名称，然后把它们读出来。

Look at the map below. Write the names of the seven continents in Chinese, then read them out.

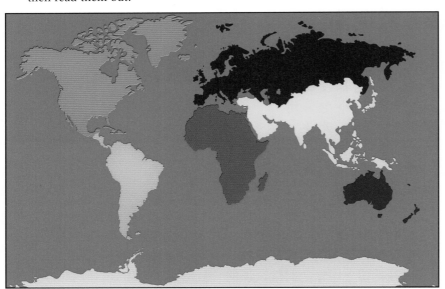

yà zhōu
亚洲 Asia

ōu zhōu
欧洲 Europe

fēi zhōu
非洲 Africa

běi měi zhōu
北美洲 North America

nán měi zhōu
南美洲 South America

nán jí zhōu
南极洲 Antarctica

dà yáng zhōu
大洋洲 Oceania

2. 看看下面的国旗。

Look at the national flags below.

a. 把它们和正确的国家名称搭配起来。

Match them with the correct countries.

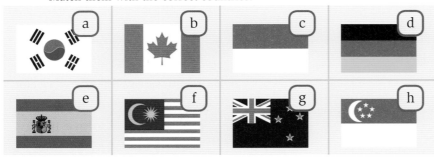

i. 新西兰　ii. 德国　iii. 马来西亚　iv. 西班牙　v. 加拿大
vi. 印度尼西亚　vii. 韩国　viii. 新加坡

xīn xī lán
新西兰 New Zealand

dé guó
德国 Germany

xī bān yá
西班牙 Spain

jiā ná dà
加拿大 Canada

hán guó
韩国 South Korea

mǎ lái xī yà
马来西亚 Malaysia

yìn dù ní xī yà   yìn ní
印度尼西亚（印尼）Indonesia

b. 和你的同学轮流说出这些国家在哪一个洲。

With a partner, take turns to say in which continents these countries are found.

3. 阅读下面的短文，然后回答问题。

Read the passage below, then answer the questions.

> 我是大卫，是德国人。德国是一个十分美丽有意思的地方。德国是一个欧洲中部的国家，是欧洲人口第二大国。这里大多数人说德语，在学校里学生必须学习英语。这里的气候是夏天热冬天冷，一年四季都很分明。这里的秋天最美丽，因为树叶有黄的，有红的，还有绿的，各种颜色，好看极了！我住在德国的南部。南部有很多高高的山和大森林，夏天你也可以来南部的山区爬山，而冬天可以来滑雪。暑假里我常常和朋友一起去山里或森林里徒步和露营。如果你来德国旅游或学习，首都柏林、南部城市慕尼黑也都是不错的选择。

a. 德国在欧洲的什么地方？主要语言是什么？

b. 德国的气候是什么样的？

c. 暑假里大卫常常做哪两个活动？

d. 冬天人们还可以去德国南部山区做什么？

4. 四个人正在谈论自己的旅游计划。先读问题，再听录音，然后选择正确的答案完成句子。

Four people are talking about their travel plans. Read the questions before you listen to the recording, then choose the right answer to complete each sentence.

a. 他们今年夏天计划去日本旅游……。
  - i. 一周
  - ii. 两周
  - iii. 三周

b. 她计划……去欧洲的法国和德国逛传统市场。
  - i. 暑假
  - ii. 秋天
  - iii. 圣诞节

c. 他要去非洲……。
  - i. 看有趣的动物
  - ii. 爬非洲最高的山
  - iii. 参观名胜古迹

d. 他觉得……。
  - i. 南美洲的风景太美了
  - ii. 南美洲的人十分热情
  - iii. 坐飞机去南美洲很累

5. 看看这个城市的照片。写下你可以在照片中看到的五样东西。

Look at this photo of a city. Write down five things you can see from this photo.

---

rén kǒu
人口 population

shǒu dū
首都 capital city

bó lín
柏林 Berlin

mù ní hēi
慕尼黑 Munich

Grammar focus p.271

二 and 两

二: used for counting things, expressing sequence, and mathematical terms

一、二、三
第二名
百分之二、二分之一

两: applied before a measure word to indicate quantity

★ 两 + measure word + object
两个例子
两样东西
两天、两周、两点

LESSON OBJECTIVE
● Describe famous landmarks of well-known cities and express your personal preferences.

1. 看看下面的地标，把它们和正确的城市搭配起来。
   Look at the landmarks below. Match them with the correct cities.

běi jīng 北京 Beijing	
mèng mǎi 孟买 Mumbai	
lún dūn 伦敦 London	
niǔ yuē 纽约 New York	
xī ní 悉尼 Sydney	
bā lí 巴黎 Paris	

i. 北京   **ii.** 孟买   **iii.** 伦敦   **iv.** 纽约   **v.** 悉尼   **vi.** 巴黎

2. 写以下词组的英文意思。
   Translate the following terms and phrases into English.

规模	地位	地理位置	特点
大 小 中等	全世界 国际 首都	东/西/南/北部 海边 中部	现代/年轻 古老/传统 有活力的/受欢迎的 吸引人的/绿色环保的 繁忙的/热闹的

3. 和你的同学轮流用第二题的词组成一句话描述下面的城市。
   With a partner, take turns to say one sentence about each of these cities, using the phrases from Activity 2.

   a. 中国的北京   **b.** 英国的伦敦   **c.** 巴西的里约

   d. 意大利的罗马   **e.** 日本的东京

bā xī 巴西 Brazil	
lǐ yuē 里约 Rio de Janeiro	
yì dà lì 意大利 Italy	
luó mǎ 罗马 Rome	
dōng jīng 东京 Tokyo	

4. 你将会听到一段关于釜山的录音。先读问题，再听录音，然后选择正确的答案完成句子。

You will hear a description of Busan. Read the questions before you listen to the recording, then choose the right answer to complete each sentence.

zhù míng de
著名的 famous; renowned
fǔ shān
釜山 Busan

a. 釜山除了有美丽的沙滩和夜景，还有这里最有名的是……。

  i. 历史博物馆

  ii. 民族艺术馆

  iii. 历史悠久的传统市场

b. 在釜山旅游……最方便。

  i. 坐公共汽车

  ii. 坐旅游巴士

  iii. 坐地铁

c. 釜山电影节已经举办了……。

  i. 十年

  ii. 十五年

  iii. 大约二十年

d. 十月在釜山可以……。

  i. 免费看很多音乐会

  ii. 见到明星、名人

  iii. 吃到各式免费的美食

5. 阅读下面的内容，然后选择正确的词语填空。

Read the following passage and choose the correct words to fill in the blanks.

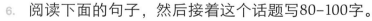

很远　觉得　东边的　地铁　买车　五年　现代化的　快

麦可已经在这个城市住了**(a)**了。他住的房子在城市的**(b)**郊区，但是离市中心不是**(c)**。他**(d)**这个城市和他的家乡很不同，家乡是一个安静的海边小城，而这里是一个**(e)**国际城市。这里最棒的就是方便的公共交通，有四通八达的**(f)**网络，去哪儿都又**(g)**又方便，因此不用**(h)**。

6. 阅读下面的句子，然后接着这个话题写80–100字。

Read the following opening sentence, then complete it by writing 80 to 100 characters on the topic.

…… 是我去过的最棒的一个旅游城市，因为……。

LESSON OBJECTIVES
- Identify various traditions and customs from around the world.
- Describe your personal experience of participating in a local festival.

1. 阅读以下句子，写下这些传统节日的时间。
   Read the sentences below and note down the correct time of each festival.

   a. 日本的樱花节是春季节日，一般是在三月到四月之间。

   b. 泰国的泼水节是在每年的四月十三日到十五日之间，是泰国的新年。

   c. 巴西里约的狂欢节是世界上最著名的，通常在每年的二月举行。

yīng huā jié 樱花节	Cherry Blossom Festival
tài guó 泰国	Thailand
pō shuǐ jié 泼水节	Songkran Festival, also known as Water Sprinkle Festival
kuáng huān jié 狂欢节	carnival

2. 阅读活动信息表，然后判断右面的叙述是对或错。
   Read the information, and decide if the statements on the right are true or false.

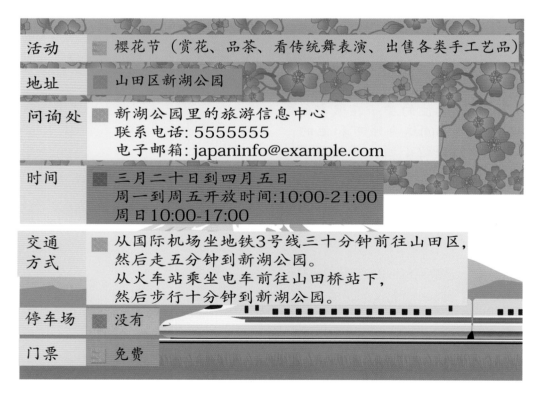

活动	樱花节（赏花、品茶、看传统舞表演、出售各类手工艺品）
地址	山田区新湖公园
问询处	新湖公园里的旅游信息中心 联系电话: 5555555 电子邮箱: japaninfo@example.com
时间	三月二十日到四月五日 周一到周五开放时间:10:00-21:00 周日 10:00-17:00
交通方式	从国际机场坐地铁3号线三十分钟前往山田区，然后走五分钟到新湖公园。 从火车站乘坐电车前往山田桥站下，然后步行十分钟到新湖公园。
停车场	没有
门票	免费

a. 樱花节在一个公园里举行。

b. 旅游信息中心就在新湖公园的对面。

c. 樱花节是一个春天里的节日。

d. 节日每天开放的时间都是从上午十点到晚上九点。

e. 从机场坐地铁到山田区只要半个小时。

f. 樱花节的门票是免费的。

3. 阅读句子，选出正确的词语填空，然后朗读。

Read the passage, choose the correct words to fill in the blanks, then read the completed passage out loud.

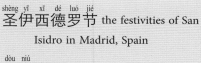

mín jiān yīn yuè jié
民间音乐节 folk music festival

住在　除了　英国　各种各样的　免费　举行　每年　票价　最受欢迎的　参加

(a) 的七月底，在(b)的剑桥城都会举行民间音乐节。剑桥民间音乐节已经 (c)了五十多次了，是英国(d)民间音乐节之一。音乐节期间，(e) 有音乐，有英格兰传统舞表演，还有(f)游戏活动，大人小孩都可以(g)。参加音乐节的人们可以选择(h) 附近的酒店，还可以选择在音乐节所在的绿地露营。音乐节成人(i)是一百五十九英镑，儿童票（五岁到十五岁）是五十英镑，五岁以下儿童(j)。

4. 先读问题，再听录音，然后选择正确的答案完成句子。

Read the questions before you listen to the recording. Then choose the correct answer to complete each sentence.

a. 马德里在西班牙的……。
　　i. 北部　　**ii.** 南部　　**iii.** 中部

b. 从圣伊西德罗节人们可以了解……。
　　i. 历史　　**ii.** 地理　　**iii.** 民俗传统

c. 圣伊西德罗节在……举行。
　　i. 5月5日　　**ii.** 5月15日　　**iii.** 5月25日

d. 节日期间人们除了可以观看传统的西班牙舞表演，还可以……。
　　i. 观看西班牙斗牛　　**ii.** 看精彩的足球比赛

e. 因为参加活动的人很多，马德里城的交通会很拥挤，所以大家最好……。
　　i. 坐地铁或走路　　**ii.** 坐出租车

shèng yī xī dé luó jié
圣伊西德罗节 the festivities of San Isidro in Madrid, Spain

dòu niú
斗牛 bullfighting

yōng jǐ
拥挤 crowded

Grammar focus p.271

最好: had better, used for making a suggestion

★ subject + 最好 + action
（在伦敦旅游）大家最好坐地铁（，因为不会堵车）。

5. 给你的网友写一篇关于参加传统活动的电子邮件，写 80-100个字。其中应该包括：

Write an email to your friend about a festival you have attended. Write 80–100 characters. It should include:

a. 你最近参加了什么特别的传统节日？　　**b.** 这个节日是哪里的传统节日？

c. 节日的时候有哪些庆祝活动？　　**d.** 你觉得这个节日怎么样？最喜欢这个节日的什么活动？

LESSON OBJECTIVES
- Identify facilities inside an airport.
- Deal with problems and make enquiries at an international airport.

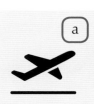

1. 看看下面的机场图标，把它们和正确的意思搭配起来。
Look at the airport signs below. Match them with the correct meanings.

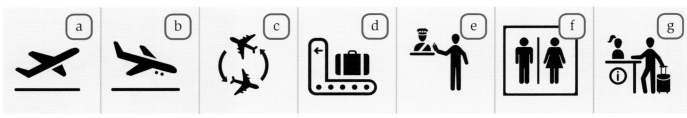

i. 海关　**ii.** 办票　**iii.** 卫生间　**iv.** 转机　**v.** 服务台　**vi.** 出发　**vii.** 到达

2. 阅读下面妈妈发给小美的手机短信，然后回答问题。
Read the message from Xiaomei's mother, then answer the questions.

> 小美：
> 妈妈现在还在机场，还没有接到林阿姨。广播说因为香港下大雨，所以林阿姨从香港到釜山的飞机晚了一个半小时，预计晚上七点到达釜山，所以你和爸爸先吃饭吧，不用等我们了。我们大约八点十五分回家。
> 妈妈

hǎi guān 海关 customs
bàn piào 办票 to check in
wèi shēng jiān 卫生间 W.C.
zhuǎn jī 转机 flight transfer
fú wù tái 服务台 help desk
chū fā 出发 to set off; departure
dào dá 到达 to arrive; arrival

a. 妈妈在哪里？做什么？

b. 林阿姨从哪个城市来？

c. 为什么飞机晚了？

d. 林阿姨乘坐的飞机会晚多长时间？

e. 妈妈要小美和爸爸先做什么？

f. 妈妈和林阿姨几点回家？

3. 先读下面的句子，再听录音，然后判断叙述对或错。
Read the sentences below before you listen to the recording, then decide if the statements are true or false.

a. 林女士把手提包忘了。

b. OUP8112次航班是从香港飞往马德里的。

c. 航班OUP8112已经起飞了。

d. OUP6886次航班登机口在二十一号。

e. OUP6886次航班预计半个小时后开始登机。

f. 希思罗机场位于罗马。

háng bān 航班 flight
dēng jī kǒu 登机口 boarding gate
dēng jī 登机 to board a plane
xī sī luó jī chǎng 希思罗机场 Heathrow Airport (London)
wèi yú 位于 to be located in

4. 阅读对话，然后选择正确的答案来完成句子。
Read the dialogue, then choose the correct answers to complete the sentences.

	wǎn diǎn

晚点 behind schedule

公斤 gōng jīn kilogram

检查 jiǎn chá to inspect

安全 ān quán safety

小　美：本杰明，是我，小美。我现在还在新加坡
　　　　国际机场，错过了转机。
本杰明：为什么？从新西兰到新加坡的飞机没有
　　　　晚点啊。
小　美：是的。但是在新加坡机场转机时，他们告诉
　　　　我我的行李超重了，有32公斤，工作人员需
　　　　要检查我的行李箱。
本杰明：你的行李箱里没有装水果或肉食吧？
小　美：没有，但是我带了五块新西兰出产的奶酪，
　　　　他们说因为食品安全问题，不可以把奶酪带
　　　　入英国。他们还在检查我的行李呢。
本杰明：那你现在打算怎么办？
小　美：我现在等着和这里的海关工作人员谈话。谈
　　　　话以后再决定吧。
本杰明：那好，在你坐上下一班去伦敦的航班以前打
　　　　电话告诉我你的航班号吧。

错过 cuò guò to miss

超重 chāo zhòng overweight

奶酪 nǎi lào cheese

班 bān measure word for a flight or train

a. 小美现在在……。
　　i. 新西兰机场　　　ii. 新加坡机场　　　iii. 伦敦机场

b. 机场工作人员告诉小美……是不可以带入英国的。
　　i. 水果　　　ii. 肉食　　　iii. 奶酪

c. 小美现在正在等着……。
　　i. 跟机场工作人员说话　　　ii. 转机去伦敦　　　iii. 办票

d. 本杰明让小美在上飞机以前……。
　　i. 吃晚饭，因为飞机上的食物不好吃
　　ii. 打电话告诉他小美坐的飞机的航班号

Grammar focus p.271

着: often used after a verb to describe an action is in progress

★ subject + verb + 着

我等着（跟海关的工作
人员谈话）。
同学们（都在教室里）
坐着。

5. 和你的同学角色扮演一个乘客和机场航空售票处的工作人
员之间的对话，轮流提出和回答下面的问题，并写下来。

With a partner, role-play a conversation between a passenger and an airline ticketing staff member. Take turns to ask and answer these questions, then write them out.

公司 gōng sī company

头等舱 tóu děng cāng first-class cabin

经济舱 jīng jì cāng economy cabin

a. 您去哪一个城市？　　　**b.** 您要单程票还是双程票？

c. 您要买几点出发的航班？　　　**d.** 您想坐哪个航空公司的飞机？

e. 您买头等舱还是经济舱？

LESSON OBJECTIVES

● Identify a variety of modes of transport.
● Describe your experiences of taking public transport.

● Express your opinion about your local public transport system.

📖 1. 先看图，再读句子，然后把它们正确地搭配起来。

Look at the pictures before you read the statements, then match them up correctly.

 a
 b
 c
 d
 e
 f

i. 伦敦最有特色的交通工具是红色的双层公共汽车。
ii. 伦敦有世界上最古老的地铁系统。
iii. 葡萄牙的里斯本以黄色的电车闻明世界。
iv. 在荷兰的阿姆斯特丹，自行车是最受欢迎的交通工具。
v. 现在越来越多的人喜欢用手机预定出租车。
vi. 不喜欢坐飞机长途旅行的人可以坐船。

> gōng gòng qì chē
> 公(共汽)车 bus
> diàn chē
> 电车 tram
> chū zū chē
> 出租车 taxi (cab)

> pú táo yá
> 葡萄牙 Portugal
> lǐ sī běn
> 里斯本 Lisbon
> hé lán
> 荷兰 the Netherlands
> ā mǔ sī tè dān
> 阿姆斯特丹 Amsterdam

📖 2. 阅读下面的内容，判断叙述对还是错。

Read the passages below, then decide if the statements are true or false.

米娜居住在一个古老的小镇，那儿有很多大大小小的河，小镇里有很多桥，除了走路外，坐船也是不错的交通方式。

思华来自新加坡，虽然他有车，但是很少开车，因为新加坡的公共交通又方便又快，坐公共交通去哪儿都方便，而且还没有停车的麻烦，所以思华更喜欢坐地铁去公司上班。

a. 米娜住的城市有世界上最忙的机场之一。

b. 米娜住的地方有很多条河。

c. 思华在新加坡很少开车。

d. 思华家附近有公车站，所以他几乎天天坐公共汽车。

> **Grammar focus** p.271
>
> 更喜欢 means like something/doing something even more
>
> ★ subject + 喜欢 + action 1,
> 但是 + 更喜欢 + action 2
> + reason
>
> 他喜欢坐火车旅游，但是更喜欢自己开车旅游，因为他觉得自己开车更方便，想去哪儿就去哪儿。

3. 先读句子，再听录音，然后选择正确答案完成句子。

Read the sentences before you listen to the recording, then choose the correct answer to complete each one.

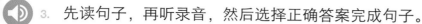

bèi bāo
背包 backpack

jiàng luò
降落 to land

shì gù
事故 accident

a. 她把……忘在出租车上了。
  i. 背包　　**ii.** 手提包　　**iii.** 手机

b. 他们坐的飞机的降落时间会……。
  i. 晚十分钟　　**ii.** 晚二十分钟　　**iii.** 晚半个小时

c. 她们坐的火车停了，因为……。
  i. 前面有红灯。　　**ii.** 火车的空调坏了。
  iii. 铁路上出了小事故。

4. 和你的同学角色扮演一个旅客和火车站的售票员之间的对话，轮流提出和回答下面的问题。

With a partner, role-play a conversation between a passenger and a ticket office staff member in a train station. Take turns to ask and answer these questions.

dān chéng piào
单程票 single ticket

zuò wèi piào
座位票 seated ticket

yìng wò
硬卧 hard sleeper

ruǎn wò
软卧 soft sleeper

a. 您好。请问您去哪儿？　　**b.** 您要单程票还是来回票？

c. 您需要买座位票、硬卧还是软卧？

d. 您要买几点出发的火车？　　**e.** 您需要买几张票？

5. 练习写汉字。按照笔画顺序写下面的字。

Practise writing Chinese. Write the characters by following the stroke order.

kāi
开 开 开 开 开
  1 2 3 4

wǎng
往 往 往 往 往 往 往 往 往
  1 2 3 4 5 6 7 8

6. 写一篇关于一次难忘的火车旅行的日记。写 120–150 个字。其中应该包括：

Write a diary entry about a memorable train journey. Use 120–150 characters. It should include:

a. 火车是什么样的？

b. 这趟火车的出发地和目的地是哪儿？

c. 旅行用了多长时间？

d. 在火车上的时候你看到了什么有趣的风景或做了什么好玩的事？

LESSON OBJECTIVES
- Describe a range of common traffic problems.
- Discuss some environmental issues caused by traffic.
- Consider the pros and cons of different modes of transport.

1. 读短句，选择正确的英文意思配对。

Read the Chinese sentences below and match them with the correct English translation.

a. 我的自行车被偷了。
b. 爸爸的摩托车坏了。
c. 姐姐坐的公共汽车出了故障。
d. 机场路出了一场小的交通事故。
e. 车站路出了车祸。

i. The bus my sister took broke down.
ii. There is a small traffic incident on Airport Road.
iii. A traffic accident happened on Station Road.
iv. Dad's motorbike broke down.
v. My bike has been stolen.

> tōu
> 偷 to steal
>
> mó tuō chē
> 摩托车 motorcycle
>
> gù zhàng
> 故障 breakdown
>
> chē huò
> 车祸 motor accident

> kāi wǎng
> 开往 to leave for; to go towards

> jué dìng
> 决定 to decide
>
> tíng
> 停 to stop

2. 先读下面的句子，再听录音，然后判断下面的叙述是对或错。

Read the statements before you listen to the recording, then decide if they are true or false.

a. 游客们可以坐船去天空岛。
b. 去天空岛的游船每个小时一班。
c. 游客们在那里可以看到很多特别的植物。
d. 岛上没有汽车。
e. 在岛上你可以骑自行车参观。
f. 天气预报说明天晚上六点开始有大风。
g. 为了安全，游船公司决定明天下午往天空岛的所有游船都不开了。

3. 练习写汉字。

Practise writing Chinese.

a. 按照笔画顺序写下面的字。

Write the characters by following the stroke order.

wū
污 污 污 污 污 污 污
  1 2 3 4 5 6

rǎn
染 染 染 染 染 染 染 染 染
  1 2 3 4 5 6 7 8

b. 设计一张海报来鼓励更多的学生走路或骑自行车上学。海报应该包括"污染"和"没有污染"这两个词语。

Design a poster to encourage more students to walk or cycle to school. Include the terms 污染 and 没有污染 on your poster.

4. 阅读下面的短文，然后回答右边的问题。

Read this short passage, then answer the questions.

> 香港电车在1904年开始在香港岛上运行，是香港历史最为悠久的交通工具之一，深受当地居民和游客们的欢迎，是香港最便宜、最方便、最环保的公共交通工具。近年来乘坐香港电车已经成为来港游客必做的旅游项目。坐在这种怀旧的双层电车上，悠闲地欣赏多姿多彩的城市景观的同时，游客们也收获了一次特别的旅行经历。

yōu jiǔ
悠久 well-established; long

huái jiù
怀旧 retro; vintage

yōu xián
悠闲 leisurely; at ease

duō zī duō cǎi
多姿多彩 colourful

a. 短文中谈到的交通工具是什么？

b. 这种交通工具为什么受到欢迎？

c. 为什么很多游客会去乘坐那种交通工具？

Grammar focus p.272

忙不忙: busy or not busy

★ stative verb + 不 + stative verb

远不远/快不快/
多不多

5. 和你的同学轮流提出和回答下面关于当地的交通问题。

With a partner, take turns to ask and answer the following questions about the traffic situation near your school.

a. 你住的城市会不会经常堵车？ **b.** 你们学校周围的交通忙不忙？

c. 学生们和老师们觉得安全吗？ **d.** 除了不安全以外，路上汽车太多还会有什么问题？

e. 你觉得学校、学生、家长还有当地的政府应该做些什么让学校周围更安全？

Cultural spotlight

zhōng guó de gāo sù tiě lù
中国的高速铁路 High-speed railway in China

高速铁路，又称为高铁。中国的高速铁路系统拥有世界上最长的高速铁路网。最近十年来，中国为了在城市和城市之间提供更经济、更快捷、更环保的交通而快速发展高速铁路。现在中国很多地方都有了高铁。

2011年北京到上海的高铁完成第一次通车，全程只需五个小时左右。这条高铁线路已经成为世界上最忙的高速铁路。中国目前已经成为像德国和日本一样的世界上最重要的高铁竞争者和出口国之一。

a. 你的国家有高铁吗？你认为高铁有哪些好处和坏处？

b. 在你居住的地方有哪些比较环保的交通工具？

LESSON OBJECTIVE

● Share your experiences of dealing with lost property.

1. 以下是一些常见的丢失的物品，写下这些词语的拼音和每个字的部首。

Here are some common items that people often misplace or lose. Write down the pinyin and radical for each character of these items.

现金　信用卡　手机　电脑　照相机　护照　背包

物品	拼音	部首
钱包	qián bāo	钱 = 钅；包 = 勹

2. 五个人都不见了一些东西。先看图，再听录音，然后把他们的名称和不见了的物品搭配起来。

Five people have each lost something. Look at the pictures before you listen to the recording, then match the correct person to the item they have lost.

a. 米娜　**b.** 本杰明　**c.** 约翰　**d.** 志军　**e.** 小美

bù jiàn le
不见了 lost

zhǎo bù dào
找不到 cannot find

jǐng chá
警察 police

xiǎo tou
小偷 thief

Grammar focus p.272

被: describes how a particular object is dealt with by somebody or something

★ object + 被 + subject + verb action

手机被小偷偷了。

3. 一名飞机乘客下机后没有取到行李箱。和你的同学角色扮演乘客和机场工作人员之间的对话，轮流提出和回答右边的问题。

A passenger is unable to find their luggage after arriving at the airport. With a partner, role-play a conversation between the passenger and an airport staff member. Take turns to ask and answer the questions on the right.

a. 您好，您叫什么名字？

b. 您是从哪个城市出发的？

c. 您的行李箱是什么颜色的？

d. 行李箱有多大？

e. 行李箱里有什么东西？

f. 您的手机号码是多少？

4. 阅读小美和妈妈的短信对话，判断下面的叙述对还是错。

Read the text messages between Xiaomei and her mother, and decide if the following statements are true or false.

小美：妈，今天我把我的钱包给丢了。

妈妈：又丢了？你今年钱包都丢了三回了！钱包里有什么？

小美：有五十元零用钱，还有我的学生卡、图书卡和公共交通卡。

妈妈：还好，钱不是很多。但是你的学生卡、图书卡、公共交通卡找不到了，那就麻烦了。你好好想一想，今天在学校里你去过哪儿？

小美：学校里我今天去过的地方，外语教室、体育馆、图书馆我都找过了，没找到。

妈妈：那学校食堂呢？吃饭的地方看过了吗？

小美：我今天中午和同学一起是去外面的餐馆吃的面条。放学后我去那家餐馆问一问。

妈妈：好的。放学后再给我打电话。没有公共交通卡、没有钱，你今天就坐不了地铁了。如果还是找不到，妈妈开车去接你。

diū 丢 to lose
má fán 麻烦 troublesome
jiē 接 to pick (someone) up

zuò bù liǎo 坐不了 cannot get on (a vehicle or mode of transport)

a. 小美今天把钱包丢了。

b. 小美的书包不见了。

c. 她今天还丢了学生卡和图书卡。

d. 小美今天去过外语教室。

e. 她只在图书馆、体育馆找过了。

f. 中午她和同学在学校餐厅吃了面条。

g. 放学后小美会去外面的一家餐馆找钱包。

h. 小美在给妈妈打电话让妈妈开车来接她。

5. 昨天你在游泳馆游完泳，在更衣室里发现你的手表不见了。写一篇关于这件事的日记。在日记里你还可以写你是怎样解决这个问题的。写100–120个字。

You went swimming yesterday, and realised you lost your watch in the changing room. Write a diary entry about this, and say how you resolved the problem. Write 100–120 characters.

1. 选择正确的词语填空。

a. 一个学生跟老师说话，她说："李老师，…… 好"。
   i. 您
   ii. 你
   iii. 他

b. 如果有人跟你说"谢谢"，你应该跟她／他说"……"。
   i. 对不起
   ii. 没关系
   iii. 不客气

c. 小明跟你说"对不起"，你会跟他说"……"。
   i. 谢谢你
   ii. 不用谢
   iii. 没关系

d. 早上起床你会和爸爸妈妈说"……"。
   i. 早安
   ii. 午安
   iii. 晚安

e. 你去朋友家里玩，要走的时候你的朋友对你说"……"。
   i. 快点走
   ii. 慢走
   iii. 对不起

2. 阅读下面的叙述，然后判断它们是对还是错。

a. 日本是一个东亚国家，东京是日本最大的城市。

b. 香港在中国的南部，那里的夏天非常热。

c. 纽约在美国的西部，是一个非常现代化的城市。

d. 澳大利亚的首都悉尼是一个海边城市。

e. 印度是世界上人口第二多的国家。

3. 写出五样你在机场带着的东西。

4. 看看下面的图片，然后写出关于每一种交通工具的特别之处，写20-30个字。

5. 重新组织下面的词语，并写出完整的句子。

a. 在 / 是最好的 / 市中心 / 旅行方式 / 走路 / 台北的 / 。

b. 去植物园 / 周末 / 我们 / 骑自行车 / 打算 / 。

c. 的 / 坐船 / 夏天 / 去年 / 我们 / 是 / 去西班牙 / 。

d. 免费的 / 公共汽车上 / 伦敦城里的 / 网络 / 有 / 。

6. 一名海关工作人员正在和旅客谈话。先读问题，再听录音，然后选择正确答案。

a. 旅客来自……。
   i. 美国
   ii. 加拿大
   iii. 澳大利亚

b. 旅客来北京……。
   i. 看名胜古迹
   ii. 看朋友
   iii. 上大学，学习汉语

c. ……游客来过北京参加夏令营。
   i. 去年夏天
   ii. 两年前
   iii. 半年前

d. 他会住在……。
   i. 国际学生公寓
   ii. 朋友家
   iii. 酒店里

e. 他的手提包里没有……。
   i. 照相机
   ii. 手机
   iii. 电脑

7. 给学校的中文杂志写一篇120–150个字的关于当地交通的短文。其中应该包括：

a. 你们当地有哪些公共交通？

b. 你对这些公共交通的想法。

c. 交通公司可以做些什么吸引更多的人乘坐公共交通？

d. 当地政府可以做些什么让当地的公共交通更好？

e. 如果我去你们当地，我坐什么最好？为什么？

8. 和你的同学聊聊不同的城市，轮流提出和回答下面的问题。

a. 你去过世界上哪些有名的城市？

b. 最喜欢哪一个？为什么？

c. 如果我去那个城市，你推荐我参观什么景点？为什么？

d. 如果我去那个城市，你觉得哪一种交通方式最方便？

e. 你以后想不想来中国？最想去哪儿？做什么？

UNIT OBJECTIVES

- Describe and discuss a variety of extracurricular activities.
- Describe and discuss what happens on a foreign school exchange programme.
- Share your experiences of organising and taking part in volunteering activities.
- Describe and discuss your preparations for university.
- Share your hopes and plans for after university graduation.
- Share facts and opinions about vocational education.

1. 翻译下面的英文句子，用中文读出来。

Translate the following sentences from English into Chinese, and read them out.

a. Mum wants me to choose two extracurricular activities next term.

b. I would like to do an online course next year.

c. My brother is very happy with his life at university.

d. Dad enjoys volunteering during the weekend.

2. 小文和劳拉正在谈话。先读问题，再听录音，然后写下答案。

Xiaowen is talking to Laura. Look at the questions before you listen to the recording, then choose the correct answers.

a. 小文想读哪一个大学专业?
   i. 计算机学
   ii. 技术培训
   iii. 网络课程

b. 为什么小文对这个专业特别感兴趣?
   i. 觉得很简单
   ii. 觉得很有趣
   iii. 觉得很期待

c. 小文没有参加哪一个课外活动?
   i. 踢足球
   ii. 网络校际交流
   iii. 去老人院做义工

wǎng luò kè chéng
网络课程 online course

dà xué shēng huó
大学生活 life at university

yì gōng
义工 volunteering

dà xué zhuān yè
大学专业 university field of study

jì shù péi xùn
技术培训 skills development and training

xiào jì jiāo liú
校际交流 interschool communications; school exchange

rù xué shēn qǐng
入学申请 university admission

jì suàn jī xué
计算机学 computer science

qī dài
期待 to look forward to

lǎo rén yuàn
老人院 old people's home

biǎo gé
表格 form

shì jiè
世界 world

3. 练习写汉字。

Practise writing Chinese.

a. 按照笔画顺序写下面的字。

Write the characters by following the stroke order.

kè

课 课 课 课 课 课 课 课 课 课 课
1 2 3 4 5 6 7 8 9 10

wài

外 外 外 外 外 外
1 2 3 4 5

huó

活 活 活 活 活 活 活 活 活 活
1 2 3 4 5 6 7 8 9

dòng

动 动 动 动 动 动 动
1 2 3 4 5 6

b. 用以上词语造句，写出一项你喜欢的课外活动。写10–20
个字。

Using the above vocabulary, write a sentence of your own about one of
your favourite extracurricular activities. Write 10–20 characters.

4. 和你的同学练习介绍自己今年参加的课外活动，轮流提出
和回答下面的问题。

With a partner, practise talking about the extracurricular activities you've
taken up this year. Take turns to ask and answer the following questions.

a. 你叫什么名字？

b. 今年你加了什么活动？

c. 你觉得这个活动怎么样？

LESSON OBJECTIVES
- Identify a range of extracurricular activities.
- Describe your past, present, and future activities.
- Share your opinion about these activities.

1. 看看下面的图片，把它们和正确的词语搭配起来。
   Look at the pictures below and match them with the correct vocabulary.

 a  b  c  d

i. 给老人讲故事　**ii.** 清洁沙滩　**iii.** 发传单　**iv.** 义卖

qīng jié
清洁 to clean

jiǎng gù shi
讲故事 storytelling

fā chuán dān
发传单 to distribute leaflets

yì mài
义卖 charity sale

2. 阅读志军的日记，然后回答问题。
   Read Zhijun's diary entry and answer the questions.

> 九月十日　星期二　天气：晴
>
> 　我以前从来没有参加过社区服务活动，今年打算试一试。听老师说今年我们可以参加的活动有：去老人院给老人讲故事、清洁沙滩、发健康知识的传单和义卖筹款。我对这些活动都感兴趣，都打算参加，但是我一个人去有点没意思，不如我明天邀请心美和小明一起参加吧！

shè qū fú wù
社区服务 community service

jiàn kāng zhī shi
健康知识 knowledge on health

chóu kuǎn
筹款 fundraising

a. 志军以前参加过社区服务活动吗？

b. 志军今年打算参加哪一些社区服务活动？

c. 志军会邀请谁一起去？

3. 心美和志军正在谈话。先读下面的问题，再听录音，然后选择正确的答案。

Sammy and Zhijun are talking. Look at the questions before you listen to the recording, then choose the correct answers.

a. 志军去年没有参加哪一个活动？
   i. 摄影   **ii.** 爬山   **iii.** 书法

b. 心美去年没有参加哪一个协会？
   i. 唱歌   **ii.** 跳舞   **iii.** 摄影

c. 心美学唱歌和跳舞学了几年了？
   i. 一年   **ii.** 两年   **iii.** 三年

d. 志军和心美今年参加什么社区服务活动？
   i. 义卖和去老人院给老人们讲故事
   ii. 义卖和清洁沙滩
   iii. 义卖和发健康知识的传单

4. 和你的同学谈你们今年参加的社区服务活动，轮流提出和回答下面的问题。

With a partner, talk about any community service activities you are taking part in this year. Take turns to ask and answer the following questions.

a. 你今年参加了哪一项社区服务活动？

b. 为什么你会参加这个活动？

c. 你参加这个活动多久了？

5. 今天你和同学一起参加了一个社区服务活动。用100–120个字写一封电邮给朋友。其中应该包括：

You took part in a community service programme with your class today. Using 100–120 characters, write an email to your friend to tell them about it. It should include:

a. 参加了什么活动？

b. 在活动中做了些什么？

c. 觉得怎么样？

d. 下次还会不会再去？

---

xié huì
协会 club, society

yǒu yì yi
有意义 meaningful

Grammar focus   p.272

1. 试一试: give it a try
   ★ subject + (verb) + verb + 一 + verb
   我(想)试一试。
   我想试一试（学跳舞）。

2. 学⋯⋯学了: have learned ... for
   ★ subject + verb + object + verb + 了 + duration
   我学中文学了两年。
   我参加这个活动参加了半年。

8.3 校际交流
GOING ON A SCHOOL EXCHANGE PROGRAMME

LESSON OBJECTIVES

- Describe the travel and living arrangements for your school exchange programme.
- Describe and discuss the activities offered on the exchange programme.
- Share your experience of being on a school exchange programme.

1. 阅读以下的情况，选择适当的交通工具。
   Read the scenarios below, and choose the best mode of transport in each case.

 a  b 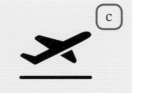 c

> jiāo huàn (xué) shēng jiāo liú shēng
> 交换(学)生/交流生 exchange student

   i. 我住在伦敦。我要去北京大学当交换生。
      我要搭什么交通工具？

   ii. 我住在香港。我要去香港大学当交换生。
       我要搭什么交通工具？

> biǎo yǎn
> 表演 to perform
> jiāo liú
> 交流 to communicate

   iii. 我住在广州，我要去北京大学当交换生。
        我买不到机票，我还可以搭什么交通工具？

2. 阅读短文，然后判断下面的叙述对还是错。
   Read the passage and decide if the following statements are true or false.

> dāng
> 当 to be; become
> jīng jù
> 京剧 Beijing opera

马克打算去北京的学校参加校际交流活动。他想当一个交换学生。他会坐飞机到那儿去。到了北京的学校以后，他会表演西方戏剧给那儿的学生看，他也会和那儿的学生一起唱中国的京剧，他还会唱歌给他们听。

马克的好朋友汤姆打算去上海的学校当交换学生，和马克一样，他也会坐飞机到上海去。到了上海的学校以后，他打算和那儿的学生一起上中文课学中文。马克和汤姆都非常期待去中国和那儿的学生交流，因为他们将会认识很多新朋友。

a. 马克打算去中国的学校当交换学生。

b. 马克会坐火车去那儿。

c. 马克会表演西方戏剧给那儿的学生看。

d. 马克会和那儿的老师一起唱中国的京剧。

e. 马克会唱歌给那儿的学生听。

f. 汤姆打算和上海的学生一起学习中文。

g. 只有马克很期待参加交流活动。

3. 玛莉和志军正在谈话。先看图片和问题，再听录音，然后选择唯一正确的答案。

Mary and Zhijun are talking. Look at the pictures and questions before you listen to the recording, then choose the correct answers.

宿舍 dormitory
sù shè

a. 玛莉会去哪儿当交换学生?

i. 　　ii. 　　iii.

b. 玛莉住哪儿?

i. 　　ii. 　　iii.

c. 玛莉坐什么交通工具去?

i. 　　ii. 　　iii.

d. 玛莉在那儿不做什么?

i. 　　ii. 　　iii.

4. 你在上海，今天是你参加校际交流活动的第二天。和你的同学轮流提出和回答下面的问题，然后用答案写一封电邮给你父母。写 80–120 个字。

You are in Shanghai. Today is the second day of your school exchange programme. With a partner, take turns to ask and answer the questions. Then use your answers to write an email to your parents. Write 80–120 characters.

a. 你是坐什么交通工具去的?

b. 你住在哪儿?

c. 你做了什么?

d. 你觉得活动怎么样?

Grammar focus p.272

1. 坐……去 : take (a vehicle) ... to
★ subject + 坐 + vehicle + 去 + location
陈明坐火车去北京。

2. 住在 : live in (verb followed by post-verb)
★ subject + 住在 + place
他住在宿舍。

LESSON OBJECTIVES
● Describe the volunteering activities you have taken part in.
● Discuss with others how you plan and organise the activities.

1. 重组以下句子。

Re-organise the words below to form complete sentences.

a. 玛莉 / 社区服务活动 / 同学 /去参加 /计划/ 带 /。

b. 心美、小明和玛莉 / 义工 / 都 / 做 / 会 /。

c. 带同学 / 打扫卫生 / 负责 / 帮老人 / 心美 / 去 / 老人院 /。

d. 沙滩 / 负责 / 去 / 清洁 / 小明 / 带同学 /。

e. 活动 / 玛莉 / 负责 / 义卖 /。

jì huà
计划 to plan
fù zé
负责 responsible for

2. 小明负责帮忙计划和组织义工活动。阅读以下他写的笔记，然后回答问题。

Xiaoming is helping to plan and organise some volunteering activities. Read the notes he has written and answer the questions.

yī gòng
一共 in total
liǎo jiě
了解 to know

义工活动笔记

● A班：四人参加，四人不参加。

● B班：五人参加，三人不参加。

● C班：八人参加，四人不参加。

● 一共十七人参加，十一人不参加。

● 去老人院给老人讲故事的有五人，参加的全都是B班的同学。参加清洁沙滩活动的同学有八人，有C班和A班的同学。

● 参加义卖的同学有四人，都是C班的学生。

● 我们什么时候去？我要先向老师了解一下。

a. A班参加义工活动的有几个人？

b. B班不参加义工活动的有几个人？

c. 参加义工活动的一共有几个人？

d. C班的同学参加了哪一些活动？

e. 小明要先向老师了解一下什么？

3. 三个人正在谈论他们的义工活动。每个叙述听两遍。先看图片和问题，再听录音，然后选择唯一正确的答案。

Three people are talking about their volunteering activities. You will hear each statement twice. Look at the pictures and questions before you listen to the recording, then choose the correct answers.

组织 to organise

 a
 b
 c

a. 约翰想带同学参加清洁沙滩活动，他得先和谁联系？

b. 海伦想组织义卖活动，然后邀请同学参加。她得先和谁联系？

c. 小华想带同学去老人院给老人讲故事，他得先和谁联系？

慈善机构 charity organisation

Grammar focus p.273

几 : how much, how many
★ subject + verb + 几 + measure word + noun + (verb)
A班有几个人(参加)?

4. 和你的同学角色扮演一位负责义工活动的老师和一个学生之间的对话，轮流提出和回答下面的问题。

With a partner, role-play a conversation between a teacher in charge of the school's volunteering programme and a student. Take turns to ask and answer the following questions.

a. 你今年会参加哪一个义工活动？

b. 你打算和谁一起参加？

c. 谁负责计划和组织这个活动？

5. 为你参加的义工活动设计一张海报。写60–80个字。海报要包括:

Design a poster about a volunteering activity of your choice. Write 60–80 characters. Your poster needs to include:

a. 学校义工团体的名字　**b.** 活动内容

c. 日期、时间、地点　**d.** 联系方法和资料

LESSON OBJECTIVES

- Identify different university fields of study.
- Share information about the subjects you are interested in studying at university.
- Explain why you would like to study these subjects.

1. 看看下面的图片，把它们和正确的学科搭配起来。
   Look at the pictures below and match them with the correct subjects.

 a  b  c  d

i. 工程系　**ii.** 心理学系　**iii.** 医学系　**iv.** 法律系

gōng chéng
工程 engineering

xīn lǐ xué
心理学 psychology

yī kē　yī xué
医科/医学 medicine

fǎ lǜ
法律 law

xì
系 faculty; department

2. 子敏想了解班里同学打算读的大学专业。她做了一个调查。阅读下面的调查结果，判断下面的叙述对还是错。

   Zimin wanted to find out what her classmates were thinking of studying at university, so she carried out a survey. Read the results and decide if the following statements are true or false.

读文科的有八人，有四个想读法律，有两个想读历史，有一个想读心理学，还有一个想读地理。

读工科有七人，全部都想读工程。

读商科的有八人，有四个想读工商管理，有四个想读市场营销学。

读理科的有六人。有两个想读数学，有两个想读计算机学，有两个想读医学。

以后打算读博士学位的有七人。

以后打算读硕士学位的有八人。

以后打算只读学士学位的有十四人。

wén kē
文科 liberal arts subject

gōng kē
工科 engineering subject

lǐ kē
理科 science subject

shāng kē
商科 business (subject)

gōng shāng guǎn lǐ
工商管理 business management

shì chǎng yíng xiāo xué
市场营销学 marketing

bó shì
博士 doctorate; PhD

xué wèi
学位 degree

shuò shì
硕士 master's degree

xué shì
学士 bachelor's degree

a. 子敏做的是一个关于了解同学参加课外活动的调查

b. 读文科的有八人。

c. 想读法律的学生都读文科。

d. 读工科的人都想读医科。

e. 读商科的有一半想读工商管理，一半想读市场营销学。

f. 读理科的有两个想读医科。

g. 以后打算读硕士的比读博士多。

h. 以后打算只读学士的最少。

3. 五个人正在谈论打算读的大学专业。每个叙述听两遍。先读句子，再听录音，然后选择正确的答案完成句子。

Five people are talking about what they hope to study at university. You will hear each statement twice. Read the sentences before you listen to the recording, then choose the correct answers to complete them.

a. 丁卡想研究＿＿＿。他希望将来可以帮助很多＿＿＿。
   i. 工程   ii. 医学   iii. 病人

b. 天伟想进大学的＿＿＿。他希望将来可以＿＿＿。
   i. 工程系   ii. 心理系   iii. 建大楼

c. 心美的哥哥打算读中国大学的＿＿＿。他希望以后可以伸张正义。
   i. 心理学系   ii. 法律系

d. 娜依玛想读＿＿＿。
   i. 心理学   ii. 法律   iii. 医科

e. 汤姆的爸爸正在读＿＿＿，他研究＿＿＿。
   i. 博士   ii. 学士   iii. 硕士   iv. 法律   v. 心理学   vi. 医学

4. 和你的同学轮流提出和回答下面关于大学专业的问题。

With a partner, take turns to ask and answer the following questions about your plans for further education.

a. 你现在读什么科？

b. 你将来想在大学读哪一个专业？

c. 为什么你想读这个专业？

d. 你将来想读硕士/博士吗？

5. 你和妈妈今天谈了你的大学计划，她不满意你想读的大学专业。用120–150字写一篇日记。其中应该包括：

You and your mother were discussing your plans for university today. She doesn't like the subject you would like to study. Using 120–150 characters, write a diary entry about this. It should include:

a. 你现在的心情怎么样？

b. 你现在读什么科？

c. 妈妈想你读哪一个专业？为什么？

d. 你想读哪一个专业？为什么？

e. 你希望妈妈怎么样？

---

yán jiū
研究 to study; research

shēn zhāngzhèng yì
伸张正义 to fight for justice

Grammar focus   p.273

1. 不……吗？ : Don't you...?
   ★ subject + 不 + verb + object + 吗？
   你不读法律吗？
   你不吃饭吗？

2. 为什么……？ : Why?
   ★ subject + 为什么 + predicate?
   陈明为什么想学中文？
   心美为什么想读法律？

Cultural spotlight

zhōng guó gǔ dài de dà xué
中国古代的大学
The university in ancient China

在现今社会，我们把大学称之为最高学府，读大学是很多中学生的首要目标。古代中国最高学府是国子监。国子监是自隋朝以后中国官方的最高学府。现在的大学生要读很多不同的专业，但是以前中国人在国子监读的课程主要以文学、历史、诗歌、哲学为主。

a. 在你的国家，大学是什么时候开始出现的？

b. 当时的大学主要提供什么课程？

LESSON OBJECTIVES

● Describe the university application process and your interview preparations.
● Discuss how well you think you have done in your interview.

1. 先读下面关于丁卡的内容，然后把表内A栏和B栏的词组搭配起来组成句子。

Read the passage about Dinkar, then correctly match the phrases in column A with those in column B to make complete sentences.

丁卡打算将来做医生，他的爸爸妈妈都非常支持他。他今年申请了大学的医学系，因为他对研究医学特别感兴趣。他希望将来能帮助很多病人治病。

他参加了大学面试。因为他认真地准备了，所以面试很顺利。他很有信心可以进大学读医科。他正在等大学给他的回复，他希望这次面试成功。

A	B
a. 丁卡申请了	i. 大学的医学系。
b. 丁卡将来想做	ii. 大学面试。
c. 丁卡对研究医学	iii. 这次面试能成功。
d. 丁卡认真地准备了	iv. 回复。
e. 丁卡的面试	v. 很感兴趣。
f. 大学还没给丁卡	vi. 医生。
g. 丁卡希望	vii. 很顺利。

miàn shì
面试 interview

zhǔn bèi
准备 to prepare for

shùn lì
顺利 smooth

xìn xīn
信心 confidence

jiāng lái
将来 in the future

zhī chí
支持 to support

xī wàng
希望 to hope

zhì bìng
治病 to treat (disease)

chéng gōng
成功 successful

2. 丽莎和安迪正在谈话。先读问题，再听录音，然后选择正确的答案。

Lisa is talking to Andy. Read the questions before you listen to the recording, then choose the correct answers.

a. 安迪刚刚交了什么？
   i. 成绩表   ii. 入学申请表   iii. 不知道

b. 丽莎昨天去哪儿面试？
   i. 大学   ii. 中学   iii. 不知道

c. 丽莎昨天的面试表现怎么样？
   i. 不好   ii. 顺利   iii. 不知道

dān xīn
担心 to worry

d. 丽莎对这次的大学申请有什么感受？

  i. 没信心   **ii.** 有信心   **iii.** 不知道

e. 丽莎叫安迪给娜依玛什么建议？

  i. 不用害怕   **ii.** 不用担心   **iii.** 不用去

3. 和你的同学角色扮演两个去完大学面试的朋友之间的对话，轮流提出和回答下面的问题。

With a partner, role-play a conversation between two friends who have both just been to university interviews. Take turns to ask and answer the following questions.

a. 你觉得刚才的面试怎么样？

b. 你对你这一次的大学入学申请有没有信心？

c. 你做了多久的面试准备？觉得怎么样？

4. 你的大学面试刚结束。用60–80字发一个短信给你的妈妈。其中应该包括：

You have just had your university interview. Using 60–80 characters, send a text message to your mother. It should include the following:

a. 觉得刚才的面试怎么样？

b. 觉得这一次的大学入学申请怎么样？为什么？

c. 如果这次面试成功，你最感谢的人是谁？为什么？

---

yǒu jī huì
有机会 to have a chance

kěn
肯 to be willing

pà
怕 to be afraid of

Grammar focus   p.273

1. 如果……就……: If ... then ...
   ★ 如果 + statement + (subject) 就 + result

   如果不好好准备，你就不能通过明天的面试。

   如果我不能进大学，就会去工作。

2. 只要……，就 : As long as ...
   ★ 只要 + condition + (subject) 就 + result

   只要下雨，她就会心情不好。

   只要有地图，我就不会迷路。

Cultural spotlight

zhōng guó xué shēng gāo kǎo xiàn kuàng
中国学生高考现况
University entrance examinations in mainland China

"普通高等学校统一招生考试"(简称"高考")是内地大学招生的主要渠道。各省或直辖市的试题一般都不同。学生可选文科或理科科目进行考试，考试科目大都为语文、外语、数学加文/理科综合。

因为每年参加高考的人数近千万，所以顶级大学的成绩要求都非常高。清华和北大是内地最顶级的大学，只有高考成绩达状元级的考生(最顶尖的千分之几)，才有机会进入这两所名校学习。

a. 在你的国家，学生是怎么样申请大学的？
b. 他们在申请大学之前要通过什么考试？

LESSON OBJECTIVES

● Describe university life and your plans after graduation.
● Discuss what you might enjoy about university life.

1. 阅读并根据以下英文句子，找出对应中文句子的错误，并写下来。

   Read each English sentence and find one error in the Chinese translation. Write out the correct answer.

   a. Jim went to a university in France as an exchange student.

   吉姆去了美国的大学当交流生。

   b. Xiaoqiang is planning to study for a doctorate in the future.

   小强打算将来读硕士。

   c. Jing'er joined the Dancing Society when she was at university.

   读大学的时候，静儿参加了绿色协会。

   d. Jiaming was living with his parents when he was at university.

   家明读大学时住在学校宿舍里。

   e. Lisa revised at home every day when she was at university.

   读大学的时候，丽莎每天到图书馆温习。

<table>
<tr><td>wǔ dǎo xié huì
舞蹈协会 Dancing Society</td></tr>
<tr><td>lǜ sè xié huì
绿色协会 Green Society</td></tr>
<tr><td>wēn xí
温习 to revise</td></tr>
</table>

2. 先读下面的内容，然后判断后面的叙述对还是错。

   Read the passage, and decide if the following statements are true or false.

   ### 我和朋友们的大学生活

   进了大学有一年多了，我和朋友们都过着不一样的大学生活。静儿参加了很多课外活动，她参加了舞蹈协会，也参加了绿色协会。她常常开玩笑说，要是毕业以后当不了舞蹈家的话，就去绿色协会当义工。奥利住在大学的宿舍，他常常和宿舍里的中国室友交流，中文进步了不少，他还打算毕业以后去中国生活呢！家明读医科，他每天都去图书馆，他读书很用功，因为他打算将来当医生。而我呢，和家明一样，每天都在图书馆温习。我打算将来大学毕业以后，去加拿大或者美国读硕士。安迪刚刚去了美国的大学当交流生，明年才回来。

<table>
<tr><td>bù yī yàng
不一样 not the same</td></tr>
<tr><td>bì yè
毕业 to graduate</td></tr>
<tr><td>yòng gōng
用功 hardworking</td></tr>
<tr><td>dú shū
读书 to study</td></tr>
</table>

<table>
<tr><td>wǔ dǎo jiā
舞蹈家 dancer</td></tr>
<tr><td>shì yǒu
室友 roommate</td></tr>
</table>

a. 我和朋友们进了大学两年多了。

b. 静儿参加了歌唱协会。

c. 奥利常常和宿舍里的美国室友交流。

d. 家明每天都在教室里读书。

e. 家明打算毕业以后当工程师。

f. 我打算大学毕业以后去美国或加拿大读硕士。

g. 安迪去了中国的大学当交流生。

3. 菲菲和小强正在谈话。先读问题，再听录音，然后选择正确的答案。

Feifei is talking to Xiaoqiang. Look at the questions before you listen to the recording, then choose the correct answers.

a. 小强到了美国多久了？
  i. 一个月　　**ii.** 两个月　　**iii.** 一年

b. 小强觉得在美国当交流生怎么样？
  i. 很没意思　　**ii.** 很有意思　　**iii.** 不知道

c. 菲菲毕业以后打算去哪儿读硕士？
  i. 中国或美国　　**ii.** 美国或英国　　**iii.** 澳大利亚或日本

d. 小强毕业以后有什么打算？
  i. 还不知道　　**ii.** 找工作　　**iii.** 读硕士

4. 练习描述你对未来大学生活的想法。

Practise describing your thoughts on your future university life.

a. 用中文写出四至五件你打算在大学做的事情。

Make a list of four to five things you plan to do if you go to university.

b. 和你的同学谈未来的大学生活，轮流提出和回答下面的问题。

With a partner, talk about your future plans for university. Take turns to ask and answer the following questions.

  i. 你期待你的大学生活吗？

  ii. 考上大学之后，你会参加哪些课外活动？

  iii. 考上大学之后，你打算到哪儿当交流生？

  iv. 考上大学之后，你会住在哪儿？

Grammar focus　p.274

1. 要是……就……: If...then...
  ★ 要是 + situation + (subject) 就 + result
  要是他不来，我们就走吧。
  要是下雨，我们就留在家。

2. 或者: or
  ★ possibility A + 或者 + possibility B
  （你可以选择）看书或者玩游戏。
  （我们可以）坐飞机或者坐船去。

kǎo lù
考虑 to consider

gōng zuò
工作 job

LESSON OBJECTIVE

● Discuss the pros and cons of online learning.

1. 先读下面的内容，然后把表内A栏和B栏的词组搭配起来组成句子。

Read the passage, then correctly match the phrases in column A with those in column B to make complete sentences.

网络学习的优点和缺点

网络课程是一种新的学习方式。它有不少优点。

第一，学生能在任何时候、任何地方学习。

第二，没有年龄限制。不同年龄的人都可以一起学习。

第三，方便分享。学生可以随时在网络上面分享不同的看法。

虽然网络课程有这些好处，但是它也有一些缺点。

第一，如果学生在不理想的环境下学习，思考很容易就会被打断。

第二，学生和老师很少有情感交流。

第三，没有真正的互动。同学们只有在网上讨论时才能互动。

fēn xiǎng
分享 to share
hù dòng
互动 interaction
tǎo lùn
讨论 to have a discussion

yōu diǎn
优点 advantage; pro
quē diǎn
缺点 disadvantage; con
xiàn zhì
限制 limitation
lǐ xiǎng
理想 ideal
sī kǎo
思考 thinking; thoughts
dǎ duàn
打断 to interrupt
qíng gǎn
情感 emotion

A	B
a. 网络课程是一种	i. 任何地方都可以学习。
b. 读网络课程的学生在	ii. 新的学习方式。
c. 网络学习可以	iii. 情感交流不多。
d. 读网络课程的学生的思考	iv. 没有真正的互动。
e. 网络课程的老师和学生	v. 容易因为不理想的环境而打断。
f. 读网络课程的学生们	vi. 让不同年龄的人一起学习。

2. 劳拉和小文正在谈话。先读问题，再听录音，然后选择正确的答案。

Laura is talking to Xiaowen. Read the questions before you listen to the recording, then choose the correct answers.

a. 谁在读网络课程？

   i. 小文爸爸   **ii.** 劳拉爸爸   **iii.** 小文

b. 读网络课程的那个人觉得网络课程怎么样？

   i. 很没意思   **ii.** 很有趣   **iii.** 不知道

c. 劳拉会读网络课程吗？

   i. 会   **ii.** 不会   **iii.** 不知道

3. 和你的同学谈网络学习的优点和缺点，轮流提出和回答下面的问题。

With a partner, talk about the pros and cons of online learning. Take turns to ask and answer the following questions.

a. 你听过网络课程吗？

b. 网络课程有什么优点？

c. 网络课程有什么缺点？

d. 你会考虑读网络课程吗？为什么？

4. 你的朋友想了解你读的网络课程。用100–120字写一个电邮给朋友解释，用第三题的答案来帮助你。

Your friend wants to understand the online course you've enrolled in. Using 100–120 characters, write an email to explain your course to your friend. Use your answers in Activity 3 to help you.

5. 为你学校的网络课程设计一个海报。用 100–120 个字。海报要包括：

Design a poster about an online learning course offered at your school. Write 100–120 characters. Your poster needs to include the following:

a. 谁可以读？

b. 这个课程开多久？

c. 读这个课程有什么好处？

d. 费用是多少？

e. 想读应该和谁联系？

miàn duì miàn
面对面 face to face

Grammar focus   p.274

1. 第（一、二、三……）：
ordinal numbers

★ 第 + number

第一，（学生在任何时候、任何地方都可以在网上学习。）

第二，（没有年龄限制。不同年龄的人都可以一起在网上学习。）

2. 只: only

★ subject + 只 + (auxiliary) verb + complete sentence

妈妈只能在晚上学习。
我们只有十块钱。

职业培训
VOCATIONAL TRAINING

LESSON OBJECTIVES
- Identify a range of vocational training programmes.
- Describe basic information about these training programmes and share your views on them.

1. 看看下面的图片，把它们和正确的词语搭配起来。
   Look at the pictures below and match them with the correct vocabulary.

 a 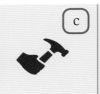 b  c  d

chuán bō hé méi tǐ 传播和媒体 media and 　　communication	
háng yè 行业 industry	
jiàn zhù 建筑 construction	
jiàn kāng hé měi róng 健康和美容 health and beauty	
yǎng lǎo hù lǐ 养老护理 elderly care	

i. 传播和媒体行业　　**ii.** 建筑行业　　**iii.** 健康和美容行业　　**iv.** 养老及护理行业

2. 阅读下面的内容，然后判断下面的叙述对还是错。
   Read the passage and decide if the following statements are true or false.

zhèng fǔ
政府 government

职业培训课程—学徒培训计划

没有读大学的学生可以选择参加学徒培训计划。它是为了打算在不同行业工作的学生而准备的。在培训的过程中，学生要学习和不同行业有关的技术，他们会一边学习，一边工作。在每个星期，他们实习工作五天然后读一天的技术培训课。现在受学生欢迎的课程有传播和媒体行业、健康和美容行业、建筑行业、养老服务行业等等。学徒的训练期通常为三至四年。政府会为参加的学生提供进修津贴。

zhí yè
职业 career; vocation
jì huà
计划 scheme
xué tú
学徒 apprentice
yǒu guān
有关 relate to
shí xí
实习 practicum; internship; work
　　placement
tí gōng
提供 to provide
jīn tiē
津贴 allowance
líng shòu
零售 retail

a. 参加学徒培训计划的学生要读大学。

b. 在培训的过程中，学生不用学习不同行业有关的技术。

c. 参加的学生会有实习。

d. 参加的学生每星期都要上课。

e. 现在零售行业课程很受学生欢迎。

f. 学徒的训练期通常为三至四个月。

g. 学校会为参加的学生提供进修津贴。

3. 六个人正在谈论职业培训。每个对话听两遍。先读问题，再听录音，然后选择正确的答案。

Six people are talking about their vocational training. You will hear each dialogue twice. Read the questions before you listen to the recording, then choose the correct answers.

a. 丽青打算参加什么？
  i. 学徒培训计划   **ii.** 学校计划   **iii.** 学徒工作计划

b. 小文每个星期要做什么？
  i. 实习工作   **ii.** 实验室工作   **iii.** 实地考察工作

c. 森姆每个星期要读什么？
  i. 中文课程   **ii.** 技术培训课   **iii.** 英文课程

d. 阿健想参加什么行业的课程？
  i. 健康和美容行业   **ii.** 传播和媒体行业
  iii. 建筑行业

e. 露西想参加什么行业的课程？
  i. 传播和媒体行业   **ii.** 养老护理行业
  iii. 健康美容行业

f. 国华想参加什么行业的课程？
  i. 传播和媒体行业   **ii.** 养老护理行业
  iii. 建筑行业

4. 两个朋友正在谈话。其中一人打算参加学徒培训计划。和你的同学角色扮演两个人之间的对话，轮流提出和回答下面的问题。

Two friends are chatting. One of them is thinking of enrolling in an apprenticeship scheme. With a partner, role-play the conversation between these two friends. Take turns to ask and answer the following questions.

a. 你对哪一个课程感兴趣？

b. 参加了计划之后，你每个星期将会做什么？

c. 你要培训多久？

5. 你刚刚去看了一个关于学徒培训计划的网页。写一篇笔记给你那个对学徒培训计划有兴趣的朋友。写 80–100 字。其中应该包括：

You have just looked up some information about an apprenticeship scheme online. Using 80–100 characters, write some notes to your friend who is interested in the scheme. Your notes should include the following:

a. 谁可以参加？   **b.** 参加之后每个星期要做什么？

c. 有哪些受欢迎的行业？   **d.** 培训期有多久？

e. 你觉得朋友应不应该参加？

Grammar focus p.274

1. 为了……而……: to do something for something's sake

★ subject + 为了 + effect + 而 + cause/means

我为了拿全班第一而努力读书。
陈明为了得到冠军而努力练习游泳。

2. 一边……一边……: one thing is done while doing something else

★ subject + 一边 + action A + 一边 + action B

你（不要）一边吃东西，一边说话。
我女儿（喜欢）一边吃饭，一边玩。

1. 翻译以下的中文词语，并用英文写下来。

   a. 给老人讲故事   b. 清洁沙滩

   c. 发传单   d. 义卖

   e. 医学系   f. 法律系

   g. 坐火车   h. 坐飞机

   i. 工程系   j. 传播和媒体行业

   k. 心理学系   l. 健康和美容行业

2. 阅读下面的电邮，判断右边的叙述对还是错。

发送	发件人:	sammy@example.com
	收件人:	xiaoming@example.com
	主题:	参加社会服务活动

亲爱的小明：

　　你好！今天我和同学一起参加了清洁沙滩这一个社区服务活动。我参加这个活动已经两年了。我觉得这个活动特别有意义。我下次还会再去参加这个活动的。

　　你呢？你又参加了哪一些社区服务活动？请告诉我。

心美

   a. 小明和心美一起参加社会服务活动。

   b. 心美觉得清洁沙滩活动特别有意义。

   c. 心美下次还会再去老人院给老人讲故事。

3. 和你的同学角色扮演两个刚刚进了大学的朋友之间的对话，轮流提出和回答下面的问题。

   a. 你会参加什么课外活动?   b. 你平时会在什么地方温习?

   c. 打算将来到哪个国家当交流生?   d. 你会住哪儿?

   e. 你打算在读大学的时候做什么特别的事情?

4. 阅读杰西卡的日记，然后写出右边问题的答案。

七月二十日　　星期五　　天气：晴

昨天太累了，没有写日记，所以今天才写。

昨天，我坐飞机到上海去参加校际交流活动。

到了上海的学校以后，我住在学校的宿舍里。

在学校里，我给那儿的学生表演了戏剧，

还给他们唱了歌。他们都很高兴，我也很高兴。

今天我将会和他们一起学中文。我很期待。

a. 杰西卡昨天坐什么去上海？

b. 到了上海学校以后，杰西卡住哪儿？

c. 杰西卡表演了什么给上海学校的学生看？

d. 杰西卡很期待什么？

5. 四个人在谈论他们的学业。每个对话听两遍。先读问题，再听录音，然后选择唯一正确的答案。

a. 吉姆现在读什么科？
　i. 文科　　ii. 理科　　iii. 工科

b. 丁卡将来想在大学读哪一个专业？
　i. 心理学　　ii. 医科　　iii. 法律

c. 汤姆为什么想读工科？
　i. 可以读心理学　ii. 可以读英文
　iii. 可以读工程系

d. 菲菲将来会读什么？
　i. 学士　　ii. 硕士　　iii. 博士

6. 你的朋友正在考虑读大学或参加学徒培训计划，他问你的意见。用 100–120 字写一个电邮给你的朋友。其中应该包括：

a. 读大学的好处；

b. 参加学徒培训计划的好处；

c. 你会介绍他参加学徒培训计划的哪个课程；

d. 为什么这个课程适合他。

UNIT OBJECTIVES
- Discuss and compare different career options.
- Describe your dream job.
- Describe what people do on their work placement.
- Discuss and compare different gap-year activities.
- Describe the steps people take when job hunting.
- Learn what to say during a job interview.

1. 看看下面的图片，把它们和正确的词语搭配起来。

Look at the pictures. Match them to the correct vocabulary.

i. 老师   **ii.** 演员   **iii.** 服务员   **iv.** 厨师   **v.** 医生   **vi.** 护士   **vii.** 警察   **viii.** 航空服务员

2. 先读问题，再听录音，然后选择正确的答案。

Read the questions before you listen to the recording, then choose the correct answers.

a. 海伦小时候想当什么？
  i. 唱歌的明星
  ii. 有名的演员
  iii. 航空服务员

b. 爸爸希望马克以后成为一名什么？
  i. 中学老师
  ii. 中学校长
  iii. 不错的厨师

c. 在中国北京旅游的时候，米娜一家人见到了谁？
  i. 香港著名电影演员
  ii. 中国有名的篮球运动员
  iii. 马来西亚最有名的羽毛球运动员

d. 谁帮助本杰明找到了他的背包？
  i. 警察
  ii. 航空服务员
  iii. 旅客

e. 今年夏天日晴和两个好朋友将去做什么？
  i. 去植物园做义工
  ii. 去老人院做义工
  iii. 去咖啡馆做兼职

> qī
> 期 a length or portion of time; period; or phase
>
> xiǎng zuò　xiǎng dāng
> 想做 / 想当 to want to be
>
> jiān zhí
> 兼职 part-time job

> zhù míng　de
> 著名(的) famous
>
> zhōu xīng chí
> 周星驰 Stephen Chow (a famous actor and director based in Hong Kong)

3. 练习写汉字。

Practise writing Chinese.

a. 按照笔画顺序写下面的字。

Write the characters by following the stroke order.

zuò

做 做 做 做 做 做 做 做 做 做 做 做
　　1　2　3　4　5　6　7　8　9　10　11

dāng

当 当 当 当 当 当 当
　　1　2　3　4　5　6

b. 填空完成下面的短文。

Complete the following paragraph by filling in the missing information.

小时候的美美喜欢唱歌，那时候她**(a)**当一名歌星。可是后来她不喜欢唱歌了，喜欢上了滑雪，又想**(b)**一名滑雪运动员，但是因为**(c)**太累了，现在她又不**(d)**做滑雪运动员了。美美今年十六岁了，她打算中学以后去大学**(e)**汉语专业，毕业以后**(f)**一名汉语老师。

读　做　想　当　训练　想

4. 阅读以下兼职广告，然后判断下面的叙述对或错。

Read the part-time job advert below, then decide if the statements on the right are true or false.

奥林匹克运动中心
"运动的夏天，健康的夏天"夏令营

运动中心需要请多名大学生做夏令营的老师。
中心现需要招游泳老师、网球老师、武术老师、画画老师、舞蹈老师和英文老师。
教五到十二岁的小学生。
夏令营每两周一期，一共三期。
第一期：七月一日到七月十五日
第二期：七月七日到七月二十二日
第三期：七月十五日到七月二十九日
感兴趣的大学生朋友们可以发
邮件给summercamp@example.com
在邮件里请说明你会教什么课和希望教哪一期的课。

zhāo
招 to recruit

wǔ shù
武术 martial arts

dì yī qī
第一期 the first phase

a. 夏令营在奥林匹克运动中心举行。

b. 夏令营需要招电脑老师。

c. 参加这个夏令营的是小学生。

d. 小朋友们可以在夏令营学习跳舞。

e. 夏令营有三期，每期为两周。

f. 感兴趣的大学生可以给奥林匹克运动中心打电话。

LESSON OBJECTIVES
- Identify the names of a range of jobs.
- Discuss the pros and cons of certain jobs.

 1. 苏菲正在谈她家人做什么工作。先读问题，再听录音，然后选择正确的答案。

Sophie is talking about her family members' jobs. Look at the questions before you listen to the recording, then choose the correct answers.

a. 苏菲的爸爸是什么？
   i. 画家　　**ii.** 音乐家　　**iii.** 建筑师

b. 她的妈妈是什么？
   i. 工程师　　**ii.** 工人　　**iii.** 导游

c. 她的爷爷以前是什么？
   i. 农民　　**ii.** 护士　　**iii.** 律师

d. 她的哥哥是什么？
   i. 兽医　　**ii.** 科学家　　**iii.** 警察

e. 她的姐姐是什么？
   i. 记者　　**ii.** 大学教授　　**iii.** 中学老师

f. 苏菲自己是什么？
   i. 服务员　　**ii.** 演员　　**iii.** 作家

dǎo yóu 导游 tour guide	
nóng mín 农民 farmer	
lǜ shī 律师 lawyer	
shòu yī 兽医 vet	
kē xué jiā 科学家 scientist	
jì zhě 记者 reporter or journalist	
jiào shòu 教授 professor	
zuò jiā 作家 writer	

jiàn zhù shī 建筑师 architect

 2. 阅读下面的描述，把它们和正确的图片搭配起来。

Read the descriptions below, then match them with the correct pictures.

a. 我喜欢小动物，现在的工作是在一家宠物医院里照顾小动物。

b. 我的工作是带着游客们去有意思的地方，参观名胜古迹，看美丽的风景。

c. 我每天都要去菜地看我种的蔬菜和水果。蔬菜和水果长熟了就会卖到城里的超级市场。

d. 我在飞机上工作，乘客们登机时我说："欢迎"，乘客叫我的时候我问："您有什么需要？"

e. 我喜欢写东西。我最近在网上写了一本网络小说，网友们都说写得不错。

 i
 ii
  iii
 iv
 v

3. 练习写汉字。

Practise writing Chinese.

> *zhuàn qián*
> 赚钱 to make money

a. 按照笔画顺序写下面的字。

Write the characters by following the stroke order.

zhuàn

赚 | 赚 赚 赚 赚 赚 赚 赚 赚 赚 赚 赚 赚 赚 赚
1 2 3 4 5 6 7 8 9 10 11 12 13 14

qián

钱 | 钱 钱 钱 钱 钱 钱 钱 钱 钱 钱
1 2 3 4 5 6 7 8 9 10

b. 用词语 "赚钱" 造句。写10-20个字。

Write a sentence of your own using the above vocabulary. Write 10-20 characters.

4. 阅读以下文字，然后回答问题。

Read the text below, then answer the questions.

> *bào dào*
> 报道 news report; article

最近有一个报道说工程师是最让人快乐的工作，而第二名和第三名是教师和护士。为什么说这些是让人快乐的职业？我们一起听一听老师们的想法。

他们觉得教师是一个快乐的职业。	但是也有人不太喜欢教师这个职业。
• 林老师说："因为我每天都和小孩子们在一起，孩子们是快乐的，所以我也觉得快乐。" • 杰克说："我是英文老师。每次上课看到同学们进步了，我很开心。" • 陈老师说："当你告诉学生们怎么做题，看到他们明白的时候，你就会感到高兴，因为你帮助了别人。"	• 麦克说："我以前在中学里当老师，三年前我换了工作。那是因为有的学生很没有礼貌。而且忙的时候，你得在周末或晚上工作。" • 张老师说："学生的考试压力大，老师的压力也很大。因为有些学生考试考得不好，会说是老师教得不好。"

a. 文中说到了哪些让人快乐的职业？写下你的回答。

b. 他们为什么觉得教师是快乐的职业？写下他们说到的三个理由。

c. 也有人说到了当老师的两个不好的方面，它们是什么？

d. 在短文中找出 "快乐" 的两个同义词。

e. 对你来说你认为找工作的时候什么最重要？为什么？写下你的回答。

理想的工作
MY IDEAL JOB

LESSON OBJECTIVES
- Talk about your past, present and future plans in relation to your dream job.
- Describe your dream job.

 1. 将英文词语翻译成中文，然后填空完成句子。

Translate the vocabulary from English into Chinese, then fill in the blanks to complete the sentences.

a. 丽丽计划 _____ 去一家有名的国际银行工作。(in the future)

b. 马克希望以后自己成为一名 _____ 的设计师。(successful)

c. 今年我们的时装店将招聘三 ___ 男售货员。(measure word)

d. 他的工作单位就在_____。(city centre)

e. 妈妈每天_____车去上班。(drives)

shòu huò yuán
售货员 salesperson

gōng zuò dān wèi
工作单位 workplace

shè jì shī
设计师 designer

zhāo pìn
招聘 to recruit

yù dào
遇到 to meet

jiàn qiáo
剑桥 Cambridge

kāng hé
康河 River Cam, a river that runs through Cambridge, UK

2. 先读问题，再听录音，然后选择正确的答案。

Read the questions below before you listen to the recording, then choose the correct answers to complete the sentences.

A	B
a. 说话的人是米娜的什么人？ 　i. 表姐 　ii. 姐姐 　iii. 祖母 b. 她以后想做一名什么？ 　i. 售货员 　ii. 时装设计师 　iii. 建筑设计师	c. 康纳在剑桥大学读什么？ 　i. 历史专业 　ii. 英文专业 　iii. 数学专业 d. 夏天康纳常常做什么？ 　i. 给游客卖咖啡 　ii. 带游客参观剑桥大学 　iii. 给游客们划船 e. 康纳喜欢做什么？ 　i. 坐船 　ii. 学外语 　iii. 遇到来自世界各地不同国家的人

3. 阅读短文，然后判断叙述对或错。

Read the following passage and decide if the statements are true or false.

> 因为爸爸是律师，所以娜依玛从小就想当一名成功的律师。今年她十六岁了，再过两年就要上大学了。娜依玛想好了大学读历史和英文，然后大学毕业后去考律师考试。为了这个理想，她这个暑假去一家律师楼做了两个月的实习生。这家律师楼在市区，离地铁站很近。娜依玛每天坐七点的地铁，坐十五分就到工作单位，很方便。实习工作比较简单，主要是在办公室帮忙和做开会的记录。那里的工作人员都十分友好，如果她有不明白的地方，同事们都会教她。娜依玛觉得这次实习对她的未来非常有帮助，给了她非常宝贵的工作经验。

a. 娜依玛再过两年就要读大学了。 **b.** 她打算大学读律师专业。

c. 她实习的律师楼在郊区，需要坐四十分钟地铁，比较远。

d. 律师楼里的同事对她很友好。

e. 她觉得这次实习对她的未来没有什么帮助，很无聊。

 5. 阅读下面的广告，然后和同学讨论右边的问题。

Read the following leaflet, then discuss the questions with a partner.

> ### 印尼巴厘岛旅游中心
> ### 招聘导游一名
>
> 地点：美丽迷人、风景秀丽的巴厘岛
> 工作时间：每周二十个小时
> 工作内容：带游客参观岛上著名景点
> 技能：必须会游泳和潜水
> 　　　　必须会流利的中文和英文
> 我们提供一千美元月薪，
> 免费提供一栋带游泳池的房子。
> 如果您感兴趣，
> 可以在www.example.com上申请。

生词

bāng máng
帮忙 to help

kāi huì
开会 to attend a meeting

tóng shì
同事 colleague

gōng zuò jīng yàn
工作经验 work experience

zuò jì lù
(做)记录 to make notes

bǎo guì de
宝贵的 precious

Grammar focus p.275

很，比较，十分: very, relatively, extremely

★ intensifier + adjectival verb or stative verb

很方便，比较简单，十分友好

jì néng
技能 skill

yuè / nián xīn
月/年薪 monthly/annual salary

nián jià
年假 annual leave

a. 以上招聘广告是关于什么的?

b. 你觉得这份工作吸引人吗? 为什么?

c. 做这份工作，你需要有哪些技能?

d. 你梦想的好工作的年薪、年假和工作地点是什么样的?

e. 你希望以后在国内还是去国外工作?

f. 你自己最想做的工作是什么? 为什么?

LESSON OBJECTIVES
- Describe what a job entails.
- Explain what you like about certain jobs.

1. 阅读下面的描述，把它们和正确的职业搭配起来。

   Read the descriptions below, then match them with the correct jobs.

   a. 医治牙疼的病人

   b. 画人物、风景、花、鸟、树木等

   c. 在百货公司、购物商场、商店里卖东西

   d. 开汽车、卡车、公共汽车等

   e. 设计房子、大楼、桥

   f. 带着游客们参观有意思的名胜古迹和风景区

   g. 给每户人家送信、寄东西

   h. 给人、给美丽的风景、有意思的古老的建筑拍照片

   i. 照顾、医治生病的动物

   j. 常常参加体育训练和体育比赛

   i. 司机

   ii. 导游

   iii. 兽医

   iv. 牙医

   v. 画家

   vi. 运动员

   vii. 摄影师

   viii. 售货员

   ix. 邮递员

   x. 建筑师

   | sī jī
司机 driver; chauffeur |
   | yá yī
牙医 dentist |
   | huà jiā
画家 painter or artist |
   | yùn dòng yuán
运动员 athlete |
   | shè yǐng shī
摄影师 photographer |
   | yóu dì yuán
邮递员 courier; postal worker |

2. 翻译以下句子，然后练习把它们读出来。

   Translate the following sentences into Chinese, then read them out loud.

   a. He is now a secondary school teacher.

   b. I teach history, but studied English at university.

   c. She is going to work in Malaysia.

3. 先看图片，再听录音，然后把图片和正确的人名搭配起来。

   Look at the pictures before you listen to the recording, then match them with the correct names.

   a. 玛莉　**b.** 迪伦　**c.** 娜依玛　**d.** 小亮　**e.** 米娜

i	ii	iii	iv	v
				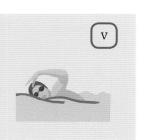

4. 阅读小月和米娜的对话，然后判断下面的叙述是对或错。

Read the dialogue between Xiaoyue and Mina, and decide if the following statements are true or false.

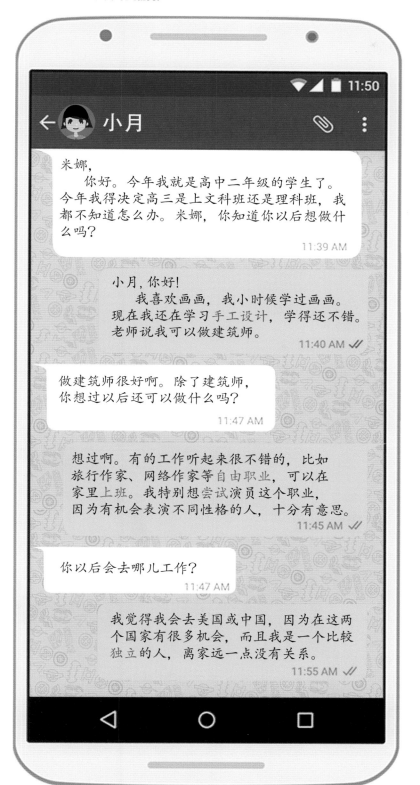

米娜，

你好。今年我就是高中二年级的学生了。今年我得决定高三是上文科班还是理科班，我都不知道怎么办。米娜，你知道你以后想做什么吗？

11:39 AM

小月，你好!

我喜欢画画，我小时候学过画画。现在我还在学习手工设计，学得还不错。老师说我可以做建筑师。

11:40 AM ✓✓

做建筑师很好啊。除了建筑师，你想过以后还可以做什么吗？

11:47 AM

想过啊。有的工作听起来很不错的，比如旅行作家、网络作家等自由职业，可以在家里上班。我特别想尝试演员这个职业，因为有机会表演不同性格的人，十分有意思。

11:45 AM ✓✓

你以后会去哪儿工作？

11:47 AM

我觉得我会去美国或中国，因为在这两个国家有很多机会，而且我是一个比较独立的人，离家远一点没有关系。

11:55 AM ✓✓

---

zì yóu zhí yè
自由职业 freelance; self-employed

shàng bān
上班 to go to work

dú lì
独立 independent

shǒu gōng shè jì
手工设计 handicraft

cháng shì
尝试 to try

Grammar focus p.275

过: used after a verb to indicate completion of a task or process.

★ subject + verb + 过 + task or process

我学过画画。
杰克参加过中文合唱队。

a. 小月是高中学生。

b. 小月已经决定高三上哪个班了。

c. 米娜小时候没有学过画画。

d. 米娜的父母说她将来可以试一试做建筑师。

e. 除了建筑师，小月想试一试表演。

f. 米娜觉得自己将来可能会去国外工作。

5. 和你的同学谈一谈未来的职业计划，轮流提出和回答下面的问题。

With a partner, have a chat about your future career plans. Take turns to ask and answer the following questions.

a. 你将来想做什么样的工作？为什么？

b. 去哪里工作？国内还是国外？为什么？

c. 要是有时间的话，你还打算学什么新的技能？

d. 你的父母支持你的决定吗？他们会怎么帮助你？

Cultural spotlight

diàn zǐ chǎn pǐn shè jì de chuàng yè zhī dōu   shēn zhèn
电子产品设计的创业之都—深圳
Shenzhen: the capital for electronic product entrepreneurs

深圳位于中国东南部的广东省，是一个现代化的大都市。这个城市现在以购物天堂、世界的制造中心、创业中心著称。近年来还发展成为来自世界各地的年轻的电子产品设计师的创业基地。可是1980年以前这里没有高楼大厦，只是一个小渔村。后来深圳设立了经济特区，慢慢地发展成为"世界电子工厂"。而如今深圳又变身为"创客之都"。因为这里有世界上最大的电子产品市场，有现成的加工工厂，如果你有任何想法，在深圳，你可以在很短的时间里制作出可以出售的电子产品。正因为这一点，深圳正吸引着来自世界各地的电子产品设计师。

a. 你听说过深圳这个地方吗？你知道为什么深圳吸引了那么多人创业？

b. 你有没有兴趣成为一名创业者？为什么？

LESSON OBJECTIVE

● Describe the preparations for and experience of going on a work placement.

1. 看看下面列出的地方。写下他们的中文拼音和英文意思。

Look at these places. Write down their pinyin and meanings in English.

a.	动物园	b.	博物馆	c.	音乐节	d.	银行
e.	汽车工厂	f.	咖啡馆	g.	医院	h.	电视台
i.	健身中心	j.	农场				

2. 先看下面的图片，再听录音，然后把它们和正确的人名搭配起来。

Look at the pictures before you listen to the recording, then match each one with the correct person.

照顾 zhào gù to look after

雅加达 yǎ jiā dá Jakarta, capital city of Indonesia

杂志社 zá zhì shè magazine-publishing house

电视台 diàn shì tái TV station

a. 杰西卡　**b.** 大海　**c.** 阿得　**d.** 日晴　**e.** 本杰明

3. 阅读以下培训项目招聘广告，然后回答问题。
Read the internship advert, then answer the questions.

新生代银行中国区大学生培训项目现招聘五名希望未来去中国工作的最后一年的在校大学生或者刚刚毕业的大学生。面试成功的大学生们将在伦敦培训两年，两年以后通过培训的学生可以选择去中国的北京、上海、广州等城市的新生代银行工作。在培训期间我们会为你提供很有吸引力的年薪和年假，努力在工作与生活中帮助你。

申请日期：每年的一月一日到五月三十一日
开始日期：每年的六月到八月

a. 面试成功以后，大学生们将培训多长时间？

b. 培训的地点在哪儿？

c. 培训完以后他们可以去哪些城市工作？列举两个城市。

d. 新生代银行在培训期间会给实习生提供什么？

e. 培训什么时候开始？

f. 谁可以申请新生代银行中国区大学生培训项目？

4. 练习写汉字。
Practise writing Chinese.

a. 按照笔画顺序写下面的字。
Write the characters by following the stroke order.

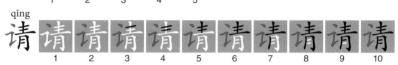

b. 用"申请"造句来描述你会申请去哪一个地方实习。写20-30个字。
Use the above vocabulary to write a few sentences to describe where you would apply for your work placement. Write 20–30 characters.

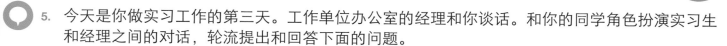

5. 今天是你做实习工作的第三天。工作单位办公室的经理和你谈话。和你的同学角色扮演实习生和经理之间的对话，轮流提出和回答下面的问题。

Today is the third day of your work placement. You are talking to the office manager. With a partner, role-play a conversation between the intern and the manager. Take turns to ask and answer the following questions.

a. 这几天你都做了什么？习惯吗？

b. 觉得我们的工作单位怎么样？

c. 你为什么来这个地方实习？

d. 你以前做过这方面的工作吗？

e. 以后五年你有什么计划？

f. 你有什么需要，请告诉我。

6. 你刚刚在一家公司做完实习，写一篇120-150字关于你的实习经历的短文。其中应该包括：

You just finished your work placement at a company. Use 120 to 150 characters to write about your experience. You should include:

a. 你在哪里做了实习？

b. 在做实习的单位需要做哪些工作？

c. 觉得实习的公司和同事怎么样？

d. 你在那里学到了哪些新的东西？

e. 你觉得中学生应不应该做实习？

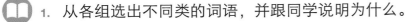

9.6 空档年
TAKING A GAP YEAR

LESSON OBJECTIVES
- Identify and express your opinion about a range of gap-year activities.
- Describe your preparations for and experience of taking a gap year.

1. 从各组选出不同类的词语，并跟同学说明为什么。

From each group, choose the term that is the odd one out, then explain why to a partner.

a. i. 做兼职	ii. 上班	iii. 下班	iv. 空档年
b. i. 笔友	ii. 牙医	iii. 演员	iv. 记者
c. i. 游客	ii. 司机	iii. 作家	iv. 警察
d. i. 说话人	ii. 运动员	iii. 邮递员	iv. 售票员
e. i. 过路人	ii. 工程师	iii. 商人	iv. 经理
f. i. 游客	ii. 顾客	iii. 乘客	iv. 找工作

> xià bān
> 下班 to finish work
> shāng rén
> 商人 businessperson
> jīng lǐ
> 经理 manager

> kòng dàng nián
> 空档年 gap year

2. 从下列词语中选出正确的动词填空，将句子写完整。

Choose the correct verbs from the list to complete the sentences.

> 找　有　发生　去　做　上　认识　读

空档年通常**(a)**在学生们**(b)**大学之前。

因为大学的学费很贵，所以我打算**(c)**一份兼职工作赚钱。

去年一年我都在一家旅行社**(d)**兼职导游。

我还有机会**(e)**中国的北京、上海和西安。

我在中国还**(f)**了一些中国朋友。

去了中国以后，我开始对中国的历史**(g)**兴趣了。

我打算在空档年之后上大学**(h)**工程系。

> **Grammar focus** p.275
>
> 是 : used for linking two noun phrases
> ★ noun phrase A + 是
> ＋ noun phrase B
> 空档年一般是在上大学之前。
> 他的哥哥是一个工程师。

3. 五个人正在谈他们对空档年的想法。先读问题，再听录音，然后选出正确的答案完成句子。

Five people are talking about their thoughts on taking a gap year. Read the questions before you listen to the recording, then choose the correct answers to complete the sentences.

a. 日晴空档年可能去……。
i. 马来西亚学习潜水　　ii. 澳洲旅游　　iii. 非洲做老师

> háng hǎi
> 航海 sailing
> làng fèi
> 浪费 to waste
> xiǎng fǎ
> 想法 opinion

b. 迪伦要去澳大利亚的东部……。

    i. 学习航海   **ii.** 冲浪   **iii.** 骑自行车旅游

c. 米娜打算去中国的一些……城市看一看。

    i. 古老的   **ii.** 现代的   **iii.** 热闹的

d. 家明认为空档年……。

    i. 浪费时间   **ii.** 非常有用   **iii.** 特别有意思

e. 心美可能不会做空档年，因为……。

    i. 没有钱   **ii.** 台湾离心美住的地方太远了

    iii. 父母不支持

4. 阅读以下短文，然后回答问题。

Read the following passage, then answer the questions.

> 很多参加空档年的学生选择做义工，包括在亚洲国家，比如印度尼西亚，教英文，或者是在南美洲参与热带雨林保护项目。有的学生选择旅游，在空档年期间尝试一些新东西，比如去美国的夏威夷冲浪，在英国南部海港学习航海，在台湾骑自行车环岛旅行等。在旅行中看世界，尝试新东西，了解不同的文化，学习不同国家的语言，认识各种各样的人。有的人因为大学学费太高而去工作，在工作中学会独立。很多年轻人都认为空档年的经历丰富了他们的生活，让他们更好地了解自己的长处，让他们成为更好的人。

xuǎn zé
选择 to choose

rè dài yǔ lín
热带雨林 tropical rainforest

xià wēi yí
夏威夷 Hawaii

fēng fù
丰富 to enrich

cháng chu
长处 strength, forte

a. 空档年的活动一般有哪三类？

b. 短文说空档年有哪些好处？列举三点。

c. 为什么有的年轻人会选择工作？

d. 短文中写道空档年选择旅行的学生可以尝试哪些不一样的活动？列举三点。

5. 和你的同学轮流提出和回答以下问题，然后做口语演示。

With a partner, take turns to ask and answer the following questions, then present your answers to the rest of the class.

a. 在你的国家，有没有空档年？   **b.** 如果有，你要做空档年，你会选择做什么？

c. 去什么地方？   **d.** 你希望自己在空档年能学到什么不一样的东西？

e. 你会做些什么准备？   **f.** 你的朋友们对你做空档年有什么想法？

g. 你的父母支持你吗？怎么支持？

LESSON OBJECTIVES
- Identify skills that are important when looking for a job.
- Describe the skills you need for a particular job.

1. 看看下面的词语，把它们和正确的英文意思搭配起来。

Match the Chinese terms with their correct meanings in English.

a.	外语	**i.**	team work
b.	电脑	**ii.**	communicating
c.	交流	**iii.**	foreign languages
d.	团队合作	**iv.**	driving
e.	开车	**v.**	computing

tuán duì
团队 team

2. 用下列动词填空，将句子写完整。

From the list below, choose the correct verb to match each of the skills and complete the sentences.

教　做　说　擅长　开　用

shàn cháng
擅长 to excel at

我会(a)一点德语。
康纳的爷爷不会(b)电脑。
康纳去年学会了(c)车。
小亮的姐姐不喜欢(d)饭。
小亮的妈妈在大学(e)历史。
我(f)团队合作。

3. 先读下面的文字，再听录音，然后选择正确的词语填空。
（提示:下面的词语多于你需要的。）

Read the text below before you listen to the recording, then choose the correct words to complete the sentences. (Hint: There are more words in the box than you need.)

> duàn liàn
> 锻炼 to train; to exercise

> néng lì
> 能力 ability

导游　售货员　义工　组织　交流　图书馆　美术馆
博物馆　　音乐节　给　电影节　西南　东北

a. 做兼职(i)和兼职(ii)的工作可以锻炼和人(iii)的能力。

b. 暑假里学生在(iv)组织活动或去(v)帮忙可以锻炼他们的(vi)
能力。

c. 小亮和爸爸一起去中国(vii)的山区做义工，(viii)山里的孩子
上英文课。

4. 康纳写了一封电子邮件给张教授，是关于一个在网上看到
的工作机会。

Connor has written an email to Professor Zhang about a job opportunity he saw on the internet.

> nǔ lì
> 努力 hardworking

> zūn jìng de
> 尊敬的 honourable
> rè ài
> 热爱 (be) passionate (about)
> xíng róng
> 形容 to describe

a. 以下这些句子来自康纳的电邮，但是它们的次序错了。请给
它们排序让邮件读起来通顺。

The content of Connor's email is in the wrong order. Arrange the parts back in order.

祝好。　　　尊敬的张教授：您好。　　To:张教授

请您把工作信息用邮件发给我，可以吗? 非常感谢！期待您的回复

我的名字是康纳，我来自英国。　　　　康纳六月一日

我今年刚刚从剑桥大学历史专业毕业。我以前在英国的游学夏令营里教过中国学生。除了教英文，我还可以教英国历史。我是一个工作认真努力的人，热爱教师工作，能很好地和学生交流，而且我还会说一点汉语。我在你学校的网站上看到你们需要两个英文老师。我对这个工作很感兴趣。

b. 再读一遍这封电子邮件，然后回答问题。

Read the email again, then answer the questions.

　　i. 康纳对什么工作感兴趣？

　ii. 他大学读了什么专业？

　iii. 他有过什么教课经验？

　iv. 他可以教哪些科目？

　　v. 他会说哪国语言？

　vi. 他是怎么样形容自己的？

> **Grammar focus**　p.275
>
> 刚刚: just
> ★ subject + 刚刚 + action
> 他刚刚结束他的实
> 习期。

5. 给一家公司写一封求职信。在信里你需要写到你为什么想得到那份工作和你擅长什么。写80–100字。

Write a letter to a company to apply for a job. State why you would like the job and what you're good at. Use 80–100 characters.

6. 和你的同学角色扮演职业培训中心的经理和来参观中心的学生之间的对话。

With a partner, role-play a conversation between a training-centre manager and a student visitor.

a. 轮流提出和回答下面的问题。

Take turns to ask and answer the following questions.

　　i. 培训完了可以找到哪些工作？

　ii. 培训需要多长时间？

　iii. 培训的地点在哪里？

　iv. 我怎么申请培训课程？

　　v. 我需要擅长什么技能？

b. 现在写下你的回答。

Now write out your response.

找工作
JOB HUNTING

LESSON OBJECTIVES
- Process information from a range of job adverts.
- Describe your strengths and personality in relation to a job.
- Reply to a job advert.

1. 以下是一些找工作的方式。

Below are some job-hunting methods.

去招聘网站	看报纸上的招聘广告
问认识的人	参加招聘会

bào zhǐ
报纸 newspaper

guǎng gào
广告 advertisement

zhāo pìn huì
招聘会 job fair

a. 写下它们的英文意思。

Write down their meanings in English.

b. 跟同学讨论每种方式有什么好处。

With a partner, take turns to name one advantage for each of these methods.

2. 看看这些词语，然后回答下面的问题。

Look at these terms, then answer the following questions.

热情	友好	亲切	有礼貌	认真

a. 写下它们的英文意思。

b. 用以上任意形容词，形容你自己的性格，并写下来。

c. 你觉得你的性格适合做什么工作？

3. 先读下面的叙述，再听录音，然后判断它们对还是错。

Read the statements before you listen to the recording, then decide if they are true or false.

a. 夏令营需要两名会唱歌和跳舞的音乐老师。

b. 四川大学需要五名年轻的英文老师。

c. 如果你对农业中心的工作感兴趣，你可以打电话给他们。

d. 警察局需要新的社区警察，要在下个月的一号开始工作。

e. 历史博物馆要找一名会说西班牙语的秘书。

mì shū
秘书 secretary

Grammar focus p.276

得 : a structure particle that provides additional meaning to an associated verb phrase

★ verb + 得 + stative verb or verb phrase

跑得快，飞得高，听得懂，听得明白

4. 阅读以下招聘广告，然后回答问题。
Read the job advert, then answer the questions.

日新百货公司
招聘售货员

a. 年龄:十八岁以上，最好有售货工作经历。擅长和客人交流，对人亲切，有礼貌，适应团队合作。对工作要有热情，认真。擅长用电脑，会普通话、粤语和一点英文。

b. 上班时间:全职周一到周五上午十点到下午五点。兼职周四和周五下午五点到晚上九点，周末上午十点到下午五点。

c. 全职提供月薪八千元人民币，年假二十天，免费住宿和每年免费去国外旅游一趟。兼职每小时三十元，提供免费午餐、晚餐，但不提供住宿。

有兴趣的朋友请跟马经理联系:
手机:19876543210
电子邮箱: contact@example.com

pǔ tōng huà
普通话 Mandarin

quán zhí
全职 full-time job

shì yìng
适应 to adapt

yuè yǔ
粤语 Cantonese

nián líng
年龄 age

dài yù
待遇 treatment, pay

Grammar focus   p.276

tàng
趟: a measure word for trip, journey; action measure similar to 次

★ subject + verb phrase + number + 趟

(今天)他去超市去了三趟。

a. 什么年龄的人可以申请这份工作？

b. 这份工作要求你会说哪三种语言？

c. 这份工作做全职的话有哪些好的待遇？列举两点。

d. 做兼职公司会提供什么？

e. 如果你对以上工作感兴趣，你可以怎么联系他们？

Cultural spotlight

zhōng guó shāng wù lǐ yí
中国商务礼仪 Business etiquette in China

彼此见面时要握手。称呼对方时，可以用对方的姓氏再加上他/她的工作职位，例如称呼某人为张总经理。跟中国人做生意，如果你会说一些简单的汉语，那会让对方很欣赏你，但是请你务必确定你说的话的意思和符不符合说话的场合。在中国交换名片是非常重要的商务礼仪之一，是十分常见的做法。通常情况下名片的一面是英文的，另一面是中文的，根据不同的区域，有的地方用简体字体，有的地方用繁体字体。

a. 你的家人是做什么工作的？用名片吗？

b. 在你居住的国家有哪些商务礼仪？

LESSON OBJECTIVES
- Understand and answer common interview questions.
- Introduce yourself briefly.
- Talk about your work experience, skills, and education background during an interview.

1. 看看下面的表格。里面是一些关于面试的词组。

Look at the table below. Inside are some terms related to job interviews.

词语	听力先后顺序	根据笔划多少
招聘		
面试		
简历		
申请表		
面试官		
报纸		
网络		
机会		

miàn shì
面试 interview

jiǎn lì
简历 CV

jī huì
机会 opportunity

miàn shì guān
面试官 interviewer

a. 听录音。每个词组听两遍。根据听力写下词语的先后顺序 (1–8)。

Listen to the recording. You will hear each term twice. Rank the terms according to the order in which they are read out in the recording (1–8).

b. 然后再根据每个词语笔划多少从大到小排列顺序 (1–8)。

Now rank the terms from 1–8, starting with the one with the highest combined number of pen strokes.

2. 先读下面的叙述，再听录音，然后判断它们对或错。

Read the statements before you listen to the recording, then decide if they are true or false.

xī zhuāng
西装 suit

a. 他是从报纸上看到这个招聘广告的。

b. 他给汽车工厂发了个人简历。

c. 没过几天汽车工厂打电话让他参加面试。

d. 面试前他一点儿都不紧张。

e. 面试那天他穿了西装。

f. 他们问了他关于未来的工作计划。

g. 他得到了那份工作。

3. 看看下面的词语。将它们重新组织，写出完整的句子。

Look at the words below. Re-arrange them to make complete sentences.

a. 专业 / 说一说 / 大学 / 读的是 / 请您 / 您 / 什么 / ?

b. 去了 / 毕业后 / 哪个 / 您 / 公司 / 工作 / ?

c. 想 / 来 / 您 / 公司 / 为什么 / 工作 / 我们的 / ?

d. 问题 / 吗 / 您 / 什么 / 有 / ?

e. 面试 / 来 / 我们 / 参加 / 谢谢 / 您 / 公司的 / 。

4. 阅读下面的广告，然后选择正确的答案完成句子。

Read the job advert below, then choose the correct answer to complete each sentence.

东风汽车工厂

招聘汽车店销售经理一名

简介：

东风汽车工厂计划新开一家汽车销售店。地点在上海郊区的现代工业园。现需要招聘一名有经验的汽车销售经理，欢迎您的加入。

职位： 全职汽车销售经理一名。

要求： 汽车工程专业大学毕业生，会开车，有两年以上汽车销售工作经验。

待遇： 年薪二十万人民币，提供免费住宿，每年去日本、德国等国培训两周。

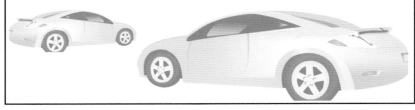

销售 sales (xiāo shòu)

相当 quite (xiāng dāng)

a. 这份工作是招聘……。
 i. 超市售货员 **ii.** 农场工人
 iii. 汽车销售经理

b. 汽车销售店在上海……。
 i. 郊区 **ii.** 海边
 iii. 市中心

c. 这份工作要求……。
 i. 你是上海人 **ii.** 你会开车
 iii. 有三年以上卖车的工作经验

d. 除了有相当好的年薪，汽车工厂还提供……。
 i. 每年免费出国旅游
 ii. 免费的汽车
 iii. 免费住宿

e. 参加工作后，你需要去日本或德国……。
 i. 参加工作培训
 ii. 参观有名的汽车销售店
 iii. 旅游

Grammar focus   p.276

还是: or
 ★ subject + verb + option A + 还是 + option B?
 你喜欢团队工作还是单独工作？

单独 individually; alone (dān dú)

---

5. 和你的同学一起练习常见的工作面试的问题，并轮流提问和回答下面的问题。

With a partner, practise asking common job interview questions. Take turns to ask and answer them:

a. 介绍一下你自己。

b. 你最大的优点是什么？你有什么技能？

c. 你最不擅长什么？

d. 你以后打算在哪里工作，做什么？

e. 在工作中你觉得什么最重要？

f. 你喜欢团队合作，还是单独工作？

g. 你有哪些兴趣爱好？

h. 你希望你的年薪是多少？

1. 看看下面关于工作的英文词语，把它们和正确的中文搭配起来。

a.	accountant	**i.**	厨师
b.	business person	**ii.**	工程师
c.	chef	**iii.**	律师
d.	driver	**iv.**	会计师
e.	engineer	**v.**	记者
f.	tour guide	**vi.**	经理
g.	journalist	**vii.**	警察
h.	lawyer	**viii.**	导游
i.	manager	**ix.**	商人
j.	police officer	**x.**	司机

2. 先看看以下人名，再听录音，然后写下他们以后想做什么工作。

> **a.** 小安　**b.** 丽丽　**c.** 阿军　**d.** 小娜　**e.** 大文

3. 先读文字，再听录音，然后选择正确答案完成句子。

a. 文化教育协会短期工作是在⋯⋯。
i. 暑假　ii. 春天　iii. 寒假

b. 短期工作时间是⋯⋯。
i. 6月到8月　ii. 7月到9月　iii. 8月到10月

c. 工作的第一天是⋯⋯。
i. 7月15日　ii. 8月15日　iii. 8月1日

d. 需要擅长什么？
i. 会做饭　ii. 唱歌和跳舞　iii. 会说流利的中文和英文

e. 文化协会的短期工招⋯⋯。
i. 15岁到18岁的中学生　ii. 在校大学生　iii. 已经毕业的大学生

4. 写下正确的词语填空。

> 想　　打算　　当　　开　　看

小的时候我 (a) 当一名飞行员。
大学毕业后如果有机会我 (b) 去亚洲工作。
他计划以后 (c) 一名会计师。
爸爸自己 (d) 了一家建筑公司。
妈妈是医生，她的工作是给病人们 (e) 病。

5. 阅读以下个人简历，然后回答问题。

尼克·李—个人简历

网站：www.exampledesign.org

电话：01234567891

电子邮件：contactnick@example.com

关于我

我来自英国伦敦，现在住在上海。

我做的是网站设计的工作。这份工作我已经做了三年了。

我有在英国和中国工作的经验。

教育

2005年—2011年：圣保罗中学

2011年—2013年：大学，计算机专业

工作经历

2013年—2015年：

● 设计建立个人网站

● 设计大学生戏剧节网站

● 设计伦敦唐人街新年活动网站及广告

2016年：在英国文化会上海办公室做网站设计

技能：网站设计，流利的中英文，摄影

爱好：艺术设计，摄影，旅游

a. 尼克是做什么工作的？

b. 他大学学的是什么专业？

c. 他在哪些国家工作过？

d. 2013年到2015年期间，他给哪两个活动设计了网站？

e. 除了网站设计，尼克还有什么技能？

f. 他有哪些爱好？

6. 尼克正在面试一家中国旅游杂志的网站设计师。和你的同学角色扮演尼克和面试官的对话，轮流提出和回答下面的问题。

a. 你好。请你先介绍一下你自己吧。

b. 请问你大学学了什么？

c. 你以前都为哪些活动/公司设计过网站？

d. 除了设计网站以外，你还有哪些其他的技能？

e. 你有什么兴趣爱好？

f. 你对未来三年的工作有什么计划？

7. 写一份你自己的中文简历，写120–150个字。你的简历应该包括：

a. 自我介绍；

b. 教育和学校；

c. 工作经历；

d. 技能和兴趣爱好；

e. 你对未来的计划。

UNIT OBJECTIVES

- Discuss and compare the seven continents.
- Learn about China's National Day and how people celebrate it.
- Learn about popular cities and tourist attractions in China.
- Discuss issues relating to international air travel.
- Discuss and compare different ways of organising a holiday.
- Discuss and compare cities and landmarks from around the world.
- Discuss and share information on ecotourism.

1. 看看下面的词语，把它们和正确的英文名称搭配起来。

   Look at the Chinese terms. Match them with their correct names in English.

不同类型的旅游	
a. 自由行	**i.** packaged tour
b. 跟团游	**ii.** ecotourism
c. 绿色旅游	**iii.** self-guided holiday

世界各大洲	
d. 亚洲	**iv.** North America
e. 北美洲	**v.** Europe
f. 欧洲	**vi.** Asia
g. 非洲	**vii.** South America
h. 南美洲	**viii.** Africa
i. 大洋洲	**ix.** Antarctica
j. 南极洲	**x.** Oceania

中国的公共假期和活动	
k. 国庆节	**xi.** Golden Week
l. 黄金周	**xii.** National Day

2. 用第一题的词语填空。

   Using the vocabulary in Activity 1, fill in the missing information to complete the sentences below.

中国在亚洲，美国在(a)，英国在(b)。

今年暑假，爸爸和我去了中国旅行，我们选择了(c)，没有跟团游。

今年寒假，我会参加(d)，去中国的农村考察，享受大自然的美景。

在中国，每年的国庆(e)会放假，很多人都利用这个长假去旅游和购物。

类型 lèi xíng type

自由行 zì yóu xíng self-guided holiday

跟团游 gēn tuán yóu packaged tour

绿色旅游 lǜ sè lǚ yóu ecotourism

国庆 guó qìng National Day

黄金 huáng jīn gold

考察 kǎo chá to observe and study

3. 汤姆和心美正在谈话。先读问题，再听录音，然后选择正确的答案。

Tom is talking to Sammy. Read the questions before you listen to the recording, then choose the correct answers.

a. 汤姆什么时候去放假？

    i. 国庆节   **ii.** 中秋节   **iii.** 春节

b. 汤姆会去哪个城市旅游？

    i. 香港   **ii.** 上海   **iii.** 北京

c. 为什么汤姆对这个地方感兴趣？

    i. 他想去那儿的动物园   **ii.** 他想去购物

    iii. 他想参加游学团

 4. 练习写汉字。

Practise writing Chinese.

a. 按照笔画顺序写下面的字。

Write the characters by following the stroke order.

huáng
黄 黄 黄 黄 黄 黄 黄 黄 黄 黄 黄 黄
  1 2 3 4 5 6 7 8 9 10 11

jīn
金 金 金 金 金 金 金 金 金
  1 2 3 4 5 6 7 8

zhōu
周 周 周 周 周 周 周 周 周
  1 2 3 4 5 6 7 8

b. 用以上词语造句，写出一至两件人们在中国的国庆黄金周期间会做的事情。写20–30个字。

Using the above vocabulary, write a sentence of your own about one or two things people might like to do during Golden Week in China. Write 20–30 characters.

 5. 和你的同学谈谈自己最近的一次旅行，轮流提出和回答下面的问题。

With a partner, talk about a holiday you've been on recently. Take turns to ask and answer the following questions.

a. 你去了哪儿旅行？

b. 你选择了跟团游还是自由行？

c. 你做了什么？

LESSON OBJECTIVE

● Share with others some facts about the seven continents, such as sizes and populations.

1. 看看下面的地图，说出七大洲的中文名称。

Look at the map below. Say the names of the seven continents in Chinese.

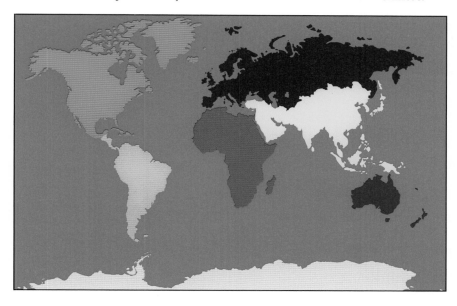

Grammar focus p.276

1. 差不多: almost the same
   ★ noun A + 和 + noun B + (situation) + 差不多
   北美洲和南美洲(的人口)差不多。

2. 比 …… 一点儿: by a little bit
   ★ noun A + 比 + noun B + stative verb + 一点儿
   亚洲比非洲大一点儿。

(约)占 yuē zhàn to take up (approximately)

百分率 bǎi fēn lǜ percentage

捕鲸队 bǔ jīng duì whaling team

定居 dìng jū settle down; permanent (settlers)

大于 dà yú bigger than

密度 mì dù density

2. 阅读短文，然后判断下面的叙述对还是错，并以文章内容说明理由。

Read the passage, then decide if the following statements are true or false, explaining your reasons with reference to the text.

七大洲介绍

亚洲是世界第一大洲。人口最多，约占世界总人口的60％。

非洲是世界第二大洲。人口比亚洲少很多，占世界总人口的12.3％。

北美洲是世界第三大洲。人口约占世界总人口的8.1％。

南美洲是世界第四大洲。占世界人口的百分率比北美洲低一点儿，约为5.6％。

南极洲是世界第五大洲。只有来自其它大陆的科学考察人员和捕鲸队会在南极洲居住一段时间，这里没有定居居民。

欧洲仅大于大洋洲，是世界第六大洲。占世界总人口的百分率和非洲的差不多，约为10.4％，是人口密度最大的一个洲。

大洋洲是世界上最小的一个洲。人口约占世界总人口的0.5％，虽然比南极洲多一点儿，但却是世界人口最少的一个洲。

a. 亚洲比非洲大。

b. 非洲人口占世界人口的百分率比北美洲多一点。

c. 南美洲比欧洲小。

d. 南极洲是人口密度最大的一个洲。

e. 大洋洲比南极洲的人口多。

3. 小明和志军正在一起看世界地图。先读下面的问题，再听录音，然后选择唯一正确的答案。

Xiaoming and Zhijun are reading a map of the world. Look at the questions before you listen to the recording, then choose the correct answers.

a. 志军认为哪一个洲有很多国家？

i. 欧洲　　ii. 北美洲　　iii. 大洋洲

b. 志军认为哪一个洲和欧洲差不多大？

i. 欧洲　　ii. 北美洲　　iii. 非洲

c. 志军认为世界上最小的是哪一个洲？

i. 大洋洲　　ii. 亚洲　　iii. 南极洲

wàn
万 ten thousand

miàn jī
面积 area
píng fāng qiān mǐ
平方千米 square kilometre

4. 和你的同学谈谈七大洲，轮流提出和回答下面的问题。

With a partner, talk about the seven continents. Take turns to ask and answer the following questions.

a. 你去过哪一个洲？

b. 哪个洲你没去过？

c. 英国位于哪个洲？

d. 肯尼亚位于哪个洲？

wèi yú
位于 to be located at
kěn ní yà
肯尼亚 Kenya

5. 你将会在课堂上演讲。用80–100个字写一篇讲稿。其中应该包括：

You're about to give a speech in class. Write a script using 80–100 characters. It should include:

a. 哪几个洲是世界上最大的三个洲？

b. 它们哪个比哪个大？

c. 每个洲有哪些国家？　（介绍其中一个）

Cultural spotlight

quán shì jiè zuì dà de zhōu　　yà zhōu
全世界最大的洲—亚洲
Asia – the largest continent in the world

　亚洲，过去译作"亚细亚洲"，是七大洲中面积最大、人口最多的一个洲。亚细亚是一个非常古老的名称，希腊人称呼他们的东方或太阳升起的地方为亚细亚。可能是来源于亚述人的名称，亚述一词在亚述的语言中也代表东方。中国是亚洲人口最多的国家，印度排第二。

a. 你住的国家位于哪一个洲？

b. 它的名字有什么特别的意思？

c. 在你住的国家那个洲还有哪些著名的国家，试着说出三个。

10.3 国庆黄金周

CELEBRATING CHINA'S NATIONAL DAY

LESSON OBJECTIVES

● Learn about China's National Day.
● Describe what people like to do during this national holiday.

1. 先看问题和图片，再听录音，然后选择唯一正确的答案。

Look at the questions and pictures before you listen to the recording, then choose the correct answers.

yóu yú 由于 due to
fán máng 繁忙 busy; bustling

yuè bīng 阅兵 parade
shēng qí 升旗 to hoist a flag
yí shì 仪式 ceremony

a. 明天是什么节日？

i.

ii.

iii.

b. 很多市民都会和家人朋友做什么？

i.

ii.

iii.

c. 北京电台提醒听众朋友们坐什么交通工具？

i.

ii.

iii.

d. 北京电台提醒听众朋友外出别忘了带什么？

i.

ii.

iii.

189

2. 阅读下面的文章。

Read the following passage.

中国国庆黄金周

中国政府宣布自一九五零年起，以每年的十月一日作为新中国宣告成立的日子，即国庆日。在国庆节当天，全国人民都会共同庆祝节日。在北京，到处都会挂起横幅，用"欢度国庆"等标语来庆祝国庆，非常热闹；大家都会一起去看阅兵仪式和升旗仪式。

国庆节假期又叫做国庆黄金周。黄金周的意思是有连续七天的假期。中国的春节和国庆节两个节日都有黄金周。国庆节七天假期叫做"十·一黄金周"。"黄金周"又叫做"长假"。

在国庆黄金周这个长假中，很多人会去不同的城市或郊区旅游和购物，交通十分繁忙，很多大城市，例如北京、上海的街上特别挤，堵车的情况特别严重。

a. 根据上面的内容，从右栏的叙述中选出搭配左边句子的叙述。（注意：右栏的叙述比需要的多。）

Referring to the passage, match the phrases in the left-hand column with those in the right-hand column to make full sentences. (Note: there are more phrases on the right than on the left.)

a. 每年的10月1日是	**i.** 用"欢度国庆"等标语来庆祝国庆。
b. 在国庆节当天，	**ii.** 新中国宣告成立的日子。
c. 在北京，人们	**iii.** 全中国的人会一起庆祝国庆节。
d. 国庆假期又叫做	**iv.** "五·一黄金周"。
	v. "国庆黄金周"。
	vi. "黄金周"又叫做"长假"。

b. 根据文章的内容，回答下面的问题。

Referring to the passage, answer these questions.

   i. 国庆黄金周连续有几天假期？

   ii. 在国庆黄金周，人们会去什么地方旅游？

   iii. 在国庆黄金周，很多大城市有什么问题？

---

tīng zhòng
听众 audience

jìn liàng
尽量 to the best of your ability

tí xǐng
提醒 to remind

---

rè nao
热闹 lively

jǐ
挤 crowded

dǔ chē
堵车 traffic congestion

yán zhòng
严重 serious

---

xuān bù
宣布 to announce

xuān gào
宣告 to declare

chéng lì
成立 establishment

héng fú
横幅 banner

biāo yǔ
标语 slogan

Grammar focus pp.276-7

1. without 的

我爸爸今年六十岁。
陈明朋友今晚不来吃饭。

2. 别 : don't

★ 别 + verb + 了, + follow-up phrase

别说了，我不想听。
别看了，明天再看吧。

3. 练习写汉字。

Practise writing Chinese.

a. 按照笔画顺序写下面的字。

Write the characters by following the stroke order.

fán

繁 繁 繁 繁 繁 繁 繁 繁 繁 繁 繁 繁 繁 繁 繁 繁 繁 繁
  1 2 3 4 5 6 7 8 9 10 11 12 13 14 15 16 17

máng

忙 忙 忙 忙 忙 忙 忙
  1 2 3 4 5 6

b. 翻译以下句子，并用中文写下来。

Translate these sentences into Chinese and write them out.

i. The traffic in Shanghai is always very busy.

ii. Beijing is a bustling city, especially during Golden Week.

4. 和你的同学谈国庆黄金周，轮流提出和回答下面的问题。

With a partner, talk about China's National Day and Golden Week. Take turns to ask and answer the following questions.

a. 在今年的国庆黄金周，你爸爸妈妈带你去哪儿玩？

b. 你们会乘坐什么交通工具？为什么？

c. 你喜欢国庆黄金周这个长假吗？

5. 明天是国庆黄金周假期的第一天。发一个短信给你的朋友，写 40-50个字。其中应该包括：

Tomorrow is the first day of Golden Week. Write a text message to your friend using 40–50 characters. It should include:

a. 去哪儿？

b. 几点去？

c. 做什么？

d. 提醒他/她带什么？

e. 乘什么交通工具？为什么？

LESSON OBJECTIVES
● Describe and plan for different activities when on holiday or travelling abroad.
● Share with others your views on a variety of such activities.

📖 **1.** 阅读下面的内容，然后回答问题。
Read the following passage, then answer the questions.

黄山旅游指南

国庆黄金周快到了，很多人打算去旅游，我们这次会介绍大家去黄山。虽然黄山没有五光十色的商区，但是风景很美。下面是一些去黄山观光旅游时要注意的事项。

行程安排：
去黄山旅游三天刚刚好。第一天可以先到风景区，建议去的景点有：翡翠谷和九龙瀑布。第二天可以去爬山，登上山以后可以住山上的宾馆。第三天下山后回机场。

旅游须知：
黄山高二千多米，山上气温偏低，早晚温差较大，游客应多注意保暖，要准备充足的防寒衣物。山上商店不多，建议多带几瓶水和一些食物。登山的时候，选择坐缆车的朋友们可以不用带头盔等爬山装备，最好多带一双备用爬山鞋。

住宿：
登山前，可以住在景点附近的家庭式旅馆，这样不但可以节省旅费，而且可以和当地人聊天，了解当地的风土人情。登上山以后，可以在宾馆住一晚，非常方便。

ān pái 安排	arrangement
huáng shān 黄山	Yellow Mountain, a well-known mountain range in southeast China
zhǐ nán 指南	guide
wǔ guāng shí sè 五光十色	colourful
shāng qū 商区	business or commercial district
guān guāng 观光	sightseeing
shì xiàng 事项	item; matter
jǐng diǎn 景点	scenic spot
fěi cuì gǔ 翡翠谷	Emerald Valley
pù bù 瀑布	waterfall
xū zhī 须知	notice
chōng zú 充足	adequate
fáng hán 防寒	to guard against the cold
lǎn chē 缆车	cable car
tóu kuī 头盔	helmet
zhuāng bèi 装备	equipment
bèi yòng 备用	back-up
jiā tíng shì lǚ guǎn 家庭式旅馆	homestay; family-run accommodation
fēng tǔ rén qíng 风土人情	local custom or practice

a. 以上文章是什么类型的文本？

b. 去黄山行程要多少天？

c. 去黄山行程可以怎样安排？

d. 黄山上的天气怎么样？要注意什么？

e. 如果想节省旅费，在登山前，游客可以住哪儿？

2. 先读下面的问题，再听录音，然后选择唯一正确的答案。

Read the questions before you listen to the recording, then choose the correct answers.

a. 丽青要去哪儿旅游？
 i. 泰山　　**ii.** 黄山　　**iii.** 华山

b. 丽青去那儿做什么？
 i. 购物和参加游学团
 ii. 看风景、爬山和拍照
 iii. 参观博物馆

c. 丽青准备了些什么？
 i. 背包　　**ii.** 一些钱　　**iii.** 一些水和食物

d. 丽青他们要带什么爬山装备？
 i. 背包　　**ii.** 头盔　　**iii.** 爬山鞋

e. 以下哪一个不是小明去北京做的事？
 i. 吃烤鸭　　**ii.** 参观博物馆　　**iii.** 爬山

3. 你打算去中国旅游。和你的同学角色扮演两个朋友之间的对话，轮流提出和回答下面的问题。

You are thinking of going to China for your holiday. With a partner, role-play the conversation between two friends. Take turns to ask and answer the following questions.

a. 你要去哪儿旅游？

b. 到了那儿，你会参观哪一些景点？

c. 除了参观景点之外，你还会做什么？

gù gōng
故宫 Forbidden City

Grammar focus p.277

一些: some; a few
 ★ 一些 + noun
 一些水果
 一些朋友

4. 练习写汉字。

Practise writing Chinese.

a. 按照笔画顺序写下面的字。

Write the characters by following the stroke order.

b. 旅游时你喜欢观光吗？为什么？用20-30个字写下你的看法。

Do you enjoying sightseeing when you go on holiday? Why or why not?
Write your views using 20–30 characters.

5. 你刚去了一次旅行。用120-150个字写一个博客。其中应该
包括：

You've just returned from a holiday. Use 120–150 characters to write a blog
post about your experience. It should include the following:

a. 你去了什么地方？什么时候去的？

b. 你和谁一起去？

c. 你在出发之前准备了什么？

d. 你做了些什么？你最喜欢哪些活动？

e. 你觉得这次旅游怎么样？

LESSON OBJECTIVES

● Identify some famous Chinese cities and tourist attractions.
● Share your views with others about various tourist attractions.

1. 小华正在和米娜谈话。先看图片和问题，再听录音，然后选择唯一正确的答案。

Xiaohua is talking to Mina. Look at the pictures and questions before you listen to the recording, then choose the correct answers.

a. 哪些是北京的景点？   **b.** 哪些是西安的景点？

c. 哪些是桂林的景点？   **d.** 哪些是拉萨的景点？

i 兵马俑	ii 故宫	iii 北海公园
iv 七星岩	v 布达拉宫	vi 长城

xī ān
西安 Xi'an, a city in northwest China

guì lín
桂林 Guilin, a city in southern China known for its landscape

lā sà
拉萨 Lhasa, a city in Tibet

běi hǎi gōng yuán
北海公园 Beihai Park, a former imperial garden

chángchéng
长城 Great Wall of China

qī xīng yán
七星岩 Seven Star Crag

bù dá lā gōng
布达拉宫 Potala Palace

2. 先读以下文字，再听录音，然后列出米娜和小华去过和将会去的景点。

Read the text before you listen to the recording again, then write down the places Mina and Xiaohua have visited and those they would like to visit.

米娜去过：北海公园、(a)、(b)的七星岩
小华去过和参观过：长城、(c)
米娜打算去参观：(d)
小华打算去：上海

3. 阅读短文，然后判断下面的叙述对还是错，并以文章内容说明理由。

Read the report, then decide if the following statements are true or false, explaining your reasons with reference to the text.

北京成为中国最热门的旅游城市

在今天早上八点左右，记者来到北京的天安门广场，这里人不多，大约有五十人左右，一群外国游客在照相。他们参加了两个星期的北京观光旅游团，昨天刚到北京，北海公园、长城、故宫等等都是他们接下来打算在北京参观的景点。

这些游客告诉记者，他们在今天早上六点左右已经到了天安门广场，因为他们对升旗仪式很感兴趣。

"北京的景点都很漂亮，就是太大了。"一位来自英国的游客说，"北京太多地方可以去，我觉得时间很不够。""我觉得在北京买东西比我们老家便宜，我爱北京！"一名来自美国的游客高兴地说。

越来越多的外国人到中国的大城市旅游。在世界旅游城市报告中，北京入选最受欢迎城市的前十位，而上海也在二十名以内。

a. 记者在天安门广场看到大约五十个中国游客在照相。

b. 北海公园、长城和故宫在北京。

c. 来自英国的游客觉得在北京参观的时间不够，因为北京有太多景点了。

d. 来自美国的游客喜欢北京是因为北京的景点太多了。

e. 北京和上海在世界最受欢迎的旅游城市中排在二十名以内。

4. 做一个关于中国旅游的调查。

Carry out a survey about tourism in China.

a. 向十位同学提出下面的问题，记下他们的答案。

Find 10 people in your class. Ask them the following questions and note down their answers.

　　i. 你去过中国的哪个城市旅游？

　　ii. 你喜欢这些城市的哪些景点？

　iii. 为什么你喜欢这些景点？

b. 用上一题的回答写一份报告。写 120–150 个字。

Write a report using the responses from your survey. Write 120–150 characters.

---

tiān ān mén (guǎng chǎng)
天安门(广场) Tiananmen Square

rè mén
热门 popular

bào gào
报告 report

rù xuǎn
入选 selected

qián shí wèi
前十位 top ten

Grammar focus p.277

1. 左右: around, approximately

★ number + measure word +左右

(这个餐厅的客人在)
五十人左右。

(今天的天气在)三十四度左右。

2. 不 + stative verb

★ noun + 不 + stative verb

(这里)人不多。

我钱不够,(不能买这本书)。

LESSON OBJECTIVE

● Describe how to prepare for international travel.

1. 看看下面的图片，把它们和正确的词语搭配起来。

   Look at the pictures below. Match them with the correct vocabulary.

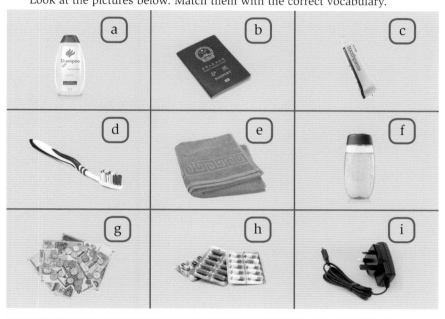

máo jīn 毛巾 towel
yá gāo 牙膏 toothpaste
yá shuā 牙刷 toothbrush

huò bì 货币 currency
gǎn mào yào 感冒药 flu medicine
zhǐ xiè yào 止泻药 anti-diarrhoeal medicine
yù yè 浴液 shower or bath gel
chōng diàn qì 充电器 charger
xǐ fà yè 洗发液 shampoo

i. 毛巾　**ii.** 牙膏　**iii.** 货币　**iv.** 护照　**v.** 感冒药、止泻药　**vi.** 浴液　**vii.** 充电器　**viii.** 洗发液　**ix.** 牙刷

2. 阅读文章，然后判断下面的叙述对还是错，并以文章内容说明理由。

   Read the article, then decide if the statements are true or false, explaining your reasons with reference to the text.

shǒu xù 手续 procedure

háng zhàn lóu 航站楼 airport terminal
zhèng jiàn 证件 identification document

国际机场旅客指南

问：旅客要到哪儿办理出发手续和接受安全检查？

答：旅客要到航站楼办理出发手续和接受安全检查。

问：旅客应该什么时候到机场？为什么？

答：旅客应该提早最少两小时到机场，以便有足够时间接受护照及安全检查。

问：要带什么证件？

答：所有国际出发的旅客必须有有效期在半年以上的护照。

问：手提行李有限制吗？

答：每件行李体积不超过20×40×55厘米(cm)，手提行李总重量不超过5公斤。手提行李中的液态物品，例如牙膏、浴液、洗发液等等，每件容积不能超过100毫升(ml)。

问：到了机场以后，如果需要寄存行李，应该找谁帮忙？

答：可以请行李寄存台的服务员帮忙。

问：过了安全检查后还可以买东西吗？

答：可以，过了安全检查以后，旅客还可以在机场的商场购物。

问：到了机场以后，如果有问题怎么办？

答：到了机场以后，如果有任何问题，请到问询台问服务员。

shǒu tí xíng li 手提行李 hand luggage	
xiàn zhì 限制 limit	
tǐ jī 体积 volume	
chāo guò 超过 to exceed	
yè tài 液态 liquid state	
róng jī 容积 volume	
jì cún 寄存 deposit	
wèn xún tái 问询台 information desk	

a. 旅客要到航站楼接受安全检查。

b. 旅客最好在登机前两小时到达机场。

c. 一位国际出发的旅客的护照和签证还有八个月才到期，他可以出国。

d. 手提行李没有大小和重量限制。

e. 到了机场以后，如果有问题可以找行李寄存的服务员帮忙。

3. 志军正在和妈妈谈话。先读问题，再听录音，然后选择正确的答案。

Zhijun is talking to his mum. Read the questions below before you listen to the recording, then choose the correct answers.

a. 志军和妈妈什么时候要到机场？
   i. 下午三点　　ii. 下午五点　　iii. 晚上七点

b. 志军想寄存行李，他要去哪儿？
   i. 航站楼　　ii. 问询台　　iii. 行李寄存台

c. 过了安全检查以后，志军还能买礼物给心美吗？
   i. 可以　　ii. 不可以　　iii. 不知道

d. 志军不知道机场的厕所在哪儿，他应该问谁？
   i. 行李寄存台的服务员　　ii. 问询台的服务员
   iii. 航站楼的服务员

Grammar focus   p.277

1. 谁: who
   ★ subject + verb + 谁?
   (请问)你找谁？
   我要问谁？

2. 哎呀: an interjection expressing frustration
   ★ 哎呀 + statement
   哎呀，我忘了带课本。
   哎呀，你真麻烦！

4. 朋友明天要出国旅游。她正在和她妈妈谈话。和你的同学
角色扮演她们之间的对话，轮流提出和回答下面的问题。

A friend is travelling abroad tomorrow. She is chatting to her mum about the trip. With a partner, role-play the conversation between mother and daughter, and take turns to ask and answer the following questions.

rì cháng yòng pǐn
日常用品 daily supplies

a. 出国旅行要带什么日常用品？

b. 出国旅行要带什么常用药吗？

c. 出国旅行要带什么证件？

d. 还要带什么？

5. 你将要出国旅游。写一份你自己的旅游备忘录，写120–150
个字。其中应该包括：

You are about to go on holiday abroad. Write your own checklist for international travel. Write 120–150 characters. It should include:

a. 要带哪些个人用品；　　b. 还要准备哪些东西；

c. 到达机场后要注意的事情。

6. 你的朋友打算去中国旅游。你和他在看地图。你正在告诉他不同城市和景点在地图上的方位。
和同学角色扮演两个朋友之间的对话，轮流提出和回答下面的问题。

Your friend is visiting China soon. You are showing him the locations of some cities and scenic spots on a map. With a partner, role-play a conversation between the two friends, and take turns to ask and answer the following questions.

北京(故宫、北海公园)

拉萨(布达拉宫)　　西安(兵马俑)　　上海 (东方明珠)

泰山

桂林(七星岩)　　黄山

a. 北京在地图上的哪一个方向？

b. 布达拉宫在地图上的哪一个方向？

c. 桂林在西安的哪一个方向？

d. 从北京和从上海去黄山，哪一个
比较远？

LESSON OBJECTIVE

- Identify and talk about the pros and cons of arranging a self-guided holiday as opposed to going on a package tour.

1. 汤姆正在和日晴谈话。先看下面的表，再听录音，然后选择正确的答案填空。

   Tom is talking to Riqing. Look at the table before you listen to the recording, then complete the table below by filling in the missing information.

	喜欢什么类型的旅游	原因	
日晴妈妈	**(a)**	• 安排行程**(b)**，不用自己计划。 • 比较**(c)**，如果是跟团游，一般旅行社安排的交通、住宿安排等都经过把关，风险较低。	bǎ guān 把关 to keep close tabs on fēng xiǎn 风险 risk tuán yuán 团员 member tíng liú 停留 to stay or remain shú xī 熟悉 to be familiar with
日晴爸爸	**(d)**	• 跟团游行程没有**(e)** • 跟团游不能选择**(f)** • 跟团游在每个景点的**(g)**也不多	

团员　　　跟团游　　　方便　　　停留时间　　　安全　　　自由行　　　自由

2. 练习写汉字。按照笔画顺序写下面的字。

   Practise writing Chinese. Write the characters by following the stroke order.

   gēn
   跟 跟 跟 跟 跟 跟 跟 跟 跟 跟 跟 跟 跟 跟
   　　1　2　3　4　5　6　7　8　9　10　11　12　13

   tuán
   团 团 团 团 才 才 才
   　　1　2　3　4　5　6

   yóu
   游 游 游 游 游 游 游 游 游 游 游 游
   　　1　2　3　4　5　6　7　8　9　10　11　12

3. 阅读文章，然后判断下面的叙述对还是错，并以文章内容说明理由。

Read the passage, then decide if the following statements are true or false, explaining your reasons with reference to the text.

跟团游 VS 自由行

每个人喜爱的旅行方式都不一样，有人喜欢跟团旅游，有人喜欢自由行。到底哪一种旅游方式合适自己呢？请看下面的介绍：

跟团游是指想去同一个地方的人在旅行社的安排下一起旅行。跟团游要交团费，团费一般包括了交通(通常包括机票和旅游车的费用)、餐饮、住宿、景点门票等，由旅行社安排行程，不用另外计划。

好处：

1. 不用花时间做行程计划。
2. 不怕语言不通。专业的导游，会在行程中详细解说。
3. 可以真正地放松，不用自己写笔记、背地图。
4. 通常团体机票和景点门票的票价都会比较便宜。

合适对象：怕麻烦、不喜欢计划行程的人。

自由行是一种自助旅游方式。机票、签证、住宿通通自己安排。

好处：

1. 旅行日期、行程、路线、旅伴都是自己决定。
2. 多了和当地人聊天的机会。
3. 行程由自己规划。由于停留时间可以由自己决定，因此对于地理位置、景点，可以有更深入的了解。
4. 可以选择自己喜欢的航空公司。

合适对象：不怕麻烦、喜欢自己计划的人。

世界上没有最好的旅游方式，只有最合适自己的旅游方式。读者们，到底哪一种最合适你们呢？

hé shì
合适 suitable

lǚ yóu chē
旅游车 tour bus

mén piào
门票 ticket

piào jià
票价 ticket price

zhù sù
住宿 accommodation

jiě shuō
解说 to explain

lù xiàn
路线 route

lǚ bàn
旅伴 travelling companion

a. 有人喜欢跟团旅游；有人喜欢自由行，每个人喜爱的旅行方式都差不多。

b. 跟团游要交团费，团费不包括交通费用。

c. 参加旅行团不用花时间做行程计划。

d. 自由行的机票、签证、住宿通通由导游安排。

e. 自由行可以让你和当地人多聊天。

f. 不怕麻烦、喜欢自己计划的人应该选择自由行。

4. 和你的同学轮流提出和回答下面关于旅游的问题。

With a partner, take turns to ask and answer the following questions about your holiday preferences.

a. 你喜欢跟团游还是自由行？为什么？

b. 你的家人喜欢跟团游还是自由行？为什么？

5. 说一说你比较喜欢跟团游还是自由行。写出两个原因，写50个字以上。

Write a few sentences on whether you prefer to go on package or self-guided holidays, giving two reasons. Write 50 characters or more.

Grammar focus   p.278

1. using 不 and 没(有)

★ 不 negates present or future actions; used with verbs, stative verbs, and adjectives

他不喜欢唱歌。
明天我不用上学。
北京离天津不远。

★ 没 negates past actions; negates the verb 有; used for making comparisons

昨天我没(有)上学。
世界上没有最好的旅游方式。

2. 到底： after all

★ 到底 + question phrase
(你)到底怎么了？
到底我们跟团游好还是自由行好呢？

LESSON OBJECTIVE
● Identify, describe, and compare landmarks in different countries.

1. 看看下面的图片，把它们和正确的中文名称搭配起来。
Look at the pictures below. Match them with their correct names in Chinese.

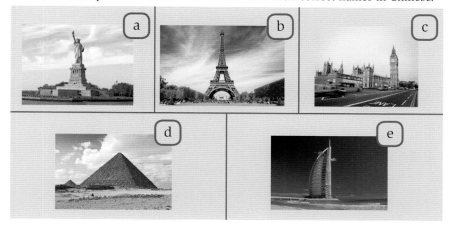

fān chuán jiǔ diàn
帆船酒店 Burj Al Arab Hotel, Dubai

dà bèn zhōng
大笨钟 Big Ben, the Houses of Parliament's iconic clock tower in London

hú fū jīn zì tǎ
胡夫金字塔 Pyramid of Khufu, Egypt

zì yóu nǚ shén xiàng
自由女神像 Statue of Liberty, New York City

āi fēi ěr tiě tǎ
埃菲尔铁塔 Eiffel Tower, Paris

i. 帆船酒店　ii. 大笨钟　iii. 胡夫金字塔　iv. 自由女神像　v. 埃菲尔铁塔

2. 阅读下面的文章。
Read the passage.

世界著名地标介绍

每个国家都有一些地标建筑令人难忘，一看到它，我们就会想起某个国家或城市。游客们，现在为您介绍一些世界闻名的地标，到了当地，别忘了去看一看。

1876年是美国独立100周年，法国在这一年向美国赠送了自由女神像作为纪念。它在美国纽约市，高46米，重200多吨，是当地著名的地标。

埃菲尔铁塔建于1889年，是法国巴黎地标之一，也是巴黎最高的建筑，一共高324米，重超过10000吨，共有1711级阶梯。

大笨钟建于1858年，是英国伦敦著名的地标。它在一座高95米的钟楼上，重14吨，时针和分针长度分别为2.75米和4.27米，每15分钟响一次。

dì biāo / biāo zhì
地标/标志 landmark

lìng rén nán wàng
令人难忘 unforgettable; memorable

wén míng
闻名 famous

zèng sòng
赠送 to gift

jì niàn
纪念 to remember or commemorate

dūn
吨 ton

jiàn yú
建于 built in

jiē tī
阶梯 steps (on stairs), ladder

xiǎng
响 to ring

203

埃及的吉萨金字塔群是世界新七大奇迹之一。其中最大的是胡夫金字塔，约4000多年前建造。它高约140米，底边长约230米，用200多万块巨石砌成。

全世界最豪华的酒店是迪拜的帆船酒店，它是世界少数的七星级酒店之一，一共有56层，321米高。酒店在一个人工岛上，是一个帆船形状的建筑。

a. 从文章的内容找出并写下以下词语的同义词。

Find synonyms of these terms from the passage, and write them down.

> **i.** 标志　**ii.** 闻名　**iii.** 一共

b. 根据文章的内容，把A栏和B栏的词组搭配起来组成句子。

With reference to the passage above, match the phrases in column A with those in column B to make complete sentences.

A	B
a. 自由女神像是	**i.** 每15分钟响一次。
b. 埃菲尔铁塔	**ii.** 法国在1876年送给美国的100周年礼物。
c. 大笨钟建于1858年，	**iii.** 是全世界最豪华的酒店。
d. 胡夫金字塔	**iv.** 是法国巴黎地标之一，共有1711级阶梯。
e. 迪拜的帆船酒店	**v.** 是埃及著名建筑物。

3. 小文正在和玛莉谈话。先读下面的叙述，再听录音，然后判断它们对还是错。

Xiaowen is talking to Mary. Read the statements below before you listen to the recording, then decide if they are true or false.

a. 自由女神像是法国著名的地标。

b. 迪拜的帆船酒店和埃菲尔铁塔的高度差不多。

c. 胡夫金字塔比自由女神像还高。

d. 埃菲尔铁塔和自由女神像差不多高。

---

^{ǎi jí}
埃及 Egypt

^{jí sà jīn zì tǎ qún}
吉萨金字塔群 Giza Pyramid Complex

^{shì jiè xīn qī dà qí jī}
世界新七大奇迹 The New Seven Wonders of the World

^{jù}
巨 huge

^{qì}
砌 to build (bricks, puzzle)

^{háo huá}
豪华 luxury, luxurious

^{dí bài}
迪拜 Dubai

^{rén gōng dǎo}
人工岛 artificial island

^{xíng zhuàng}
形状 shape

Grammar focus　p.278

米，吨： metre, ton (units of measurement)

自由女神像有四十六^{mǐ}米高。

这头大象有两^{dūn}吨重。

4. 练习描述一个世界著名的地标。

Practise describing a famous landmark.

a. 做一个课堂报告，给同学们介绍一个世界著名的地标。其中应该包括：

Give a class presentation on a famous landmark. You should include:

i. 它叫什么名字？ 　　　　**ii.** 它建于哪一年？

iii. 它在哪个国家和城市？ 　**iv.** 它有多高？

v. 它有多重？ 　　　　　　**vi.** 它还有什么特点？

vii. 你喜欢它吗？为什么？

b. 用以上资料写一个关于该地标的旅游介绍。写120–150个字。

Using information from the above activity, write a passage about the landmark you spoke about in your presentation. Write 120–150 characters.

Cultural spotlight

dōng fāng de āi fēi ěr tiě tǎ　　dōng fāng míng zhū guǎng bō diàn shì tǎ
东方的埃菲尔铁塔—东方明珠广播电视塔
The Eiffel Tower of the East – The Oriental Pearl Radio & TV Tower

东方明珠广播电视塔是中国上海浦东著名的地标，它是国家首批5A级旅游景点。塔高大约468米，建筑面积大约7.3万平方米。它于1991年7月开始兴建，1995年5月投入使用。它能够覆盖整个上海市及邻近80公里半径范围内的地区，建成后大幅度地改善了广播和电视节目的收听收视质量。当游客们站在塔上的时候，还可以观赏到黄埔江两岸的美景。

塔内有太空舱、旋转餐厅、上海城市历史发展陈列馆等设施。东方明珠广播电视塔在1995年被列入上海十大新景观之一。

a. 在你的国家或以前住过的地方，有没有一些闻名的地标？

b. 这个地标有什么特别的地方？请分享一下。

LESSON OBJECTIVES
- Describe a range of activities related to ecotourism.
- State your preferences regarding the types of eco-activities you have taken part in.

1. 阅读下面的传单，然后判断下面的叙述对还是错，并以文章内容说明理由。

Read the flyer below, then decide if the following statements are true or false, explaining your reasons with reference to the text.

zǔ zhī	
组织 organisation	
jiě shì	
解释 to explain; explanation	

shēng tài	
生态 ecology	
yuǎn zú	
远足 hiking	
guān chá	
观察 to observe	
kūn chóng	
昆虫 insect	
yǐng xiǎng	
影响 influence	
tàn pái fàng	
碳排放 carbon emission	
huàn jù huà	
换句话 in other words	

"环保绿游游" 绿色旅游活动

各位同学，听到"绿色旅游"，大家会想到哪些活动呢？去郊外生态旅游，还是骑自行车去旅行？对，这些都是绿色旅游。同学们，那参观文化古迹或者跟团购物游又算不算是"绿色旅游"呢？

根据世界旅游组织的解释，绿色旅游既包括我们经常说的生态旅游，比如去乡村远足、观察昆虫和动物活动；也包括环保的旅游方式。台湾绿色旅游协会认为：绿色旅游是尽量减低对环境造成不良影响的一种旅游方式，既要节约能源也要减少碳排放。换句话说，绿色旅游可以说是一种重视环保的旅行态度，既要求人们在旅游的时候不破坏环境，减少对当地社区的不良影响，也希望尽量可以为当地的环境和人带来好处！

如果大家对绿色旅游感兴趣，请立即参加绿色旅游协会的"环保绿游游"活动！

如有任何问题，请联系绿色旅游协会大使美美，谢谢。

a. 绿色旅游包括去郊外生态旅游和骑自行车。

b. 只有到郊外远足、观察昆虫活动才算是绿色旅游。

c. 绿色旅游不是节约能源和减少碳排放的旅游方式。

d. 绿色旅游要求人们一定要为当地的环境和人带来好处。

e. 对绿色旅游感兴趣的同学可以参加学生会举办的"环保绿游游"的活动。

2. 先看下面的表格，再听绿色旅游大使的电台录音，然后用正确的词组填空。

Look at the table before you listen to the radio broadcast by the ambassador of the ecotourism society, then fill in the missing information to complete the table.

活动	负责老师	报名地点	名额	截止报名日期	费用
第1个活动：远足	黄老师	(e)	10个	(h)	请向 (i) 查询
第2个活动：(a)	(c)	2楼图书馆	(g)		
第3个活动：(b)	(d)	5楼(f)	20个		

自行车郊外旅行　李老师　3楼办公室　陈老师
观察昆虫　体育馆　负责老师　10月10日　15个

3. 你刚听完关于"环保绿游游"的宣传广播，和你的同学轮流提出和回答下面的问题。

You have just listened to the advert from the ecotourism society on campus radio. With a partner, take turns to ask and answer the following questions.

a. 想参加哪个绿色旅游活动？

b. 找谁报名？　　**c.** 去哪儿报名？

4. 根据第二题表格中的内容，设计一个海报。写120–150个字。其中应该包括：

Use the information in the table of Activity 2 to design a poster. Write 120–150 characters. It should include:

a. 哪个协会负责这个活动？

b. 举办什么活动？有几个活动？

c. 谁带你们去？

d. 名额有多少个？

e. 去哪儿报名？报名费用是多少？

f. 什么时候去？什么时候截止报名？

bào míng
报名 to sign up

míng é
名额 quota

jié zhǐ
截止 closing (for applications)

chá xún
查询 to enquire

xiào yuán diàn tái
校园电台 campus radio

Grammar focus　p.278

1. 到: arrive/to go to
★ subject + 到 + place
我刚到学校。
同学们(请)到三楼办公室。

2. 既……也……: it is … but also …
★ subject + 既 + A + 也 + B
绿色旅游既要节约能源也要减少碳排放。
她既是我妈妈也是我朋友。

复习
PROGRESS CHECK

1. 看看下面的图片，把它们和正确的中文名称搭配起来。

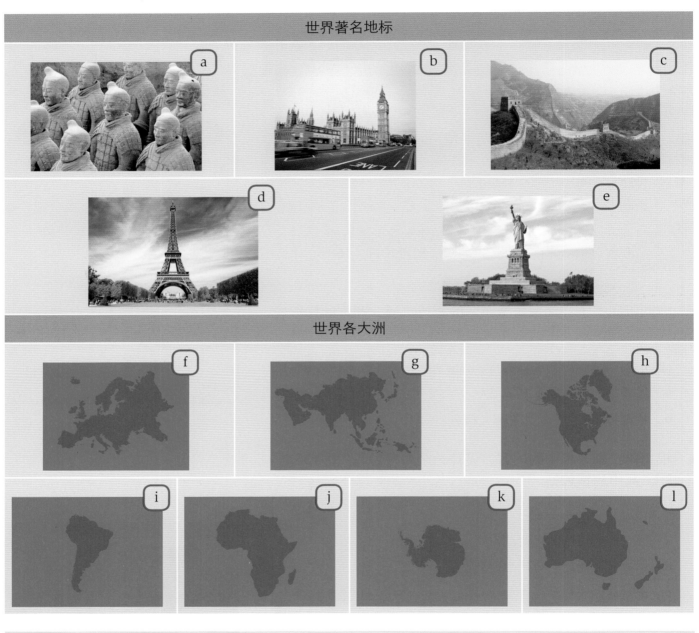

世界著名地标

世界各大洲

i. 自由女神像　ii. 欧洲　iii. 兵马俑　iv. 长城　v. 非洲　vi. 大洋洲　vii. 南极洲
viii. 埃菲尔铁塔　ix. 大笨钟　x. 北美洲　xi. 亚洲　xii. 南美洲

2. 根据下面对话的内容，把A栏和B栏的词组搭配起来组成句子。

心美：汤姆，你去了中国游学差不多一个月了，最近还好吗？假期有什么计划？
汤姆：还不错，下星期一是中国的国庆节，一共有七天假期，我还在想着去哪儿旅游呢！
心美：太好了。听说在中国，人们把这几天假期叫做黄金周，他们会在假期去不同地方旅游和购物，在北京、上海这些大城市里，人特别多。对了，你打算去哪儿旅游？
汤姆：我打算去香港。我对这个城市特别感兴趣。
心美：为什么你对这个城市感兴趣？
汤姆：听说香港是购物天堂。我想去那儿购物！

A	B
a. 汤姆打算在国庆节去	i. 一个月了。
b. 国庆黄金周假期一共有	ii. 香港旅游。
c. 汤姆对香港	iii. 特别感兴趣。
d. 汤姆去了中国游学差不多	iv. 购物天堂。
e. 有人认为香港是一个	v. 特别多。
f. 黄金周时大城市里人	vi. 七天。

3. 阅读以下的讲稿，然后写出答案回答下面的问题。

老师、各位同学：

大家好，我是心美。今天我会介绍世界上最大的三个洲。世界上最大的洲是亚洲；非洲比亚洲小，是第二大的洲；北美洲比非洲小，是第三大的洲。中国位于亚洲，肯尼亚位于非洲，美国位于北美洲。我今天的演讲完毕，谢谢大家。

a. 心美介绍了世界上最大的几个洲？

b. 哪一个是世界最大的洲？　　c. 美国位于哪一个洲？

4. 先读句子，再听录音，然后用下列词组填空。

头盔	爬山	参观	爬山鞋	观光	拍照

志军打算去中国的黄山(a)旅游。他会(b)翡翠谷和九龙瀑布。他也会在那儿和朋友一起(c)和(d)，他会带(e)、(f)和相机。

10

5. 阅读下面的问题，再听录音，然后选择唯一正确的答案。

    a. 小明去过中国的哪个城市旅行？
       i. 西安   **ii.** 上海   **iii.** 北京

    b. 心美最喜欢北京的哪一个景点？
       i. 故宫   **ii.** 天安门广场   **iii.** 北海公园

    c. 丽青最喜欢西安的哪一个景点？
       i. 天安门广场   **ii.** 兵马俑   **iii.** 故宫

    d. 为什么丽青喜欢到西安旅游？
       i. 因为西安很好玩   **ii.** 因为她想参观新建筑   **iii.** 因为她喜欢参观古迹

6. 你要出国旅游，用 100–120个字写一个旅游备忘录。其中应该包括:

    a. 带什么个人用品？   **b.** 在哪儿换当地货币？

    c. 带什么药品？   **d.** 带什么证件？   **e.** 带哪些充电器？

7. 你打算和家人一起去旅游，你的家人不知道选择自由行好还是跟团游好。和你的同学角色扮演你和家人之间的对话，轮流提出和回答下面的问题.

    a. 自由行有什么好？   **b.** 自由行有什么不好？

    c. 跟团游有什么好？   **d.** 跟团游有什么不好？

    e. 你喜欢自由行还是跟团游？为什么？

8. 你是绿色旅游协会的大使，你正在校园电台做关于绿色旅游的宣传。其中应该包括:

    a. 你们举办什么活动？   **b.** 为什么要举办这个活动？哪些老师负责？

    c. 名额有多少个？   **d.** 去哪儿报名？报名费用多少？

    e. 什么时候去？什么时候截止报名？

可以用以下句子开始和结束:

> 各位同学：
> 大家好！欢迎收听校园电台的活动宣传广播。我是绿色旅游协会的大使……
> ……欢迎大家参加！

UNIT OBJECTIVES

- Discuss the pros and cons of studying abroad.
- Learn the facts behind some Chinese wedding traditions.
- Understand the history and customs of the Mid-Autumn Festival.
- Understand the history and customs of the Dragon Boat Festival.

- Learn about a range of festivals from around the world.
- Describe and discuss table manners from around the world.
- Share with others your views on social networking.

1. 下面是五个国家的名称。写下他们的拼音和英文名称。

Below are the names of five countries. Write down their pinyin and English names.

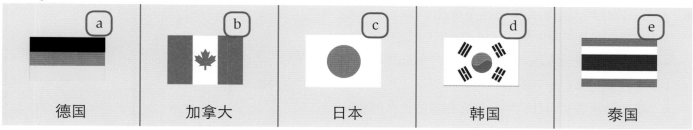

a	b	c	d	e
德国	加拿大	日本	韩国	泰国

2. 先读下面的文字，再听录音，然后把地方名称和正确的活动搭配起来。

Look at the text below before you listen to the recording, then match the places with the correct activities.

a. 日本
b. 韩国
c. 德国
d. 加拿大
e. 澳大利亚

i. 参加音乐节
ii. 爬火山
iii. 看不一样的动物
iv. 看传统的面具舞
v. 尝试各种各样的美食

3. 先读句子，然后选择正确的答案回答问题。

Read the sentences, then choose the correct answer for each question.

a. 今天是二月八日。日晴在广州的爷爷奶奶家过中国新年。
他们正在看春节晚会。
日晴在谁的家里过年?
i. 爷爷奶奶   **ii.** 爸爸的朋友   **iii.** 妈妈的妹妹

b. 下周三九月二十日为了庆祝中秋，中午午餐时间学校将在食堂举行吃月饼的活动。
中秋节学校举行什么活动?
i. 吃月饼   **ii.** 做中国灯笼   **iii.** 穿中国传统服装

c. 今天十二月十三号了，离圣诞节只有十二天了。台北市的购物中心、百货大楼都挂起了彩灯迎接圣诞。

什么节日快到了？

i. 复活节　　**ii.** 中秋节　　**iii.** 圣诞节

d. 每年的七月和八月期间，爱丁堡都会举行夏季艺术节。

爱丁堡每年夏天举行什么节？

i. 音乐节　　**ii.** 艺术节　　**iii.** 戏剧节

e. 泼水节在泰国也被称为宋干节。宋干节是泰国的新年，通常是在每年的四月。

泰国的泼水节在什么时候？

i. 三月　　**ii.** 四月　　**iii.** 五月

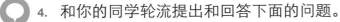
sòng gàn jié
宋干节 Songkran Festival (marking the Thai New Year)

4. 和你的同学轮流提出和回答下面的问题。

With a partner, take turns to ask and answer the following questions.

a. 中国最重要的传统节日有哪些？一般在什么时候？

b. 中秋节是哪个季节的节日？

c. 泰国泼水节又叫什么？一般在每年的什么时候？

d. 你参加过泼水节吗？如果没有，想参加吗？

5. 练习写汉字。

Practise writing Chinese.

a. 按照笔画顺序写下面的字。

Write the characters by following the stroke order.

tè
特 特 特 特 特 特 特 特 特 特 特
　1　2　3　4　5　6　7　8　9　10

bié
别 别 别 别 别 别 别 别
　1　2　3　4　5　6　7

b. 选择词语填空完成句子。

Complete the following sentences by filling in the missing information.

伦敦是一个**(a)**大都市，居住着来自**(b)**不同文化的人。这是一座多元**(c)**、多种族的城市，是**(d)**十分有意思，也十分**(e)**的地方。

世界各地	特别	文化
一个	国际化	

LESSON OBJECTIVES
- Discuss the pros and cons of studying abroad.
- Share your views on why some people choose to study abroad.

1. 看看下面的国家和大学名称。
Look at the names of these countries and universities.

a.	中国	**i.**	悉尼大学
b.	美国	**ii.**	多伦多大学
c.	日本	**iii.**	慕尼黑大学
d.	英国	**iv.**	清华大学
e.	新加坡	**v.**	哈佛大学
f.	德国	**vi.**	南洋理工大学
g.	加拿大	**vii.**	牛津大学
h.	澳大利亚	**viii.**	东京大学

a. 写下它们的英文名称。
Write them out in English.

b. 把国家和大学名称正确地搭配起来。
Match each country with the correct university.

2. 和你的同学谈谈中学毕业以后你是否会上大学。如果上的话，你打算读什么专业？
With a partner, discuss whether or not you would like to go to university after leaving school, and if so, which subject you would like to study.

3. 阅读短文，然后判断下面的叙述是对、错还是未提及，并以文章内容说明理由。
Read the passage, then decide if the following statements are true, false, or not mentioned. Explain your reasons with reference to the text.

niú jīn dà xué
牛津大学 University of Oxford
yī liú
一流 excellent; first-rate
sài tǐng
赛艇 rowing

　　牛津大学是英国最古老的大学，世界十大学府之一。牛津大学由三十八个独立的学院组成，有的学院已经有七百多年的历史了。大学以一流的教学和悠久的历史吸引着成千上万的年轻人来这里学习。牛津大学的学生来自世界一百五十多个不同的国家和地区。
　　牛津大学的课程，无论是文科还是理科，都由导师自己选学生。学生们经过三年的学习，取得学士学位。大学不仅给学生们提供一流的课程，还有各种各样的学生协会。牛津大学的船队世界闻名。如果有一天你去牛津留学，你可以试一试参加大学里的赛艇协会。

a. 牛津大学是英国历史最悠久的大学。

b. 大学里一共有三十五个学院。

c. 有的学院非常古老，已经有七百多年历史了。

d. 这里的学生来自世界上一百五十多个城市。

e. 牛津大学的学生们学习三年就可以取得学士学位。

f. 大学里参加赛艇协会的学生人数最多。

4. 用下列词组填空，将句子写完整。
Using the terms below, fill in the missing information to complete the sentences.

xiāng chǔ
相处 to get along

来　开始　习惯　相处　明白　做兼职工作　读书　世界各地　打电话　的时候

a. 去年八月我(i)在美国纽约的一所中学(ii)。刚到那儿的时候，因为英文不好，上课时有很多东西都听不(iii)。我也不喜欢学校食堂的饭菜，我觉得一点都不好吃。

b. 牛津大学的学生来自(i)。在那里留学(ii)，我除了学会了友好地和同学们(iii)，还了解了很多不同的文化，认识了一些国际朋友。

c. 我是今年夏天(i)澳大利亚留学的。因为学习成绩好，得到了奖学金，不仅不用付学费和住宿费，每个月我还有一些零花钱，所以不用像别的同学那样边读书边(ii)。

d. 我刚刚到德国留学的时候，因为不太会说德文，也不太(i)德国的生活和饮食，所以特别想家。还好现在的智能手机很方便，可以用手机上的一些社交软件给家人免费(ii)，经常保持联系。

5. 先读问题，再听录音，然后写下答案。

Read the questions before you listen to the recording, then write the correct answers.

liú xué shēng
留学生 student studying abroad

a. 他来北京多久了？

b. 他的妈妈住在哪个国家？

c. 在北京大学里他住在哪里？

d. 他喜欢住那儿吗？为什么？

e. 他觉得食堂的饭菜怎么样？

f. 他的留学生朋友们来自哪些国家？

6. 练习写汉字。

Practise writing Chinese.

a. 按照笔画顺序写下面的字。

Write the characters by following the stroke order.

liú

留 留 留 留 留 留 留 留 留 留
1 2 3 4 5 6 7 8 9 10

xué

学 学 学 学 学 学 学 学
1 2 3 4 5 6 7 8

b. 写短句回答问题，然后练习把句子读出来。

Answer each question by writing a short sentence, then practise reading your answers out loud to a partner.

i. 你觉得上大学重要吗？

ii. 你会不会去国外留学？可能会去哪个国家留学？

iii. 你打算学什么专业？为什么？

iv. 你认为出国留学有哪些好处？有哪些不太好的方面？

LESSON OBJECTIVES
● Learn the facts behind some Chinese wedding traditions.
● Describe your experience of attending a wedding.

1. 看看这张中国传统婚礼的图片，然后选择正确答案回答问题。

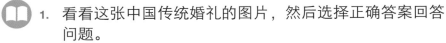

hūn yàn
婚宴 wedding banquet

Look at this picture of a typical Chinese wedding banquet, then answer the following questions.

a. 中国传统婚礼上最主要的颜色是……。
i. 红色　　ii. 白色　　iii. 黄色

b. 中国婚宴上人们用……吃饭。
i. 刀叉　　ii. 筷子　　iii. 勺子

c. 图片中参加婚宴的客人……。
i. 只有年轻人　　ii. 只有老年人　　iii. 每个年龄段的人都有

d. 图片中参加婚宴的客人们看起来……。
i. 很高兴　　ii. 很伤心　　iii. 觉得很无聊

2. 翻译小文给朋友发的手机短信。

Translate the following text that Xiaowen sent to his friend.

> Today my cousin got married! She looked beautiful. The wedding was held at a big hotel in the city centre. Over 100 guests came. It was so lively!

3. 阅读下面的短文，然后判断下面的叙述对还是错，并以文章内容说明理由。

Read the passage, then decide if the statements are true or false. Explain your reasons with reference to the text.

> 　　我的表姐刘文上个月和一个美国华侨结了婚。我们一家人都去参加了她的婚礼。婚礼那天傍晚的时候我们来到市区最有名的国际酒店参加婚宴。进去的时候，按照中国婚礼习俗，妈妈给了新郎新娘一个大红包，并祝他们快乐。这是一场传统的中式婚宴，所以到处都贴着大红的"喜"字，我觉得婚礼现场又漂亮又喜庆。婚宴的时候新郎和新娘穿着大红色的中式礼服给客人们敬酒表示感谢。我以前没有参加过中式婚礼，所以这对我来说是一次很有趣的经历，我觉得太有意思了。

a. 表姐是上个月结的婚。

b. 新郎是英国华侨。

c. 我们全家人都去了表姐的婚礼。

d. 参加中国人的婚宴时给新人红包是习俗。

e. 表姐的婚礼是中式婚礼。

f. 婚宴期间新娘新郎穿的是红色的中式礼服。

g. 虽然这是我第三次参加中式婚礼，但是我还是觉得很有意思。

4. 先读问题，再听录音，然后选择正确的答案。

Read the questions before you listen to the recordings, then write the correct answers.

录音A

a. 广告中的婚宴场所叫什么？
 i. 世纪酒店　　**ii.** 半岛酒店　　**iii.** 国际酒店

b. 这家酒店在哪里？
 i. 火车站附近　　**ii.** 城市花园旁边　　**iii.** 城市广场附近

c. "龙凤新人堂"在酒店的哪层？
 i. 最高层　　**ii.** 六十八层　　**iii.** 二十八层

---

huá qiáo	
华侨	overseas Chinese
àn zhào	
按照	according to

bàng wǎn	
傍晚	early evening
xīn láng	
新郎	groom
xīn niáng	
新娘	bride
xiàn chǎng	
现场	on site
xǐ qìng	
喜庆	joyous
lǐ fú	
礼服	formal wear
jìng jiǔ	
敬酒	to toast

Grammar focus p.279

又……又……: describes two features of one thing, often used with stative verbs and verbs

★ 又 + description A + 又 + description B

(他)又冷又饿。
(这道菜)又好看又好吃。

lóng fèng	
龙凤	dragon and phoenix (traditional symbol of a harmonious marriage)
hūn jiè	
婚戒	wedding ring

录音B

d. 广告中的"龙凤新人"是一家什么？

    i. 办婚宴的酒店   **ii.** 摄影公司   **iii.** 婚礼服务公司

e. 除了婚宴、婚车服务，"龙凤新人"还会给新人们提供什么？

    i. 安排新婚旅游   **ii.** 买婚戒   **iii.** 送免费结婚礼物

5. 和你的同学谈参加婚礼的经历，轮流提出和回答下面的问题。

With a partner, talk about your experiences of going to weddings. Take turns to ask and answer the following questions.

a. 你参加了谁的婚礼？

b. 参加婚礼的客人多不多？

c. 婚礼在哪里举行的？ 在酒店里、教堂里，还是在户外？

d. 你觉得婚礼热闹吗？ 大家是不是都吃得很开心？ 玩得也很开心？

e. 你觉得什么是那场婚礼最令人难忘的部分？

Cultural spotlight

zhōng shì hūn yàn xí sú
中式婚宴习俗 Chinese wedding customs

在中国人的婚宴上，客人们会给新人们装有钱的红包。很多地方会在新房里放很多枣、花生、桂圆、莲子或栗子。这是一个非常有意思的传统：因为"枣"和"早"读音相同，"桂"和"贵"读音相同，这四种水果放在一起"枣、生、桂、子"的意思其实是"早生贵子"，表示预祝新人们早点生小孩。

在婚宴时客人会祝贺新人新婚快乐，新人们也会一桌一桌地向客人们敬酒。现代婚宴上很多新娘都会先穿西式婚纱入场，然后又会换上传统的中式红裙。

a. 你的国家有什么特别的婚礼习俗？

b. 你在婚宴上吃过最特别的食物是什么？

11.4 中秋节
MID-AUTUMN FESTIVAL

LESSON OBJECTIVES

● Develop a deeper understanding of this important festival, celebrated by Chinese communities around the world.

● Identify food and activity vocabulary related to the festival.

1. 看看下面的图片，把它们和正确的中文词语搭配起来。

Look at the pictures. Match them to the correct Chinese vocabulary.

> tuán yuán fàn
> 团圆饭 reunion meal

 a
 b
 c
 d

i. 月饼　**ii.** 团圆饭　**iii.** 灯笼　**iv.** 赏月

2. 阅读以下短文，然后回答问题。

Read the passage below, then answer the questions.

> yuán
> 圆 round
>
> yuè liàng
> 月亮 moon
> jù shuō
> 据说 It is said that ...
> xiàngzhēng
> 象征 to symbolise
> qí jù yī táng
> 齐聚一堂 get or gather together
> shāo kǎo
> 烧烤 barbeque

　　每年农历8月15日是东亚各国的重要传统节日——中秋节。有的地方也称它"月节"。这是一个和月亮有关的节日，据说这一天的月亮是一年中最大最圆最亮的。中秋节这天家人、朋友会在家里吃团圆饭，一边吃美味可口的月饼，赏月，一边聊天。中秋节吃月饼是因为月饼是圆的，象征团圆。近年来有些地方（例如香港和台湾）家人朋友齐聚一堂，会一起烧烤，也是一种团圆的象征。

a. 哪些地方庆祝中秋节？

b. 中秋节是一个和什么有关的节日？

c. 人们怎样庆祝中秋节？

d. 为什么中秋节人们要吃月饼？

e. 近年来有的地方的中秋节有了什么新的活动？

3. 和你的同学轮流提出和回答下面关于中秋节的问题。

With a partner, take turns to ask and answer these questions about the Mid-Autumn Festival.

a. 你有没有过过中秋节？在哪里过的？

b. 你有没有吃过月饼？在哪里吃的？觉得好吃吗？

219

4. 先读句子，再听录音，然后判断它们是对、错还是未提及。

Read the statements before you listen to the recording, then decide if they are true, false, or not mentioned.

jié shù
结束 to end or finish

a. 九月三日到十七日的每天晚上都会举行中秋节晚会。

b. 晚会在城市的大剧院里举行。

c. 晚会从晚上八点开始到晚上十点三十分结束。

d. 中秋晚会上可以看到京剧表演。

e. 除了有京剧表演，晚会还有传统民族舞表演。

f. 中秋节市区的交通会很拥挤，所以最好坐公共交通。

g. 您需要坐地铁五号线去看晚会。

h. 您也可以坐306路巴士去城市广场站。

5. 将以下段落翻译成中文并写下来。

Translate the following passage into Chinese and write it down.

Mid-Autumn Festival is one of the most popular and oldest Chinese festivals. People celebrate Mid-Autumn Festival on the fifteenth day of the eighth month in the Chinese calendar. This festival is not just celebrated by the Chinese; Koreans and many other countries in Asia also celebrate it.

On this day, families and friends will gather together for a reunion meal, go moon-gazing, and eat mooncakes.

Cultural spotlight

cháng é bèn yuè
嫦娥奔月 Chang'e flies to the moon

　　中秋节是具有悠久历史的传统节日，就像其他传统节日一样，有着很多美丽的传说故事。嫦娥奔月就是中秋最有名的传说了。

　　听说很久很久以前，天上出现了十个太阳，天干地热，人们都无法生活了。这时候出现了一个十分厉害的弓箭手名叫后羿。为了帮助人们，他把其中九个太阳射了下来。因为后羿救了人们，天上的神给了他一颗能长生不老的药。后羿打算和他的妻子嫦娥一起吃这颗药，这样两个人都可以长生不老。但是嫦娥自私地吃掉了这颗药，结果她飞到了月宫，不能回来。后羿每年就在农历的八月十五日这一天对着月亮摆出圆饼来表达对妻子的思念。现在"嫦娥工程"是中国进行的航天探月工程的名字。

a. 你还知道别的中秋习俗的传说和由来吗？
b. 你觉得过中秋节有哪些意义？

LESSON OBJECTIVES
- Identify key words related to this festival.
- Describe some activities that take place during this festival.

1. 下面是一些关于端午节的词语和图片。
   Below are some words and pictures related to the Dragon Boat Festival.

xiāng bāo
香包

zòng zi
粽子

xiónghuáng jiǔ
雄黄酒

wén chóng
蚊虫

a. 选择正确的英文意思。
Find the correct meaning in English for each one.

- **i.** scented bag / scented water
- **ii.** dumpling with rice / dumpling made of wheat flour
- **iii.** realgar wine / red wine
- **iv.** snakes / mosquitoes

b. 把正确的动词和词语配对，组成端午节期间的活动。
Match the verbs with the correct terms to form five customs during Dragon Boat Festival.

a. 吃   i. 雄黄酒

b. 喝   ii. 香包

c. 看   iii. 草药浴

d. 做   iv. 粽子

e. 洗   v. 龙舟比赛

lóng zhōu bǐ sài
龙舟比赛 dragon boat race

cǎo yào yù
草药浴 herbal bath

2. 先读句子，再听录音，然后选择唯一正确的答案。
Read the sentences before you listen to the recording, then choose the correct answers.

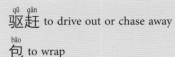
qū gǎn
驱赶 to drive out or chase away
bāo
包 to wrap

a. 在她住的地方，端午节也叫……。
　　i. 四月节　　**ii.** 五月节　　**iii.** 六月节

b. 端午节到了，……也就到了。
　　i. 春天　　**ii.** 夏天　　**iii.** 秋天

c. 端午节这一天人们除了用草药洗澡，还会……。
　　i. 做香包　　**ii.** 吃饺子　　**iii.** 赏月

d. 今年我们会……。
　　i. 从超市买粽子　　**ii.** 去酒店吃粽子　　**iii.** 在家里包粽子

e. 我和……跟妈妈学包粽子，觉得特别有意思。
　　i. 弟弟　　**ii.** 妹妹　　**iii.** 姐姐

3. 练习写汉字。
Practise writing Chinese.

a. 按照笔画顺序写下面的字。
Write the characters by following the stroke order.

bǐ
比　比　比　比　比
　　1　2　3　4

sài
赛　赛　赛　赛　赛　赛　赛　赛　赛　赛　赛　赛　赛　赛
　　1　2　3　4　5　6　7　8　9　10　11　12　13　14

b. 选择正确的动词，把短文中的句子写完整。
Choose the correct verbs to complete the sentences in the passage.

| 参加 | 举行 | 比赛 | 了解 | 到 | 让 |

六月初，一年一度的端午节**(a)**了。社区活动中心为了**(b)**年轻人更好地**(c)**中国的传统文化，**(d)**了品尝粽子的活动。粽子的种类很多，有肉的，也有素的，很多年轻人都**(e)**了吃粽子的活动。除了吃粽子和包粽子，社区居民还可以自己组队**(f)**划龙舟。

4. 阅读对话，然后判断下面的叙述是对或错。

Read the dialogue, then decide if the following statements are true or false.

明华：下周四是端午节。你知道端午节都有哪些
　　　活动吗？

艾米：知道。端午节的活动有包粽子和龙舟比赛。

明华：是的。那你知道这两个习俗是怎么来的吗？

艾米：不知道。请你给我讲一讲。

明华：两千多年前有一个受人尊敬的大臣屈原，他热
　　　爱自己的国家楚国和人民。当秦国灭了楚国
　　　后，屈原非常伤心，跳江死了。人们听说屈原
　　　跳江了，争先恐后地划船去救他，但是都太迟
　　　了。为了不让鱼吃他的身体，人们就往江里丢
　　　饭团。从那以后每年端午就有了包粽子和龙舟
　　　比赛的习俗。

艾米：我明白了。端午节就是纪念屈原的节日。在
　　　英国我们也有纪念日。为了纪念在战争中死
　　　去的人，英国把十一月十一日作为阵亡将士
　　　纪念日。

a. 端午节就在下个星期。

b. 端午节和纪念嫦娥有关。

c. 月饼是端午节的传统食物。

d. 龙舟比赛是端午节很重要的活动。

e. 英国也有有纪念意义的节日，那就是十一月十一日的阵亡将
　　士纪念日。

f. 根据短文写道的内容，包粽子和龙舟比赛的习俗开始于两千
　　多年前。

5. 和你的同学轮流提出和回答下面的问题。

With a partner, take turns to ask and answer the following questions.

a. 你听说过端午节吗？有没有过过端午节？

b. 你知道端午节是纪念谁的节日？有哪些传统习俗？

c. 你有没有看过龙舟比赛？在哪里看的？

d. 在你的国家，有没有纪念某一个人的节日？

e. 节日的时候会有什么庆祝活动？

jiù	
救	to save

shòu rén zūn jìng de	
受人尊敬的	respectable
dà chén	
大臣	minister
Qū Yuán	
屈原	Qu Yuan (a well-respected Chinese government minister, 340 BCE–278 BCE)
chǔ guó	
楚国	State of Chu, a state in China (c. 1030 BCE–223 BCE)
qín guó	
秦国	State of Qin, a state in China (c. 900 BCE–221 BCE)
miè le	
灭了	destroyed
zhēng xiān kǒng hòu	
争先恐后	fighting to be the first; fearing to be the last
diū fàn tuán	
丢饭团	to throw rice balls
sǐ qù de	
死去的	deceased
zhèn wáng jiàng shì	
阵亡将士	fallen soldiers

11.6 亚洲国家的节日和习俗
OTHER ASIAN FESTIVALS AND CUSTOMS

LESSON OBJECTIVE

● Identify and describe some festivals and customs observed by Asians around the world.

1. 阅读下面的叙述，把它们和正确的节日搭配起来。

   Read the statements below. Match them with the correct festivals.

   a. 这一天是妈妈们的节日，一般在五月。请送给你的妈妈一束花，并跟她说"我爱你，妈妈"。

   b. 中国有一个节日，一般在十月。这一天很多人会到爷爷奶奶家陪他们过节，和他们聊天。

   c. 这是一个春天的传统节日，一般在四月。为了纪念祖先这一天很多人都会去扫墓。节日前后也是喝春茶的最好的时候。这个节日不仅是中国人的节日，也是日本、新加坡等国的传统节日。

   i. 清明节　**ii.** 母亲节　**iii.** 重阳节

祖先 zǔ xiān ancestor
扫墓 sǎo mù to sweep the tomb of one's ancestor
清明节 qīng míng jié Tomb-Sweeping Day
重阳节 chóng yáng jié Double-Ninth Festival

2. 先读问题，再听录音，然后写下答案。

   Read the questions before you listen to the recordings, then write the answers.

   广告**A**

   a. 这个星期天是什么节日？

   b. 国际酒店星期天有什么活动？

   广告**B**

   c. 为了庆祝重阳节，文化公园将举办什么活动？

   d. 除了有演出活动，文化公园还会给老人们提供什么？

   e. 这个节日庆祝活动的时间是什么时候？

3. 阅读下面这篇关于新加坡开斋节的短文，然后回答问题。

   Read this passage about Eid al-Fitr celebrations in Singapore, then answer the questions.

   新加坡是一个多元文化的国家。这里有华人、欧亚裔、印度裔、马来人等。马来人是最早开始在新加坡生活的居民。大多数马来人都是穆斯林。斋戒月期间，穆斯林在日出到日落这个时间段是不能吃喝的，他们用大部分时间来敬拜、行善举。斋戒月结束以后

裔 yì descendant
穆斯林 mù sī lín Muslim
斋戒月 zhāi jiè yuè Ramadan
日出 rì chū sunrise
日落 rì luò sunset
敬拜 jìng bài to worship
行善举 xíng shàn jǔ to do good deeds
开斋节 kāi zhāi jié Eid al-Fitr, meaning the end of the fast
伊斯兰教 yī sī lán jiào Islam
标志着 biāo zhì zhe marked

就是开斋节(在新加坡被称为 Hari Raya Puasa)，这是伊斯兰教最重要的传统节日之一，标志着30天左右的斋戒月的结束。

　　这一天穆斯林会跟家人、朋友聚在一起享受美食。如果被邀请参加开斋节宴会，你就可以吃到像辣肉 (Rendang)、马来粽 (Ketupat) 这样的美食。除了美食，开斋节当天最大的特色就是人们会穿着他们最美丽的传统服装庆祝节日。这些五颜六色的传统服装成为了节日特别的风景。

a. 为什么说新加坡是一个有多元文化的国家？

b. 这篇短文是关于哪一个节日的？

c. 这个节日的传统美食有哪些？举两个例子。

d. 这个节日除了美食，另外一个特色是什么？

4. 和你的同学角色扮演两个电台节目主持人之间的对话，介绍你的家乡最重要的节日。

With a partner, role-play a conversation between two radio presenters as they introduce the most important festival in your culture.

5. 先读文字，再听录音，然后选出正确的答案完成句子。

Read the text before you listen to the recordings, then choose the correct answers to complete the sentences.

对话A

a. 父亲节快到了，就在……。

　　i. 两个星期以后　　ii. 下个月　　iii. 下个星期

对话B

b. 她明白清明节是……的节日。

　　i. 举行龙舟比赛　　ii. 纪念祖先　　iii. 吃月饼

对话C

c. 因为这些天……，所以她中午没有去聚餐。

　　i. 是斋戒日　　ii. 她肚子不舒服　　iii. 她非常忙

shì qù de
逝去的 gone; passed away

Grammar focus p.279

知道 (know) vs 明白(understand)
我知道中国人春节要吃饺子，但是我不明白为什么要吃饺子。

6. 写一篇80-100字的短文介绍清明节。其中应该包括：

Do some research on Tomb-Sweeping Day. Write 80–100 characters about it. You can include the following:

a. 清明节是什么时候？

b. 人们为什么过清明节？

c. 清明节的传统食品有哪些？

d. 清明节时人们怎样纪念祖先？

e. 除了纪念祖先，清明节还有哪些其他的活动？

LESSON OBJECTIVES
- Identify different festivals from around the world.
- Describe how people celebrate a special festival.

1. 看看下面的图片，把它们和正确的中文名称搭配起来。
Look at the pictures. Match them with the correct names in Chinese.

pái dēng jié
排灯节 Diwali

fān qié zhàn
番茄战 La Tomatina

a

b

c

i. 新年　　**ii.** 排灯节　　**iii.** 番茄战

2. 选择正确的词语，把短文中的句子写完整。
Choose the correct words to complete the sentences in the passage.

shù yǐ wàn jì
数以万计 tens of thousands

开始　　传统　　称作　　来自　　最后　　历史

番茄战，也(a)西红柿战，是西班牙东部小镇Buñol在每年八月的(b)一个星期三举行的节日。每年都有数以万计的(c)世界各地的人们参加番茄战。据说番茄战是从1944年(d)的，到现在已经有70多年的(e)了，已经成为这个小镇的特色(f)了。想去西班牙旅游的人们可以去试一试这个特别的番茄大战。

3. 阅读下面的短文，然后选择正确的答案完成句子。

Read the passage below about Diwali, then choose the correct answers to complete the sentences.

排灯节是印度人最重要的传统节日之一。排灯节一般在每年的十月到十一月之间，一共有五天。每年排灯节时世界各地的印度家庭都会点上油灯，在自己家房子的周围、花园等地方挂上美丽的彩灯，有着希望生活美好光明的意思。除了挂彩灯，他们还会在房门上画下美丽的图画。当然穿新衣服、互送礼物和分享甜甜的传统点心也都是排灯节重要的庆祝活动。

diǎn shàng
点上 to light

yóu dēng
油灯 oil lamp

a. 排灯节是……的节日。
   i. 春天   **ii.** 夏天   **iii.** 秋天

b. 在家的周围挂上彩灯是……。
   i. 让家变得热闹
   ii. 因为晚上太黑了
   iii. 希望生活美好光明

c. 除了挂彩灯，排灯节时人们还会……画下美丽的图画。
   i. 在门上   **ii.** 在桌子上   **iii.** 在手上

d. 排灯节的传统点心……。
   i. 是咸的   **ii.** 是甜的   **iii.** 是酸的

e. 人们还会互送……庆祝排灯节。
   i. 礼物   **ii.** 红包   **iii.** 彩灯

Grammar focus   p.279

上、下、进、出、来、去: directional words, used after verbs to show the direction of the action

★ verb + directional complement

点上, 挂上, 画下

4. 和你的同学轮流提出和回答下面的问题。

With a partner, take turns to ask and answer the following questions.

a. 你参加过的最有趣的节日是哪一个？

b. 这个节日是哪里的节日？是什么时候的？

c. 你是和谁一起过的这个节？

d. 节日时有哪些活动？

e. 你觉得这个节日怎么样？

5. 来自西班牙的玛丽亚和来自澳大利亚的史蒂文谈庆祝新年。先读问题，再听他们的对话，然后写下答案。

Maria from Spain is chatting to Steven from Australia about their new year celebrations. Read the questions before you listen to their conversation, then write the answers.

a. 他们在哪一个城市？

b. 玛利亚新年那天会和父母去哪里？

c. 史蒂文年末那一天会和谁一起去外滩参加新年派对？

d. 新年派对上有什么特别的活动？

e. 参加完派对以后，史蒂文还要去做什么？

pú tao 葡萄 grape
wài tān 外滩 the Bund, an embankment in Shanghai
pài duì 派对 party
mǎ dé lǐ 马德里 Madrid
Xú jiā huì tiān zhǔ dà jiào táng 徐家汇天主大教堂 Xujiahui Catholic Church
mí sā 弥撒 mass
yān huā 烟花 fireworks

6. 在西班牙旅行手册中写一篇关于番茄战的短文，用 80–100 个字。其中应该包括：

Write a passage of 80–100 characters about La Tomatina for a travel brochure on Spain. It should answer the following questions:

a. 番茄战是哪儿的节日？在一年中的哪一天？

b. 这个节日是怎么开始的？

c. 是免费的吗？还是需要门票？

d. 番茄战有哪些活动？

e. 如果要参加番茄战，你建议人们穿什么衣服，或带什么？

LESSON OBJECTIVES
- Identify vocabulary related to table manners.
- Describe and discuss table manners from around the world.

1. 写下这些词语的拼音和英文意思。

Write down the pinyin and English meanings of these words.

a. 筷子　**b.** 刀叉　**c.** 谢谢　**d.** 请给我　**e.** 说话　**f.** 有礼貌　**g.** 吃得很快

2. 先读文字，再听录音，然后选择正确的答案完成句子。

Read the text before you listen to the recording, then choose the correct answers to complete the sentences.

a. 小亮吃饭的时候……。
　i. 说话声音很大　**ii.** 爱唱歌　**iii.** 不用刀叉

b. 欧文吃饭时习惯……。
　i. 用手拿食物　**ii.** 看电视　**iii.** 玩游戏

c. 米娜吃饭……。
　i. 吃得太快　**ii.** 每次都吃不完　**iii.** 只吃肉，不吃蔬菜

d. 杰克去爷爷奶奶家吃饭的时候要……。
　i. 用筷子　**ii.** 说 "谢谢" 和 "请"
　iii. 说话声音小一点

e. 新兰吃饭……。
　i. 吃不完，浪费食物　**ii.** 常常说不好吃　**iii.** 不用筷子

xí guàn
习惯 to be used to

làng fèi
浪费 to waste

dà shēng de
大声地 loudly

chī wán
吃完 to finish eating

Grammar focus p.279

不要: don't
★ 不要 + action
不要大声说话。
不要浪费食物。

3. 阅读短文，然后回答问题。

Read the short passage, then answer the questions.

中国基本餐桌礼仪

现代中国社会的基本餐桌礼仪包括：坐下时要把上座给客人或者老人坐；开始吃的时候，要等重要的客人或者老人开始吃以后才可以吃；用公筷来保持卫生；吃完饭后，应该坐在座位上聊一会儿天再离开；吃饭的时候，不应该敲筷子；发出声音（例如打饱嗝）的时候应该要说 "对不起" 或 "不好意思" 等。

jī běn
基本 basic

gōng kuài
公筷 chopsticks used for serving (when dining with a group of people)

dǎ bǎo gé
打饱嗝 to burp

a. 在中国人的餐桌上，什么人可以坐在上座？

b. 吃饭的时候，为了保持卫生，人们会怎么做？

c. 短文中讲到吃饭的时候不可以做哪些事情？举两个例子。

4. 美美被邀请和朋友吃日本菜，她向日本留学生询问日本的餐桌礼仪。阅读他们的对话，然后判断下面的叙述是对或错，并以文章内容说明理由。

Mimi has been invited to a Japanese meal, so she is asking an exchange student from Japan for information on Japanese table manners. Read the dialogue, then decide if the following statements are true or false, explaining your reasons with reference to the text.

美美

山本，你们吃饭时要注意什么？

山本

我们日本人开始吃饭前会说"我开始吃了"。吃完了会说"谢谢您的款待"。

美美

这些跟我们这儿很像，我们也那样说，应该不会有问题。还有别的应该注意的地方吗？

山本

在日本家庭或餐馆一起吃饭的时候，你应该用公筷从大盘子里夹一些食物放到自己的盘子里吃但不能给其他人夹菜。

美美

我明白，这是为了保持卫生。我们中国人吃饭也会用公筷。

山本

吃饭时不要打饱嗝，因为这样别人会觉得你很没有礼貌。

美美

好的，这个我记住了。我是不是应该把食物都吃完？

山本

对，你应该吃完你盘子里的食物，不要浪费。

款待 kuǎn dài treat or hospitality

夹 jiā to pick

a. 日本人在吃饭前会说"谢谢您的款待"。

b. 在日本只有在餐馆吃饭时人们才会用公筷。

c. 吃饭的时候打饱嗝是没有礼貌的。

d. 在日本家庭或餐馆聚餐时，你最好吃完盘子里的食物。

5. 先读下面的句子，再听录音，然后选择正确的词语填空。
   (提示：下面的词语多于你需要的。)

   Read the sentences below before you listen to the recording, then choose the correct words to fill in the missing information. (Hint: There are more words in the box than you need.)

餐具	甜点	勺子	菜	汤	说话	不能	吃完了	能	刀	叉	饱

英国人吃饭一般都用刀叉和勺子，一般应该是右手拿(a)或(b)，左手拿(c)。家庭聚餐一般包括三道(d)，开胃菜，主菜，还有(e)。

英国人常常以喝一小碗(f)作为一餐的开始，然后是主菜，最后以甜点结束。吃不同的东西要用不同的(g)。喝东西时(h)发出很大的声音！还有嘴里有东西时不要(i)。当你吃完了就要把刀叉一起放到盘子的中间，表示你(j)。

kāi wèi cài
开胃菜 appetiser or starter

6. 和你的同学讨论餐桌礼仪，轮流提出和回答下面的问题。

   With a partner, have a discussion on table manners. Take turns to ask and answer the following questions.

   a. 中国和日本的餐桌礼仪有什么不同之处？

   b. 英国和中国的餐桌礼仪有什么不同之处？

   c. 日本和英国的餐桌礼仪有什么相同之处？

7. 练习写汉字。

   Practise writing Chinese.

   a. 按照笔画顺序写下面的字。

   Write the characters by following the stroke order.

zhù
注

yì
意

   b. 设计一张"十条餐桌礼仪"海报，告诉留学生同学中国的一些基本餐桌礼仪。

   Design a "Top 10 Dining Rules" poster to inform exchange students of some basic table manners in China.

LESSON OBJECTIVES

- Compare different social networking sites.
- Express your views on social networking, and the pros and cons of making friends online.

1. 下面是一些网络用语的缩写。把它们还原成完整的形式，用中文写出来，然后翻译成英文。

Below are some abbreviations commonly used on the internet. Write out their full meanings in Chinese, then translate them into English.

a 网友(网络 + 朋友)

b 电邮(电子 + 邮件)

c 微博 (微型+博客)

d 网游 (网络+游戏)

博客 blog
(bó kè)

2. 你希望加入一个叫"网络友谊"的社交网站。在下面的表格里写下你的个人信息。

You would like to join a social networking site called *Online Friendships*. Write down your personal information as if you were filling in the form.

"网络友谊" 社交网站

姓名	
年龄	
性别	
居住城市	
家乡	
爱好	
性格	
最新个人计划	

确认

3. 先读下面的叙述，再听录音，然后从每组选择唯一正确的句子。

Read the statements before you listen to each recording, then choose one correct statement from each group.

录音**A**

a. 她常在脸书上和朋友分享信息。
b. 她只有周末的时候才会上脸书看看。
c. 她不经常用脸书。

录音**B**

a. 他喜欢社交网，因为他觉得很有意思。
b. 他觉得上社交网对学习也有好处。
c. 有的人沉迷社交网，如果他们上不了社交网，就会觉得非常不舒服。

录音**C**

a. 他在国外留学，离家人很远。
b. 他不用微信跟家人视频，因为太贵了！
c. 微信让他可以和在新加坡的家人每天都通话。

录音**D**

a. 她常常在博客上写一些有意思的东西。
b. 她没有上传照片到博客上。
c. 她的博客几乎没有人看。

liǎn shū
脸书 Facebook
fēn xiǎng (xìn xī)
分享(信息) to share (news)
chén mí
沉迷 to be addicted to
wēi xìn
微信 WeChat (a popular social
networking app for smartphones in
China)
shì pín
视频 to make a video call
tōng huà
通话 to chat
shàngchuán
上传 to upload
jǐ hū
几乎 almost

4. 和你的同学谈关于社交网的话题，轮流提出和回答下面的问题。

With a partner, have a discussion about social networking. Take turns to ask and answer the following questions.

a. 你知道"脸书"和"推特"是哪两个社交网吗？

b. 你用不用脸书或推特？你用社交网做什么？

c. 你会在社交网上和朋友们交流学习吗？

d. 你觉得在网上交朋友安全吗？

e. 你喜欢自己在网上查信息学到新的东西，还是更喜欢上社交网和朋友交流而得到新的知识？

5. 阅读以下短文，然后回答问题。
Read the passage below, then answer the questions.

社交媒体已经成为人们特别是年轻人生活的一个非常重要的部分。有的人每天都要在社交媒体平台上传自拍照片，看脸书上的通知，每时每刻都要看一看他们的智能手机，不看就不舒服，完全沉迷于网络世界。

虽然社交媒体有不好的方面，但是对年轻人来说它还是有很大的好处的。我个人喜欢用社交媒体和家人还有世界各地的朋友保持联系，看他们上传的有趣的照片和阅读他们精彩的冒险故事。这些社交媒体上的图片和冒险故事让我了解了不同的国家和文化，学到很多新的知识。

社交媒体让我们很好地了解新闻故事。我们还可以用它组织各种重要的活动，例如慈善活动。所以我个人认为社交媒体还是非常不错的。

a. 你觉得这篇短文是电子邮件还是博客？

b. 人们一般在社交媒体平台上做什么？

c. 有的人沉迷于网络世界。如果他们看不了他们的社交媒体，他们会觉得怎么样？

d. 作者喜欢用社交媒体做什么？举两个例子。

e. 人们通过社交媒体了解新闻，还用它做什么？

tōng zhī 通知 to inform	

shè jiāo méi tǐ 社交媒体 social media	
píng tái 平台 platform	
zì pāi 自拍 selfie	
wán quán 完全 completely	
bǎo chí lián xì 保持联系 to keep in touch	
mào xiǎn gù shi 冒险故事 adventure story	

6. 练习写汉字。
Practise writing Chinese.

a. 按照笔画顺序写下面的字。
Write the characters by following the stroke order.

chén
沉 沉 沉 沉 沉 沉 沉 沉
  1 2 3 4 5 6 7

mí
迷 迷 迷 迷 迷 迷 迷 迷 迷
  1 2 3 4 5 6 7 8 9

b. 回答以下问题，并用20-30字写下来。
Write 20-30 characters to answer the question below.

你觉得自己有没有沉迷社交网？为什么？

1. 选出以下这些词语的近义词。

a. 旅游	b. 不但	c. 高兴	d. 漂亮	e. 亲切	f. 打算
i. 开心	ii. 美丽	iii. 友好	iv. 计划	v. 不仅	vi. 旅行

2. 用第一题中的词语填空完成句子。

   a. 跟家人朋友一起吃烧烤是很_____的事情。

   b. 印尼有很多_____的海岛，是旅游的好地方。

   c. 他_____以后去美国留学。

   d. 那个小村子里的人非常_____。

3. 先读问题，再听录音，然后写下答案。

   录音A

   a. 这个广告是关于什么节日的？

   b. 这是哪一样食品的广告？

   c. 儿子在国外做什么？

   录音B

   d. 中国留学生可以去哪家饭店预订粽子？预订电话是多少？

   e. 如果要去那家饭店，你可以乘坐哪种公共交通？在哪里下车？

   f. 你可以买到哪两种粽子？

4. 先读通告，然后判断下面的叙述是对或错，并以文章内容说明理由。

cān sài zhě
参赛者 contestant

端午节龙舟比赛

为了庆祝传统节日端午节，今年六月九日华人社区将在城市公园的湖上举行龙舟比赛。比赛时间在六月九日上午十点到十二点之间。龙船由华人社区提供。欢迎大家组队参加。每一队人数十个人，参赛者的年龄要在十六岁以上，一定要会游泳。龙舟比赛结束以后参赛者还可以一起去唐人街的"金龙"中国餐馆聚餐。

a. 华人社区将举行龙舟比赛庆祝端午节。

b. 比赛将在一条大河上举行。

c. 比赛在六月九日的上午。

d. 每个队可以有十二人参加比赛。

e. 参赛者必须会游泳。

f. 比赛完了大家会去唐人街中餐馆聚餐。

5. 重新组织下面的词语，并写出完整的句子。

a. 英国的牛津大学 / 打算 / 哥哥 / 去 / 留学 / 中学毕业以后 / 。

b. 数学专业 / 去那里 / 他 / 学习 / 希望 / 。

c. 一座座 / 世界一流的 / 不仅有 / 还有 / 牛津大学 / 牛津城里 / 古老的建筑 / 。

d. 游客 / 吸引了 / 每年都 / 成千上万的 / 这座城市 / 。

e. 来自 / 这些 / 世界各地 / 游客们 / 。

6. 和你的同学角色扮演学生和老师之间的对话，轮流提出和回答下面的问题。

a. 同学，请问你是哪一班的学生？

b. 你擅长哪些科目？喜欢哪些科目？

c. 你打算大学读什么专业？

d. 你想去哪个国家留学？

e. 你希望去哪所大学留学？

7. 用 80–100个字写一篇关于你国家的博客，列出关于这个国家的一些有趣的东西。
其中应该包括：

a. 国家的名字、首都、人口、气候等等；

b. 国家的传统节日和节日活动；

c. 你们国家餐桌上不能做的事情；

d. 那儿最受欢迎的社交网站。

1. 汤姆的叔叔结婚了。他的客人来自不同的国家。先看图，再听录音，然后选择唯一正确的答案。

   a. 他来自哪个国家？   **b.** 她来自哪个国家？
   c. 他来自哪个国家？   **d.** 她来自哪个国家？

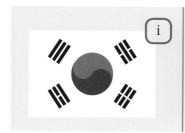 i
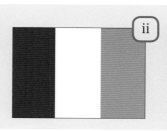 ii
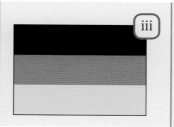 iii
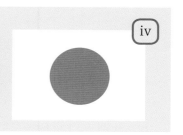 iv

2. 阅读短文，然后为下面的问题选择正确的答案。

> 　　汤姆的叔叔住在中国，他就要结婚了。汤姆一家人坐飞机去参加他的婚礼。结婚宴会在一家五星级酒店里举行。参加结婚宴会的客人很多，听说有两百人，他们来自亚洲、欧洲的不同国家，包括日本、韩国、法国、德国等等。这个酒店的餐厅很大，听经理说这儿一共有三百多个座位。餐桌上的饭菜种类很多，有韩国的烤肉，中国的海鲜—水煮鱼和酸辣汤，还有澳洲的牛排，也有日本的生鱼片和加拿大羊肉等等，色香味都不错，大家都很喜欢。
>
> 　　汤姆最爱吃中国的酸辣汤，因为他喜欢吃辣的食物。这道菜闻起来特别香，吃起来又爽滑可口，是那天晚上的亮点。他弟弟最爱吃肉，所以他吃了好多澳大利亚牛排，他说做得真是太好吃了。他爸爸妈妈对世界各地的食物都很喜欢，他们吃了中国的水煮鱼、日本的生鱼片，还有加拿大的羊肉。
>
> 　　因为好吃的东西太多了，汤姆吃得很饱，所以他吃不下酒店在最后给每位客人的甜点—冰淇淋了。

   a. 婚礼在哪儿举行？

   i. 　**ii.** 　**iii.**

   b. 汤姆最喜欢哪一道菜？

   i. 　**ii.** 　**iii.**

c. 甜点是什么？

i. 　　**ii.** 　　**iii.**

 3. 写下最少两道在汤姆叔叔婚礼上你最想吃的和最不想吃的菜，并用20–30个字造句。

4. 在宴会中，汤姆和弟弟讨论刚吃过的菜。先读问题，再听录音，然后写出下面问题的答案。

a. 弟弟觉得中国是哪一个洲的国家？
　　i. 亚洲　　　**ii.** 欧洲　　　**iii.** 南美洲

b. 亚洲人口最多的是哪一个国家？
　　i. 中国　　　**ii.** 印度　　　**iii.** 美国

c. 哪一道菜是中国有名的菜？
　　i. 生鱼片　　　**ii.** 牛排　　　**iii.** 水煮鱼

d. 弟弟觉得加拿大是哪一个洲的国家？
　　i. 北美洲　　　**ii.** 南美洲　　　**iii.** 亚洲

5. 宴会过后的第二天，汤姆和叔叔正在谈话。和你的同学角色扮演他们之间的对话，轮流提出和回答下面的问题。

a. 平时吃中餐还是西餐？为什么？

b. 上一次和家人去餐馆吃饭是什么时候？吃了什么菜？

c. 你会推荐你的朋友去那家餐馆吗？为什么？

d. 今天晚上你打算带我们去中餐厅还是西餐厅吃饭？吃什么？

 6. 汤姆一家在中国。参加叔叔的结婚宴会后的第二天，汤姆要写一封邮件感谢叔叔邀请他们一家参加宴会。写100–120个字。邮件中应该包括：

a. 对叔叔表示感谢；

b. 宴会那天做了什么？喜欢哪些食物？为什么？

c. 未来的这几天有什么计划？会不会邀请叔叔和他们一起玩？

1. 阅读短文，然后用下列词组填空。

> 昨天小文的奶奶和家人一起去郊区玩，但是昨天天气很冷，风很大。因为奶奶的衣服不够暖和，所以她今天早上起来的时候头疼得厉害，而且好像还发烧了，她觉得自己应该是感冒了。

| 天气 | 郊区 | 衣服 | 头痛 | 暖和 | 发烧 | 重感冒 | 家人 |

> 奶奶头痛得厉害，她得了(a)。
>
> 奶奶和家人一起去郊区玩的时候忘了穿(b)的衣服。
>
> 奶奶今天早上起来好像还(c)了。
>
> 昨天(d)很冷。

2. 奶奶生病了，她去看了医生。先读问题，再听录音，然后写下答案。

a. 奶奶有什么不舒服？　　b. 医生叫奶奶去哪儿取药？

c. 医生建议奶奶做什么？　　d. 奶奶的药应该在什么时候吃？

3. 阅读下面的短文，然后回答问题。

> 奶奶吃完医生开的药后，还是觉得不舒服。她病了好几天了，爸爸很担心，听说郊区医院的传统中医治疗不错，医院里的中医陈医生很有名，所以他把奶奶送到医院让陈医生来治疗她。小文打算去医院看奶奶，但是医院在郊区，离家有点儿远，得坐火车。听爸爸说，来回票比较便宜，所以他买了一张去医院的来回火车票。可是中途火车停了，因为前方的铁路出了小事故，通知说铁路上出现了两头牛。因为这个意外，小文下了火车，改坐公共汽车去医院。可是他又坐错车，在美术馆附近下了车。结果他找不到医院，也迷路了，只好请路人帮忙指路。

a. 奶奶吃了药后觉得怎么样？

b. 为什么小文要买火车来回票？

c. 为什么小文不能坐火车去医院？

d. 小文最后在哪下了车？

4. 先读问题，再听录音，然后选择唯一正确的答案。

   a. 医院在动物园的哪个方向？
      i. 东边   ii. 南边   iii. 北边

   b. 去医院要先顺着哪个地方一直走？
      i. 美术馆   ii. 公园   iii. 动物园

   c. 从十字路口向北走多少米就会看到医院？
      i. 一百米   ii. 五百米   iii. 一千米

5. 小文到了医院，他看到了奶奶。和同学角色扮演小文和奶
   奶之间的对话，轮流提出和回答下面的问题。

   a. 今天觉得怎么样？

   b. 出院/住院的感觉怎么样？

   c. 习不习惯医院的饮食？

   d. 出院以后最想做什么？

6. 小文在医院迷路了。他正在向医院的职员问路。先看下面
   的图片，然后和你的同学进行角色扮演，轮流提出和回答
   下面的问题。

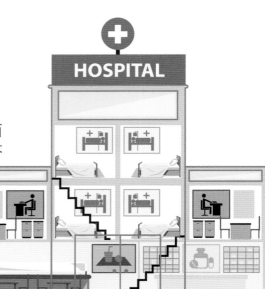

   a. 请问从病房到药房怎么走？

   b. 请问从病房到办公室要怎么走？

   c. 请问从医院大门到食堂怎么走？

7. 奶奶出院了，她想写一张感谢卡给陈医生。想象你是奶
   奶，用50-60个字写感谢卡。其中应该包括：

   a. 对陈医生表示感谢；

   b. 身体恢复得怎么样；

   c. 你以后会怎样保持健康。

1. 阅读下面本杰明的课程表，然后选择正确的答案填空。

星期一	
8:20	点名
第一节	经济
第二节	英文
10:30	休息
第三节	数学
第四节	历史
12:10	午休
第五节	中文
第六节	中文
第七节	美术
15:20	放学

心美： 本杰明，你今天上什么课？

本杰明： 让我先看看课程表吧！早上(a)点名。第一节和第二节，我先上经济课，然后上(b)课。下课后就是(c)时间。休息后，在第(d)节和第四节，我先上(e)课，然后上历史课。(f)后是两节中文课，(g)以前是美术课。到了下午(h)点(i)分就放学了。放学后，我们一起玩网上游戏好吗？

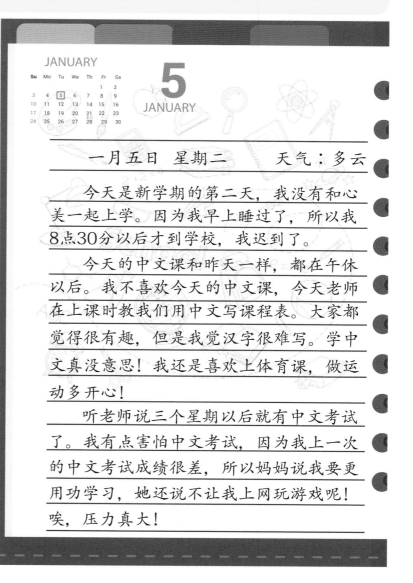

JANUARY

5
JANUARY

Su	Mo	Tu	We	Th	Fr	Sa
					1	2
3	4	5	6	7	8	9
10	11	12	13	14	15	16
17	18	19	20	21	22	23
24	25	26	27	28	29	30

一月五日　星期二　　　天气：多云

　　今天是新学期的第二天，我没有和心美一起上学。因为我早上睡过了，所以我8点30分以后才到学校，我迟到了。

　　今天的中文课和昨天一样，都在午休以后。我不喜欢今天的中文课，今天老师在上课时教我们用中文写课程表。大家都觉得很有趣，但是我觉汉字很难写。学中文真没意思！我还是喜欢上体育课，做运动多开心！

　　听老师说三个星期以后就有中文考试了。我有点害怕中文考试，因为我上一次的中文考试成绩很差，所以妈妈说我要更用功学习，她还说不让我上网玩游戏呢！唉，压力真大！

2. 阅读右边本杰明写的日记，然后判断下面的叙述对还是错，并以文章内容说明理由。

a. 今天本杰明和心美一起上学。

b. 心美今天迟到了。

c. 昨天的午休以后是中文课。

d. 本杰明今天教心美用中文写课程表。

e. 本杰明觉得虽然写汉字特别难，但是特别有趣。

f. 妈妈不让本杰明上网玩游戏。

3. 在学校，本杰明正在和心美谈话。先读问题，再听录音，
然后选择正确的答案。

a. 心美正在准备什么？
    i. 中文考试
   ii. 数学考试
  iii. 英文考试

b. 为什么心美在考试前特别注意自己的饮食？
    i. 因为她特别喜欢喝果汁
   ii. 因为考试快到了，她不想生病
  iii. 因为考试压力特别大

c. 心美为什么不吃快餐？
    i. 快餐的食物大多是油炸的，热量很高
   ii. 快餐的食物大多是不健康的，热量不高
  iii. 快餐的食物特别难吃

4. 先听录音，根据心美在考试前会做的活动，选择正确的
图片。

5. 写出最少五种你觉得可以帮助保持身体健康的运动，并用
20–30个字造句，说说你喜欢和不喜欢哪些运动。

6. 本杰明刚刚收到中文考试成绩。他正在给他的好朋友写电
子邮件。想象你是本杰明，用100–150个字写这封邮件。
其中应该包括：

a. 这次考试难不难？
b. 这次考试你的分数是多少？

c. 你觉得自己的成绩怎么样？
d. 你觉得考试压力大不大？

e. 你觉得哪位同学读书最用功？

7. 本杰明正在和心美谈话，他们正在谈生活习惯和考试压力。
和你的同学角色扮演本杰明和心美，轮流提出和回答下面
的问题。

a. 你一般睡几个小时？
b. 你每天花多少时间做功课和温习？

c. 你觉得这样健康吗？为什么？
d. 压力大的时候，你通常喜欢做什么来减少压力？

e. 为了保持健康，你会怎样做？

12.4 我们毕业了！
WE ARE GRADUATING!

1. 安吉拉和朋友们刚考完毕业考试，他们收到了成绩单。先看图、读问题，再听录音，然后选择正确的图片。

a. 安吉拉哪一科考得最好？　　**b.** 阿俊哪一科考得最好？

c. 娜依玛哪一科考得最好？　　**d.** 天伟哪一科考得最好？

2. 写下最少两门你最喜欢和最不喜欢读的学科，并用20–30个字造句。

3. 安吉拉和朋友们正在谈他们打算在大学读的专业。先读问题，再听录音，然后把他们的名字和正确的图片搭配起来。

a. 安吉拉　　**b.** 阿俊　　**c.** 天伟　　**d.** 娜依玛　　**e.** 子敏

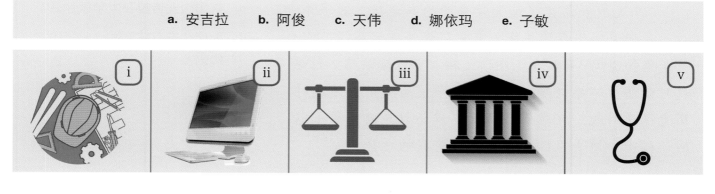

4. 和你的同学谈将来的打算，轮流提出和回答下面的问题。

a. 你将来想做什么样的工作？为什么？

b. 去哪里工作？国内还是国外？为什么？

c. 如果有时间，你还打算学什么新的技能？

243

12

 5. 安吉拉的哥哥安迪去了美国大学当交流生。阅读安迪和朋友丽莎的对话，根据文章选择三个正确的叙述。

 丽莎

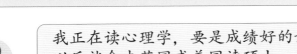
安迪，你去了美国一个多月了，还好吗？

还不错。我觉得在美国当交流生很有意思。这里的老师和同学都很好。丽莎，听说你最近读书很用功，将来有什么打算？
 安迪

丽莎
我正在读心理学，要是成绩好的话，我毕业以后就会去英国或美国读硕士。读完硕士后可能还会读博士。你呢？将来有什么打算？

我下一年可能到中国或日本当交流生。还没有想到毕业以后的打算。等回来再说吧！不过，我爸爸说要是我毕业以后不读硕士的话，就会考虑让我去找工作。
 安迪

a. 安迪去了美国一个多月了。

b. 安迪觉得在美国当交流生很有趣。

c. 安迪觉得美国的老师和同学都不错。

d. 丽莎将来打算去日本读心理学。

e. 丽莎将来打算只读到硕士。

f. 安迪将来不读硕士，毕业后会找工作。

6. 阅读下面的信件，然后回答右边的问题。

亲爱的妈妈：

　　今天我和您谈了读大学专业的事之后，我很不开心。我知道您想我读法律，您觉得读法律容易找工作。可是您知道吗？虽然我现在读文科，可以读法律，但是我对读法律不感兴趣。我想在大学读历史，因为我对历史很感兴趣，我想研究历史，我还打算读完学士以后读硕士和博士呢！希望您能尊重我的选择。

女儿 安吉拉

十月十日

a. 安吉拉想在大学读什么？

b. 安吉拉现在在高中读什么科？

c. 妈妈想安吉拉在大学读什么？

d. 为什么安吉拉要写这封信给妈妈？

 7. 安吉拉毕业后，写了一封电子邮件给张先生，是关于一个在网上看到的工作机会。想象你是安吉拉，用120-150个字写这封电邮。邮件中应该写到：

a. 你想做什么工作？　　**b.** 你有什么工作经验？　　**c.** 你的性格为什么适合这个工作？

d. 除了你的专业之外，你还有什么其他的技能？　　**e.** 请张先生回复你的电子邮件。

1. 天伟和他的朋友们正在谈他们的兴趣爱好。先读问题，再
   听录音，然后把他们的名字和正确的图片搭配起来。

a. 天伟　　b. 丁卡　　c. 劳拉　　d. 小文　　e. 约翰　　f. 娜依玛

i　　ii　　iii　　iv　　v　　vi

2. 写出最少三种你喜欢和不喜欢的兴趣爱好。并用20–30个字
   造句。

3. 根据第二题的答案，说一说：

   a. 你最喜欢哪一种兴趣爱好？为什么？

   b. 你最不喜欢哪一种兴趣爱好？为什么？

   c. 哪些兴趣爱好可以帮助我们保持身体健康或心情愉快？
      为什么？

4. 先读问题，再听录音，然后选择正确的答案。

   a. 天伟要参加社区义工活动，他想帮忙举办社区自行车比赛，
      他要先和谁联络？
      i. 学校的体育老师　　iii. 老人院的职员
      ii. 社区服务组织的职员

   b. 一共有多少人参加自行车比赛？
      i. 20人　　ii. 25人　　iii. 30人

c. 天伟在自行车比赛中帮忙做什么？
 i. 联络老师 **ii.** 放警告标牌 **iii.** 联络同学

d. 除了天伟以外，还有谁帮忙计划和组织这个活动？
 i. 学校的老师 **ii.** 小文和娜依玛 **iii.** 社区服务组织的职员

5. 帮忙设计自行车比赛的海报。写100–120个字。海报中应该写到：

a. 活动的名称； **b.** 活动的目的； **c.** 谁负责这个活动；

d. 活动日期、时间、地点； **e.** 名额有多少个；去哪儿报名；

f. 报名费用多少；什么时候截止报名。

6. 阅读下面的短文，然后回答下面的问题。

>   天伟星期天去给自行车比赛当义工，活动地点在公园。那天的天气有点冷，没有太阳，阴天多云，参加比赛的人都穿了外套和长裤，他们也戴了手套和头盔。因为是星期天，所以人很多。
>   比赛的时候下雨了。因为子敏没有看清楚路上左边标牌上"注意安全"的警告，所以她不小心从自行车上摔了下来。天伟带她到急诊室看医生。
>   到急诊室以后，子敏发觉钱包丢了。她很着急，所以想打电话找警察帮忙。但是天伟告诉子敏说他捡到她的钱包了，是在刚才她跌倒受伤的时候捡到的。子敏拿回了她的钱包，她很高兴。
>   虽然那一天天伟很忙，但是他很高兴，因为他帮助了别人。他希望以后能继续帮忙举行自行车比赛活动，他也希望以后会有更多人参加。只要注意安全，骑自行车不但可以使人保持身体健康，而且可以使他们心情愉快。

a. 比赛那天的天气怎么样？ **b.** 参加比赛的人都穿什么、戴什么？

c. 路上左边标牌上写着什么？ **d.** 为什么子敏想给警察打电话？

e. 为什么天伟觉得很高兴？

7. 子敏和她的爸爸正在谈上星期日的自行车比赛。和你的同学角色扮演他们之间的对话，轮流提出和回答下面的问题。

a. 自行车比赛在哪儿进行？ **b.** 为什么你喜欢骑自行车？

c. 在比赛中发生了什么事？ **d.** 骑自行车要注意什么？要戴什么？

e. 下次你还想参加自行车比赛吗？为什么？

1. 黄老师要带学生参加春节义工活动。他们要去老人院跟老人聊天和给他们讲故事。先读问题，再听录音，然后写下答案。

   a. 学校附近的银行在哪儿？

   b. 黄老师想买什么给老人院的老人们？

   c. 李老师为什么要去银行？

2. 黄老师在百货商店。她要去买一些东西送给老人们。看看下面楼层的标牌，然后把它们和正确的中文句子搭配起来。

   a. 4/F   **b.** 2/F   **c.** 3/F
   d. 5/F   **e.** B P   **f.** G

   i. 银行在五楼。   **ii.** 运动部在四楼。   **iii.** 文具部在三楼。

   iv. 鞋部在二楼。   **v.** 食品区在一楼。   **vi.** 停车场在地下一层。

3. 黄老师和李老师在百货商店。根据第二题的答案，和你的同学角色扮演两位老师在百货公司的对话，轮流提出和回答下面的问题。

   a. 银行在百货商店的哪儿？   **b.** 肚子饿了可以去哪儿吃东西？

   c. 买钢笔应该去哪层楼？   **d.** 停车场在哪儿？

4. 一位杂志记者正在访问黄老师。听下面的对话，然后选择正确的答案。

   a. 黄老师来过百货商店几次了？
   i. 一次   **ii.** 两次   **iii.** 很多次

   b. 黄老师觉得百货商店怎么样？
   i. 是一个购物天堂   **ii.** 是一个美食天堂   **iii.** 经常在打折

   c. 黄老师的学生打算到老人院做什么？
   i. 打球   **ii.** 跳舞   **iii.** 讲故事

5. 海伦跟黄老师一起去老人院看望老人。她正在介绍自已。
阅读下面的介绍，然后把A栏和B栏的词组搭配起来组成
句子。（注意：B栏的叙述比需要的多。）

> 大家好！我叫海伦。我今年十六岁。我来自英国，我是在伦敦出生的。我家有四口人：爸爸、妈妈、姐姐和我。因为爸爸工作的原因，我们全家搬来了上海。我们是去年来上海的。我很高兴能来给你们拜年。我是一个爱笑，爱聊天，活泼开朗的人。我有很多爱好，最大的爱好就是听音乐。除了听音乐外，我今年也开始喜欢做运动。我上个月才刚刚参加过学校举行的自行车比赛。我也常常和朋友去健身房做运动。我喜欢吃菜，不喜欢吃肉。很高兴认识你们！

A	B
a. 海伦今年	i. 参加学校举行的自行车比赛。
b. 海伦出生在	ii. 十六岁。
c. 因为海伦爸爸要到上海工作，	iii. 英格兰的南部。
d. 海伦喜欢和朋友	iv. 所以他们全家去年离开了伦敦。
	v. 去健身房做运动。
	vi. 不喜欢吃肉。
	vii. 最喜欢听音乐。

6. 大海在老人院。他正在问老人们一些问题。和你的同学角色
扮演他们在老人院的对话，轮流提出和回答下面的问题。

a. 您的生日是什么时候？　　b. 您是在哪里出生的

c. 您以前在哪里居住过？　　d. 您有什么爱好？

7. 你和朋友会一起负责计划和组织你们班的义工活动，你希
望在春节时探访老人院。用40-50个字发一个短信给你的朋
友。其中应该包括：

a. 会组织什么义工活动？会做什么？

b. 有多少人参加？　　c. 有多少人不参加？

d. 谁负责联络？　　e. 和谁联络？

1. 志军和爸爸今天要去博物馆参观。他们在网上看博物馆的地图。看看下面的图片，然后选择正确的地点填空。

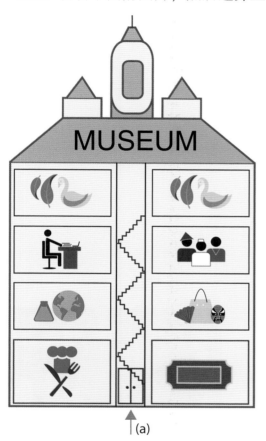

从(a)一直走就看到售票处了，进博物馆之前要先在那儿买票。

(b) 在四楼，里面有一些关于环境保护的展览。

文化厅在三楼，在(c)的右边。

志军会先去二楼的(d)，因为他对科学特别感兴趣。

志军想去(e)，他想买一份礼物给妈妈。

爸爸想去(f)，他想在哪儿吃早餐。

2. 志军和爸爸在博物馆看到不同的标牌。看看下列词组，然后给这些标牌上的图片搭配正确的名称。

i. 请勿拍照   ii. 咨询中心   iii. 禁止停车   iv. 禁止入内   v. 危险

3. 志军在博物馆的文化厅。他在听不同国家的节日的介绍。
先读问题，再听录音，然后填空。

地点	节日	时间
日本	樱花节	春季：(a)月到(b)月之间
泰国	泼水节	泰国的(c)：四月十三日到十五日之间
(d)里约	狂欢节	每年的(e)月

4. 志军和爸爸在自然环境厅，他们在听一个关于环境保护的
讲话。先读问题，再听录音，然后回答问题。

   a. 陈老师教哪一科？

   b. 陈老师的学生在上课时学过什么环境问题？

   c. 为什么会有环境问题？

   d. 在哪儿可以看到社区环保活动的最新消息？

5. 志军的爸爸正在向博物馆的职员问路。根据第一题提供的
地图，回答他的问题。

   a. 请问从办公室到纪念品商店要怎么走？

   b. 请问从办公室到自然环境厅要怎么走？

   c. 请问餐厅怎么走？

6. 志军正在听爸爸和博物馆的职员谈话。志军想把他们说的
路线信息记下来，方便以后使用。参考第五题的口语练
习，写60–70个字。

7. 志军参观博物馆后，写了一篇博客介绍博物馆。写120–150
个字。其中应该包括:

   a. 你什么时候参观了博物馆？　　**b.** 博物馆有什么（参考上面的博物馆地图)？

   c. 做了什么？　　**d.** 你买了什么纪念品？

   e. 你觉得博物馆的哪一个地方最有趣？为什么？

1. 哈里刚刚和父母从加拿大搬到了中国，他们住进了新房子。看右边的句子，然后选出正确的那一张图。

哈里的新房子有两层楼。
二楼有两个卧室和一个厕所。
一楼有客厅、饭厅和厨房。
外面有花园和车库。

2. 哈里在新学校读书。他正在向同学们介绍他住的地方。阅读他的介绍，然后回答问题。

同学们：

　　大家好，我是哈里。最近我和父母刚搬家到上海的市中心。今天我会向大家介绍我们家的新房子和周边的环境。

　　我们很幸运在市中心的小区租到了一栋独立的老房子。我们喜欢住在这里，因为小区的环境很好，外滩公园就在我家的前面。每天吃完饭，我们和父母会去河边散步。我们以前住在郊区，上学很不方便。现在我们住在市中心，离我的学校一点儿都不远，坐地铁两站就到了。

　　我们的新房子有两层楼，我的房间在二楼，我的新房间特别大，以前的没现在的大。我很喜欢我们的新房子。

a. 这是一篇：
　i. 信　　ii. 演讲稿　　iii. 日记

b. 根据文章，选出三个正确的叙述。
　i. 哈里一家刚搬进新家不久。
　ii. 哈里家住的房子在上海的郊区。
　iii. 哈里家有三层楼。
　iv. 从哈里家坐地铁到他的学校需要坐两站路。
　v. 小区的后面有一个公园。
　vi. 哈里父母的新房间特别大。
　vii. 哈里以前住在郊区，上学没有现在方便。
　viii. 哈里以前的房间比现在的大。

3. 哈里要向同学介绍他的家乡。先读问题，再听录音，然后回答问题。

   a. 哈里的家乡是哪一个城市？

   b. 这个城市在加拿大的哪个方向？

   c. 那个城市的周边有哪三个地理景观？

   d. 为什么说那是一个多元文化的地方？

4. 哈里刚介绍完自己以前住的地方，现在轮到他问同学一些问题。和你的同学角色扮演哈里和他的同学，轮流提出和回答下面的问题。

   a. 你的家乡在哪里？是一个什么样的地方？

   b. 你的家乡的周边有哪些地理景观？

   c. 你喜欢你的家乡吗？为什么？

5. 放学以后，哈里的表姐露西打电话给哈里，他们正在谈哈里的新房间。先读问题，再听录音，然后选择唯一正确的答案。

   a. 哈里的新房间没有什么家具？
      i. 冰箱　　**ii.** 衣柜　　**iii.** 椅子

   b. 哈里的房间有多少面镜子？
      i. 没有　　**ii.** 一面　　**iii.** 两面

   c. 谁最喜欢照镜子？
      i. 哈里　　**ii.** 露西　　**iii.** 没有人

6. 根据上一题的答案，用中文写出在哈里新房间你会看到的五样东西。然后用其中三个词语造句，写20–30个字。

7. 回家以后，哈里要做功课。老师要他用中文给朋友写一封电邮，用120–150个字介绍自己住的小区。其中应该包括：

   a. 你的小区在市中心还是郊区？

   b. 你的小区里有哪些体育设施？

   c. 小区的绿化怎么样？树多不多？草坪大不大？

   d. 小区的交通方便吗？为什么？

   e. 你喜欢这个小区吗？

1. 小明和心美在学校，他们正在谈这个周末的计划 。先读问题，再听录音，然后写下答案。

a. 星期六的天气怎么样？　　　　**b.** 小明邀请心美去他家做什么？

c. 为什么小明没有邀请苏菲去他家？　　**d.** 小明打算怎样联系苏菲？

2. 小明的朋友都准备带一样食物到小明家参加派对。看下面的句子，选择正确的图片。

a. 米娜打算带饼干到小明家。米娜打算带什么到小明家？

b. 志军打算带热狗到小明家。志军打算带什么到小明家？

c. 汤姆打算带薯片到小明家。汤姆打算带什么到小明家？

d. 心美打算带年糕到小明家。心美打算带什么到小明家？

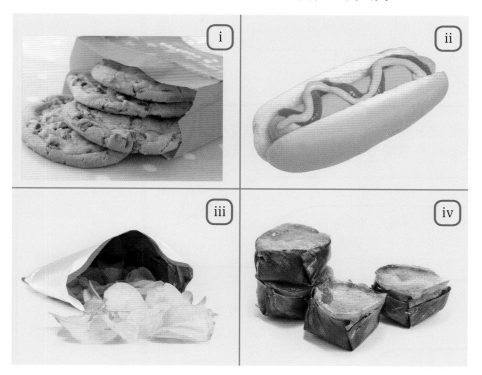

3. 小明和心美正在谈星期六的派对。根据下面的对话，从右栏的叙述中选出搭配左边句子的叙述。（注意：右栏的叙述比需要的多。）

对了，小明，我们什么时候到你家去？

八点半吧，早一点路上车少，可以快点到。

那好，我八点半来。对了，听说你刚搬家了，新家在哪儿？

在公园附近的小区，一会儿我用手机短信把地址发给你。

谢谢！
那我要不要带吃的东西？

可以呀。

我可以带水果和三明治。

谢谢！我的哥哥喜欢买东西，我可以请他帮忙准备饮料和其他的食物。我也叫会来的同学们每人都准备一样食物。对了，我们在派对上玩什么？

你们几个男生应该喜欢玩电子游戏，但是我不喜欢玩电子游戏。我可以带一些音乐来，这样你们玩游戏的时候，我可以跳舞。

没问题。心美，别担心，我们还可以一起听音乐。那好，我们星期六早上见！

嗯，星期六见！

心美

小明

a. 小明的新家在
b. 心美会带
c. 小明的派对在
d. 小明会叫他哥哥

i. 八点到小明家。
ii. 八点半到小明家。
iii. 公园附近的小区。
iv. 音乐和电子游戏到小明家。
v. 水果和三明治到小明家。
vi. 星期六举行。
vii. 看书。
viii. 准备饮料和食物。

4. 小明的哥哥正在超级市场。他打算给周末的派对买一些食物和饮料。先看图片，再听录音，然后选择哥哥打算买的东西。

5. 小明邀请你参加他家的派对。写下最少三样你会带去的食物和饮料，并用30–50个字造句。

6. 小明的朋友都在派对上。他们在聊一些周末会做的活动。和你的同学角色扮演他们，轮流提出和回答下面的问题。

a. 你有什么爱好？
b. 上个周末你做了什么有意思的事情？
c. 下个周末你打算做什么？
d. 你最喜欢哪一个周末活动，为什么？

7. 苏菲今天没有去小明的派对。写一个短信给小明，用60–80字说一说：

a. 感谢小明的邀请；
b. 为什么今天不能去他家；
c. 下次如果小明再邀请会不会参加；
d. 和小明说对不起。

1. 约翰刚从台湾交流回来一个月，他在和苏菲聊天。阅读对话，然后判断下面的叙述是对或错，并以文章内容说明理由。

> 你最近还和台湾交流营的同学们联络吗？

> 是的，我最近都在和他们联络。上个星期，我才刚给其中一位台湾的朋友写信，不过他还没回复我。

> 不会吧，现在哪还有人写信！

> 有啊，我就喜欢写信。我喜欢收信的一刻！还有，我觉得写信更有意思，因为可以练习用手写汉字呢！苏菲，如果我们经常用中文写信，中文一定会进步的。

> 其实你可以跟朋友在网上聊天，既可以练习说中文，又可以及时和国外的朋友联络。这比写信或发电邮方便多了。我就常常用手机和说中文的朋友在网上聊天。

> 我知道网上聊天很方便。不过，我还是喜欢写信！

苏菲

约翰

a. 约翰上个星期给台湾的朋友写了信。   b. 约翰觉得写信比网上聊天有意思多了。

c. 苏菲常常跟台湾的朋友在网上聊天。   d. 苏菲觉得网上聊天比写信方便多了。

2. 苏菲在学校礼堂。她正在演讲。她在介绍现代智能生活。先读问题，再听录音，然后回答问题。

a. 以前我们怎样联络国外的朋友？   b. 现在我们怎样联络国外的朋友？

c. 连上网络的手机可以做什么？   d. 除了发短信、上社交网络之外，还有哪些事情可以上网完成？

3. 写出你平时在网上喜欢做的四件事情，并用40–60个字造句。

4. 约翰在网上看到一篇和他在台湾交流营活动有关的文章。阅读这篇文章，然后回答问题。

| 主页 | 关于我们 | 服务项目 | 联系我们 |

现代人的网络生活

网络将世界各地的人连在一起。今天我们邀请了刚从英国来到台湾参加交流营的约翰，谈谈他对网络的看法。

记者：约翰，可以告诉我们你来台湾做什么吗？

约翰：可以！我是今年七月来到台湾学习中文的。我将会在这儿住一个月。

记者：你是怎样和英国的家人保持联系的？

约翰：我常常上社交网站，看我的家人和朋友们上传的照片和信息，了解他们生活中最近发生的事。我会和他们在网上聊天，也会读网上的新闻，让我可以知道多一些英国的事。

记者：除了这些以外，你还会上网做什么？

约翰：网上的娱乐活动也很多，我常常看网络电视，或者上网听歌，这可以让我好好地放松。

记者：谢谢你接受访问。

约翰：不客气！

a. 这篇文章是
   i. 一个采访
   ii. 一篇日记
   iii. 一个广告
   iv. 一封信

b. 约翰在台湾是
   i. 老师
   ii. 学生
   iii. 记者
   iv. 歌手

c. 写出网络的其中三个好处。

5. 和你的同学分享网上购物的经验，轮流提出和回答下面的问题。

a. 你从什么时候开始在网上购物？

b. 你会在网上买什么东西？

c. 你觉得网上购物有什么好处？

6. 苏菲的妈妈打算用网上银行业务，她正在问用过网上银行业务的爸爸一些问题。和你的同学角色扮演苏菲的父母，轮流提出和回答下面的问题。

a. 你什么时候开始使用网上银行业务的？

b. 使用网上银行业务有什么好处？

c. 除了使用网上银行业务外，你还会上网做什么？

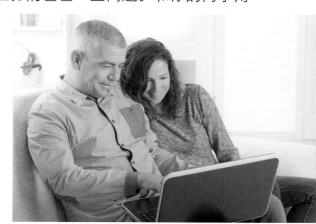

7. 苏菲打算和她的朋友分享她和她家人的网上活动经验。参考第五和第六题的内容，选择下面其中一个网上活动，用100–150个字替苏菲发一个电邮给朋友。

a. 玩网络游戏
b. 网上购物
c. 网上聊天

Unit 1

Grammar focus 1.1   p.2

正在: used before verbs to express that an action is *ongoing* or *in progress*.

★ subject + 正在 + action

最近爸爸正在写一本新书。

Following the grammatical structure above, translate these sentences into Chinese.

a. I have been learning Chinese recently.

b. When Mum came home, I was surfing the internet.

c. We were having our English lesson when he arrived.

Grammar focus 1.2   p.5

除了…… 以外，还: apart from … also; in addition; as well as

★ subject + 除了 + A + 以外，还 + B.

他除了喜欢打篮球以外，还喜欢踢足球。

Rewrite these sentences following the grammatical structure above.

a. 本杰明长得又高又帅。本杰明很聪明。

b. 他喜欢游泳。他喜欢听音乐。

c. 我喜欢玩电子游戏。我喜欢和宠物玩。

Grammar focus 1.3   p.7

是……的: is (used to emphasise a detail from an event)

★ subject + 是 + description + 的

陈丽是五年级时开始喜欢玩电子游戏的。

Rewrite these sentences by using the grammatical structure above. (Remember to emphasise the phrases in bold.)

a. 莉莉从美国来。

b. 马克五岁时开始打网球。

c. 她在中国学会了打篮球。

Grammar focus 1.5   pp.10–11

1. 量词: measure words

★ number + measure word + noun

一只鸟，一条虫，一匹斑马

Identify the error in each sentence and write it out in full correctly.

a. 我们家里养了两条绿色的鸟。

b. 她家的农场里有三个马。

c. 我以后想养一匹白色的小猫。

Grammar focus 1.5   pp.10–11

2. 看上去: looks as if

★ subject + 看上去 + stative verb

你爸爸看上去(非常) 严厉。

Expand these sentences following the grammatical structure above.

a. 他瘦了。

b. 米娜的新衣太漂亮了。

c. 朋友做的饭菜好吃极了。

Grammar focus 1.5   pp.10–11

3. 给: for (preposition to indicate an action as being done for someone)

★ subject + 给 + recipient + verb + object

爸爸给我买了一本新书。

Following the grammatical structure above, translate these sentences into Chinese.

a. Grandfather cooked dinner for us.

b. She sang a song for me.

c. He bought two goldfish for his son.

Grammar focus 1.6   p.13

1. 了: often used directly after a verb to indicate that an action has been completed or has already happened.

★ subject + verb + 了 + action

周末小文和爸爸妈妈一起去了海边。

今天她画了一幅中国山水画。

Complete these sentences by choosing the correct verbs and using them in the context of the above grammatical structure.

滑	去	看	收

a. 生日那天 / 他 / 很多礼物。

b. 他们 / 今年秋天 / 中国的北京。

c. 去年冬天 / 我和同学们 / 在日本 / 雪。

d. 上个周末 / 我和好朋友 / 一起 / 电影。

Grammar focus 1.6　　p.13

2. 最: most

★ subject + 最 + stative verb

在他们班上他最聪明。

上海的冬天冷，北京的冬天更冷，哈尔冰的冬天最冷。

★ subject + 最 + verb + action

我最讨厌唱歌，因为我唱得很难听。

我喜欢跑步，更喜欢打羽毛球，最喜欢爬山。

Answer these questions following the grammatical structure above.

a. 周末你最喜欢做什么事情？

b. 你觉得哪一种运动最好玩？

c. 在你们家谁长得最高？

Grammar focus 1.6　　p.13

3. 不: not (to express a negative action or statement)

★ subject + 不 + verb

我不打网球。

她不会说中文。

★ subject + 不 + stative verb

那个地方不远。

他不高。

Following the grammatical structure above, reorder the words to make proper sentences. Translate these sentences into English.

a. 不去 / 这个周末 / 爸爸 / 郊外 / 了 / 拍照 / 。

b. 有很多 / 所以 / 作业 / 他 / 不看电视 / 今天 / 了 / 。

c. 唱得不好听 / 因为 / 所以 / 她 / 不唱歌了 / 。

Grammar focus 1.7　　p.14

完: to complete or finish

★ activity A + 完 (以后)，subject + activity B

骑完自行车以后，他们去了一家咖啡馆喝茶聊天。

吃完饭以后，他们就走路回家了。

Identify the grammatical error in each sentence, then write the sentence out correctly.

a. 她看了一会儿电视，做完作业以后。

b. 他想画完画以后去钓鱼河边。

c. 去音乐厅看了一场音乐会，米娜逛完街以后。

Grammar focus 1.8　　pp.16–17

1. 要: be going to; be planning to

★ subject + 要 + verb

这个周末我们要去森林公园骑自行车。

今年冬天心美要去日本滑雪。

Write out these sentences in Chinese following the grammatical structure above.

a. We are going to Hong Kong to visit my grandparents next summer.

b. She is going to watch a concert this weekend with her family.

Grammar focus 1.8 pp.16–17

2. Verb–object compounds

★ verb + noun

划船 (rowing) = 划 (to row) + 船 (boat)

滑冰 (ice staking) = 滑 (to slide, to skid) + 冰 (ice)

周末哥哥喜欢和朋友一起去划船。

小时候她没学过滑冰，现在她也不会滑冰。

Some of these sentences contain incorrect verb–object compounds. Find them, then write these word compounds out correctly.

a. 他们在山上听美丽的风景。

b. 放学以后我和同学一起打了网球。

c. 爷爷经常周末去河边跳鱼。

d. 他的爱好是打足球。

e. 他们一边吃东西，一边聊天，聊得很开心。

Grammar focus 1.8 pp.16–17

3. 吧: used to indicate a sentence as a suggestion, in a similar context as 'Let's...'

★ command + 吧

晚饭后我们去散步吧！

有空我们一起去山上看美丽的星空吧！

Following the grammatical structure above, write a suitable suggestion for each of these scenarios in Chinese.

a. After going shopping, you would like to watch a film.

b. After school, you would like to play basketball.

Grammar focus 1.9 p.19

了: used with 快／快要／要 to indicate something is about to happen

★ Subject + 快/快要/要 + action / description +了。

爷爷的生日快到了。

音乐会快要开始了。

天很冷，看上去要下雪了。

Complete these sentences by first choosing the correct verbs or stative verbs, then rewrite them following the context of the grammatical structure above.

迟到　　黑　　回国

a. A: 现在几点了？

B: 现在八点十五分。我们要快点走。我们_____！

b. A: 圣诞节快到了，儿子_____。

B: 我们一起去机场接他吧。

c. A: 天_____。我们回家好吗？

B: 好的，我们走吧。

Unit 2

Grammar focus 2.2 p.25

1. 也: also

★ subject + verb phrase A, 也 + verb phrase B

她喜欢美术课，也喜欢外语课。

★ subject A + verb, subject B + 也 + verb

玛莉觉得物理很难。小文也觉得物理非常难。

Following the grammatical structures above, reorder the words to make proper sentences.

a. 喜欢 / 也喜欢 / 读德语 / 读中文 / , / 我 / 。

b. 觉得 / 有趣 / 有意思 / 觉得 / 她 / 。 / 生物课 / 她的好朋友 / 也 / 生物 / 很 / 。

c. 化学 / 昨天 / 考了 / , / 也 / 考了 / 数学 / 他 / 。

Grammar focus 2.2   p.25

2. 很: very (used before stative verbs or psychological verbs)

★ subject + 很 + stative verb

(我觉得)化学很容易。

学校里的学生很多。

★ subject + 很 + psychological verb

我很想念我的家人。

他很不喜欢上政治课。

Following the grammatical structures above, reorder these words to make proper sentences.

a. 觉得／作业／德语／我／难／很／。

b. 很／新／漂亮／校园／我觉得／。

c. 她／去／上大学／美国／很想／。

Grammar focus 2.3   p.27

1. ……先……，然后……: … first, then ….

★ subject + 先 + verb phrase A, 然后 + verb phrase B

我们先去踢足球，然后去看书。

Following the grammatical structure above, translate these sentences into Chinese.

a. We visited the assembly hall first, then saw the classrooms.

b. After school, he often does his homework first, then he goes out to play.

c. During our PE lesson, we ran first for 10 minutes, then we played football for 20 minutes.

Grammar focus 2.3   p.27

2. 因为: because

★ situation B, + 因为 + situation A

她不喜欢中文课，因为她觉得写汉字太难了！

Following the grammatical structure above, complete these sentences using words of your own.

a. 我喜欢＿＿＿＿，因为＿＿＿＿。

b. 我不喜欢＿＿＿＿，因为＿＿＿＿。

Grammar focus 2.4   p.29

1. 比……更: even … than

★ subject A + 比 + subject B + (更) + stative verb

(心美的语言天分高。)日晴的语言天分比心美的(更)高。

2. 最: the most

★ subject + particle + object + 最 + stative verb

哥哥学校的设施最好。

★ subject + verb + 最 + stative verb

(我喜欢读中文，) 我觉得学中文最有趣。

Read the following scenarios. Write a new sentence by comparing the subjects mentioned in each scenario, following the grammatical structures above.

Example:

Scenario: 他们班有30个学生。我们班有34个学生。

Sentence: 他们班有很多学生，但是我们班的学生比他们班的学生更多。

a. 米娜英语说得很流利。小文英语说得还可以。

b. 我们学校的设施很多，有图书馆、音乐厅，还有游泳池。但是他们学校没有音乐厅，也没有游泳池。

c. 苏菲中文考试考了99分，米娜中文考试考了88分，本杰明中文考试只考了60分。

Grammar focus 2.5   p.30

1. 之前 : before

★ time + 之前 + action

放学之前的一节课是英文课。

2. 之后: after

★ time + 之后 + action

英文课之后是午休。

Study Sammy's timetable on page 30, then complete the sentences using 之前 or 之后.

a. 美术课＿＿＿＿是中文课 。

b. 午休＿＿＿＿是历史课。

c. 英文课＿＿＿＿是经济课。

Grammar focus 2.6   p.33

1. ……在哪儿？ : Where is…?
- ★ place + 在哪儿？
  你的卧室在哪儿？

2. …… 在…… : … is located at …
- ★ place + 在 + adverb
  我的卧室在书房右边。

Following the grammatical structures above, translate these sentences into Chinese.

a. My bedroom is upstairs.
b. Our living room and study are downstairs.
c. There is a small garden in front of the house.
d. There is a very big garden behind the house.
e. The garage is next to the house.

Grammar focus 2.7   p.35

1. 的: to indicate possession
- ★ subject + 的 + object
  我的电脑(在书桌上边。)

2. 有: to have
- ★ subject + 有 + object
  陈明有好多书。

3. 没有: to not have
- ★ subject + 没有 + object
  志军的房间没有镜子。

Following the grammatical structures above, translate these sentences into Chinese.

a. This house doesn't have a garage.
b. My bedroom is next to the bathroom.
c. The house that has five bedrooms is really big.
d. Because there is no air conditioning, my room gets very hot in the summer.

Grammar focus 2.8   p.37

1. 多少: how many
- ★ subject + verb + 多少 + noun?
  你有多少本练习本？

2. 什么时候: when
- ★ subject + 什么时候 + verb + action?
  你什么时候下课？

Complete these questions by filling in the missing words.

什么时候　　多少

a. 暑假以后你们_____开学？
b. 开学你们收到_____本新的课本？
c. 你们家有_____台电脑？
d. 今天你_____上中文课？
e. 文具盒里有_____支黑色的笔？

Grammar focus 2.9   p.39

1. 给: to / for
- ★ person A + 给 + person B + action
  妈妈给我们做饭。

Following the grammatical structure above, make full sentences using the actions in brackets.

a. 他 → 他弟弟 （写信）
b. 姐姐 → 我 （发电邮）
c. 心美 → 陈明 （复习功课）

Grammar focus 2.9   p.39

2. 的时候: when
- ★ person A + time + 的时候 + action
  爸爸吃饭的时候看电视。

Following the grammatical structure above, reorder the words to make proper sentences.

a. 五岁 / 开始学中文 / 的时候 / 陈明 / 。
b. 的时候 / 学上网 / 十岁 / 志军 / 开始 / 。

Unit 3

Grammar focus 3.2   p.45

1. 经常/常常: often
   - ★ subject + 经常/常常 + action (verb)

   我经常去那家面馆吃面。

   妈妈常常去那个市场买菜。

Following the grammatical structure above, translate these sentences into Chinese.

a. We often have rice, vegetables, and some meat for supper.

b. At the weekends, I often go window-shopping with my friends.

c. They often watch a film on Saturday night.

Grammar focus 3.2   p.45

2. 通常: usually
   - ★ subject + 通常 + action

   他们家通常都吃中餐。

Following the grammatical structure above, reorder the words to make proper sentences.

a. 爸爸 / 她们家 / 做饭 / 是 / 通常 / 。

b. 家 / 西餐 / 杰明 / 吃 / 通常 / 。

c. 星期五 / 做 / 晚上 / 通常 / 中餐 / 妈妈 / 。

d. 通常 / 尝试 / 在家里 / 下雨天 / 他 / 会 / 做蛋糕 / 。

Grammar focus 3.3   pp.46–47

1. 量词: measure words

   一碗白饭，一瓶汽水，一勺盐，一杯水，一双筷子，一壶热水

Choose the correct measure words to complete the sentences below.

a. 请给我来一_____青菜面。

b. 天太热了！他喝了两_____冰红茶。

c. 您好。我要一_____黑咖啡，不加奶，但要_____糖。谢谢。

d. 在广州喝早茶时，人们都会要一_____茶。

e. 海伦送给她的英国朋友一_____好看的筷子。

f. 爸爸从法国回来时买了两_____有名的红酒。

Grammar focus 3.3   pp.46–47

2. 您和你: you
   - ★ 您: a polite and respectful form of address, reserved for the elders, teachers, strangers

   王老师，您好。
   - ★ 你: a form of address for people your age (or younger) and friends

   米娜，你会不会去小文的生日聚会？

Choose either 您 or 你 to complete the question in each scenario.

a. 你在咖啡店工作。你每天对客人说："_____要什么？"

b. 你是老师。你和你的学生说："_____的作业在哪儿？"

c. 你和你妈妈的朋友第一次见面。你和阿姨说："阿姨，_____想吃什么菜？"

d. 你问你的同学："_____喜欢吃意大利面吗？"

Grammar focus 3.5   p.51

地 : particle word used directly after a stative verb to turn it into an adverb, which then appears before a verb to describe an action
   - ★ stative verb + 地 + verb (action)

   一口一口地吃，一步一步地走

Rewrite the sentences following the grammatical structure above.

Example:

Original sentence: 她吃饭的时候很开心。

New sentence: 她很开心地吃饭。

a. 儿子走路走得很慢。

b. 他学做饭的时候很认真。

c. 她说中文说得很流利。

Grammar focus 3.6   p.53

得: particle word used directly after a verb or stative verb but before an adverb to add descriptive information to the action, or to indicate the extent of an action
   - ★ subject + verb/stative verb + 得 + adverb

   汤姆的病好得很快。

的, 得, 地 are pronounced the same, but they are used differently in sentences. Look at these sentences. Choose the correct character to complete each one.

a. 中文老师经常说：你们要好好_____学外语，认真_____做外语作业。

b. 兔子可以跑_____很快。

c. 公园里有很多高高_____树，美丽_____花。

d. 海伦生病时，妈妈每天给她做鸡汤喝，让她好好休息，这样就好_____快一点。

e. 因为弟弟吃太多甜的东西，所以他_____牙齿不太好。

f. 喝汤的时候，一定要轻轻_____喝，千万不要发出很大的声音，因为那样很没有礼貌。

Grammar focus 3.7   p.54

应该: should

★ subject +应该 + action

为了健康我们应该有均衡的饮食。
如果你去西安玩，你应该尝一尝西安有名的小吃。

Use the grammatical structure above to complete the following sentences.

a. 你的朋友吃很多甜食。他常常牙疼。你对他说：_____。

b. 陈丽要去巴西玩。巴西有各种各样的热带水果。你对陈丽说：_____。

c. 小明生病了，但是他还想玩游戏。爸爸和妈妈对他说：_____。

Grammar focus 3.8   p.56

为了: for the purpose of, in order to

★ 为了+ purpose, subject + action

为了有健康的身体，我打算新学期多去健身房。

Rewrite the sentences following the grammatical structure above.

Example:

Original sentence: 她早早地就来到市场里逛。她买最新鲜的鱼。

New sentence: 为了买到最新鲜的鱼，她早早地就来到市场里逛。

a. 我们除了应该有好的饮食，还应该经常运动。我们有健康的身体。

b. 跑步比赛前杰西卡会听一会儿音乐。她让自己放松，不紧张。

c. 他学习很认真。他考试考得好。

Unit 4

Grammar focus 4.2   p.64

······月······日/号 : month / day

★ number +月+ number +日/号

我们将在11月20号一起吃晚饭。

Answer these questions.

a. 今天是几月几日？

b. 你什么时候过生日？

c. 暑假什么时候开始？

Grammar focus 4.3   p.67

1. 把 : word used to focus on the result or influence of an action

★ person + 把 + object + verb + particle

我把行李准备好了。

Reorder the words to make proper sentences according to the grammatical structure above.

a. 爸爸 / 修理好 / 了 / 车子 / 把 / 。

b. 把 / 老师 / 了 / 这一课 / 教完 / 。

c. 打扫干净 / 房间 / 了 / 把 / 我 / 。

Grammar focus 4.3   p.67

2. 们 : to indicate a plural noun

★ noun/pronoun + 们

约翰假期里跟家人们一起去了中国旅游。

Choose the correct term from the options to complete each sentence.

a. [长辈／长辈们]

春节期间_____会给小孩子们红包。

b. [男孩／男孩们]

那个十一、二岁的＿＿＿＿＿自己一个人坐飞机去英国呢。

c. [同学／同学们]

假期里我和班上的五个＿＿＿＿＿一起参加了汉语夏令营。

Grammar focus 4.4　p.69

1. 例如: such as / for example; used to introduce a list

★ sentence + 例如 + noun 1 + noun 2 + 和 + noun 3

我喜欢吃水果，例如苹果、香蕉和梨。

动物园里有很多动物，例如老虎、大象和马。

Use these words to make proper sentences according to the grammatical structure above.

a. 喜欢吃的春节的食物: 饺子／汤圆／年糕

b. 中国的节日: 春节／中秋节／端午节

c. 经常做运动: 骑自行车／游泳／打网球

Grammar focus 4.4　p.69

2. 呢/吗: modal particles used at the end of questions

★ 呢 has a very similar meaning to 'What do you think?'

我穿什么衣服去参加聚会呢？

★ 吗 has a very similar meaning to 'Will you...?'

你可以把这本书借给我吗？

Choose the correct modal particles to complete the sentences below.

吗　　呢

a. 我去过中国，你知道 ＿＿?

b. 我的玩具 ＿＿?

c. 你带钱包了 ＿＿?

d. 你今晚会打电话给我 ＿＿?

Grammar focus 4.5　p.71

1. 和: and

★ subject 1 + 和 + subject 2

铅笔和橡皮

2. 一起: together

★ plural subject + 一起 + action

陈明和心美一起上中文课。

Choose the correct words to complete the sentences below.

和　　　一起

a. 我的房间有桌子 ＿＿ 椅子。

b. 陈明 ＿＿ 妈妈 ＿＿ 去看电影。

c. 我的笔 ＿＿ 练习本在哪儿？

d. 你 ＿＿ 我放学后 ＿＿ 去图书馆吧!

Grammar focus 4.6　p.73

1. 不用: no need

★ 不用 + verb + noun

汤姆去英国旅行不用办签证。

Answer these questions using the grammatical structure above.

a. 你明天要上学吗？

b. 你要借我的手机发电子邮件吗？

Grammar focus 4.6　p.73

2. 有没有: to have or not

★ subject + 有没有 + object?

你有没有铅笔？ 我要写字。

Following the grammatical structure above, work out what each question should be based on the response.

a. 问:＿＿＿＿?

答: 我没有地图。

b. 问: ＿＿＿＿?

答: 我有行程表。

c. 问: ＿＿＿＿?

答: 我有从北京到台湾的机票。

Grammar focus 4.7   p.75

1. 虽然……但是……: although ... but / yet ...
   ★ 虽然 + subject + 但是 + contrary reaction
   陈明虽然想去游学团，但是他没有报名。

Following the grammatical structure above, turn the short phrases into full sentences.

a. 努力温习 / 考试不及格
b. 中国人 / 英文说得很好

Grammar focus 4.7   p.75

2. 不多/不少: not much/not less
   ★ subject + verb + particle + (object) + 不多 / 不少
   会说中文的美国人不多。
   不少人到台湾读书。

Use 不多 and 不少 to write four sentences about what you have at home.

Grammar focus 4.8   p.77

1. 不但……而且/还……: not only… but also…
   ★ subject + 不但 + description A, 而且/还/也 + description B
   他不但喜欢吃中国菜，而且还会做中国菜。

Following the grammatical structure above, turn the short phrases into full sentences.

a. 唱中文歌 / 跳中国舞
b. 说中文 / 写毛笔字

Grammar focus 4.8   p.77

2. 都: also, both, all
   ★ subject A + subject B + 都 + action
   约翰和米娜都去过上海。
   他们三个人都住过北京饭店。

Translate these sentences into Chinese. Remember to apply the word 都 to the sentences correctly.

a. We all want to book a hotel that has a swimming pool.
b. My friend and I both want to visit the Great Wall of China.
c. While staying in that hotel, they all went to the gym.

Grammar focus 4.9   p.79

1. 大概/可能/好像: approximately / probably / likely
   ★ 大概 / 可能 / 好像 + situation
   心美大概八点回到学校。
   汤姆考试可能不及格。
   天好像快要下雨了。

Following the grammatical structure above, first choose the correct approximation term, then use the words in brackets to write a full response to each question.

大概   可能   好像

a. 妈妈在哪儿？（好像 / 书房）
b. 你知道陈明有多高吗？（大概 / 一米七）
c. 心美喜欢台湾吗？（可能 / 喜欢吧）
d. 明天会下雨吗？（好像 / 下雨）

Grammar focus 4.9   p.79

2. 因为……所以……: because ... so ...
   ★ 因为 + complete sentence (cause),
   所以 + complete sentence (consequence)
   因为下大雨，所以我们没有去打篮球。

Following the grammatical structure above, turn the short phrases into full sentences.

a. 小华 / 丢了钱包 / 很不高兴
b. 春节 / 孩子们 / 穿红色的衣服

Unit 5

Grammar focus 5.1   p.83

的: a particle word that can be used as a possessive indicator

★ pro (noun) A + 的 + noun B

他的家

It can be omitted when a pronoun is followed by a noun that describes a relationship, or when a pronoun is followed by a place noun to which the person is closely associated.

我爸爸，她妈妈，你朋友，我们老师
我们家，他们学校，你们班

Identify whether or not 的 has been added or omitted correctly in these sentences.

Example: 我喜欢他的家，因为他家的花园很大。 (T)

a. 这是我姐姐的公寓。
b. 这是我的朋友电脑。
c. 他们家在北京的郊区。
d. 城市的中心有好几家很不错的美术馆。

Grammar focus 5.2   p.85

动词的重叠: two-syllable, duplicated verbs

★ verb + verb + noun

Choose the correct phrase to complete each sentence.

吃吃　　走走　　逛逛　　喝喝
聊聊　　尝尝　　来来往往

a. 在釜山旅游时，你可以去那里的传统市场 _____。
b. 去广州玩儿，你一定得 _____ 那里有名的广式早茶。
c. 吃完晚饭，我们去公园里 _____ 吧。
d. 清早七八点钟进城的公路上汽车 _____，特别忙。
e. 周末我最喜欢做的事情就是和朋友 _____ 饭，_____ 咖啡和 _____ 天。

Grammar focus 5.3   p.87

第: used before a number to form an ordinal number, which shows a sequence

★ 第 + number

图书馆是这座城市第二大旅游点。

Following the grammatical structure above, reorder these words to make full sentences.

a. 第二大 / 这座城市 / 是 / 旅游城市 / 英国 / 受欢迎的 / 。
b. 第二长的 / 黄河 / 河 / 是 / 中国 / 。
c. 是 / 高楼 / 第一 / 这座建筑 / 伦敦的 / 。

Grammar focus 5.4   p.88

得 : to have to

★ subject + 得 + action

我每天得等半个小时的公共汽车去上学。

Following the grammatical structure above, reorder these words to make full sentences.

a. 得 / 到 / 开车 / 最近的超市 / 二十分钟 / 。
b. 父亲和母亲 / 我 / 看看 / 回家 / 得 / 我的 / 今年春节 / 了 / 。
c. 她 / 女儿 / 我们 / 看看 / 病了 / 得 / 带 / 去医院 / 。

Grammar focus 5.5   p.90

的: added between a modifier and a noun

★ modifier (stative verb) + 的 + noun

蓝蓝的天，人山人海的大街

Following the grammatical structure above, translate the following phrases into Chinese.

a. a beautiful place
b. a quiet library
c. an ancient small town
d. a modern building
e. a lively street

Grammar focus 5.7   p.95

1. Money expressions in Chinese

★ number + measure word + currency

五百块人民币, 三千镑英镑, 九十九美元

Read the sentences first, then answer the questions.

a. 在法国买一瓶葡萄酒大约需要十欧元。三瓶葡萄酒是多少欧元?

b. 在英国买两份鱼和薯条大约需要十六英镑。一份鱼和薯条是多少英镑?

c. 在中国四个人吃一顿普通中餐大约需要四百块人民币。两个人吃中餐要多少人民币?

d. 在美国买三双运动鞋可能只需要两百美元。买六双运动鞋要多少美元?

Grammar focus 5.7   p.95

2. 两 and 二

★ Both mean "two" and are used in number expressions.

二十, 二百, 两瓶水, 两个小时

See 7.3 for further examples and practice activities.

Grammar focus 5.8   p.97

就 : just/only/right (for emphasis)

★ noun + 就 + verb phrase

图书馆就在火车站对面。
美术馆就在城市广场的那边。

Identify the grammatical error in each sentence, then write it out correctly.

a. 妈妈刚刚就做完晚饭, 爸爸到家了。

b. 那个小区在就城市的中心, 很方便。

c. 她刚从中国回来, 又要就去英国了。

Grammar focus 5.9   p.99

希望: to wish/to hope (to indicate future desires)

★ subject + 希望 + action

他希望有机会到中国旅游。

Translate these sentences into Chinese following the grammatical structure above.

a. She hopes to go to Singapore to study in future.

b. When I was little, I hoped to be a basketball player.

c. He hopes to go to live in Shanghai one day.

d. I wish to be happy every day.

Unit 6

Grammar focus 6.2   p.105

1. Using 昨天／今天／明天 in a sentence

昨天我去了图书馆。
今天下午我会去踢足球。
明天我不需要去学唱歌。

Following the grammatical structure above, translate these sentences into Chinese.

a. Yesterday he went swimming.

b. Today I have to study.

c. Today the weather is very good. We are going hiking.

d. Tomorrow is Sunday. I will visit my grandmother.

e. Tomorrow I am having dinner with my dad.

Grammar focus 6.2   p.105

2. 在 + location: in/at a location

★ subject + 在 + location + action

他在加拿大看雪。

Following the grammatical structure above, answer these questions by turning the words in brackets into full sentences.

a. 阿里在家中做什么?　　　　　(玩电脑游戏)

b. 心美在百货商店做什么?　　　(买东西)

c. 小明放学后在球场上做什么?　(踢足球)

Grammar focus 6.3　　p.107

1. 根据 : according to
   ★ 根据 + noun, + complete sentence
   根据地图，运动中心就在附近。

Following the grammatical structure above, expand these phrases into full sentences.

a. 根据 / 下雨 / 下星期 / 天气预报
b. 完成功课 / 老师的要求 / 志军 / 根据
c. 食物 / 这家餐厅 / 根据 / 姐姐的建议 / 味道最好

Grammar focus 6.3　　p.107

2. 星期（一至六）；周末（星期六、星期日）: days of the week
   今天是星期一，我放学后要踢足球。
   星期日是假期，我不用上学。

Following the grammatical structure above, write a sentence about one thing you do each day of the week.

Grammar focus 6.4　　p.108

1. Measure words for items of clothing
   一条裙子，一件大衣，一双运动鞋

Match the items of clothing with the correct measure words.

一件，	一条，	一双

a. ＿＿＿ 衣服
b. ＿＿＿ 围巾
c. ＿＿＿ 雨衣
d. ＿＿＿ 裤子
e. ＿＿＿ 袜子

Grammar focus 6.4　　p.108

2. 会: will
   ★ subject + 会 + action
   明晚会下雨。

Following the grammatical structure above, translate these sentences into Chinese.

a. It will be foggy tomorrow.
b. I will play tennis next Monday.
c. Mum and Dad will not be at home on Friday.

Grammar focus 6.5　　p.111

1. 从: from one place to another
   ★ 从 + location 1 + 到 + location 2
   从运动中心到图书馆要走十五分钟路。

Following the grammatical structure above and referring to the information below, write out the questions and answers in full.

a. 学校→机场?　　　（坐大巴车，三小时）
b. 学校→心美的家?　（走路，二十分钟）
c. 台湾→北京?　　　（坐飞机，三小时）

Grammar focus 6.5　　p.111

2. 往: to (for direction)
   ★ 往 + direction + verb
   往教学楼的方向一直走，你会看到食堂。

Following the grammatical structure above, reorder these words to make proper sentences.

a. 前边 / 走五分钟 / 你 / 就可以到 / 往 / 食堂 / 。
b. 博物馆方向 / 往 / 坐一站地铁 / 就到 / 百货商店 / 。
c. 南边 / 骑车 / 就到 / 半个小时 / 往 / 森林公园 / 。

Grammar focus 6.6   p.112

1. 怎么: how to
   ★ subject + 怎么 + verb?
   博物馆怎么走?

Complete the questions based on the responses given.

a. 问：_____?
   答：从这儿一直往前走就到学校了。
b. 问：_____?
   答：坐101号巴士，半小时就到机场了。

Grammar focus 6.6   p.112

2. 这儿/那儿: here, there
   ★ place noun + 在 + 这儿/那儿
   ★ 这儿/那儿 + verb + noun
   运动中心在这儿。美术馆在那儿。
   这儿是市区最大的书店。
   那儿有全亚洲最大的游乐园。

Translate these sentences into Chinese using the characters 这儿 and 那儿.

a. Here is the best hotel in the city.
b. According to the map, the zoo is right here.
c. The world's longest river is there.
d. The oldest building in Beijing is there.

Grammar focus 6.7   p.115

什么: what
   ★ subject + verb + 什么 + object
   美术馆里有什么东西?

Translate these sentences into Chinese.

a. Q: What animals are there in the zoo?
   A: In the zoo, there are pandas, tigers, and monkeys.
b. Q: What facilities are there in the sports centre?
   A: In the sports centre, there is a swimming pool, a gym, and a basketball court.

Grammar focus 6.8   p.117

将/将会/将要: be going to
   ★ subject + 将/将会/将要 + imminent event
   我将参加社区组织去山区种树的活动。
   很多人将会参加明天的音乐会。

Rearrange these words to make proper sentences.

a. 动物园一日游 / 同学们 / 参加 / 将要 / 明天 / 。
b. 将会 / 飞机 / 降落 / 在十五分钟以后 / 。
c. 汤姆的生日聚会 / 心美 / 和 / 将会 / 我 / 去 / 。

Grammar focus 6.9   p.119

1. Duplication of single-word stative verbs
   志军喜欢快快地步行。
   弟弟小时候长得胖胖的。

Choose the correct phrase to complete these sentences.

高高的	慢慢地	胖胖的	急急地

a. 在爱丁堡动物园里游客们可以看到_____ 大熊猫。
b. 这个城市里处处都是_____ 大楼。
c. 阿里早上_____出了门。
d. 爷爷老了，他总是_____ 步行。

Grammar focus 6.9   p.119

2. 只有: only
   ★ 只有 + subject + action
   (在教室里)只有老师可以使用手机。

Turn these phrases into full sentences using只有. Translate the sentences into English.

a. 在我们家 → 妈妈会开车
b. 在我们班里 → 我去过南美洲
c. 那么多朋友里面 → 杰克是素食者
d. 到法国旅游时 → 大卫要签证

Unit 7

Grammar focus 7.2   p.125

是……的: used to emphasise or confirm an action

★ subject + 是 + action + 的

他们是每星期六一起打网球的。

Following the grammatical structure above, write out full answers to these questions.

a. 你们什么时候认识的？

b. 你和谁一起去马来西亚？

c. 你们怎样去马来西亚？

d. 你来香港做什么？

Grammar focus 7.3   p.127

二 and 两

二: used for counting things, expressing sequence, and mathematical terms

我有二十二元。

我是第二个到达的人。

两: normally applied before a measure word to express there are two of something

我有两条鱼。

请给我两勺糖。

Use 两 or 二 to complete these sentences.

a. 这是他们第＿＿＿次去西安玩儿。

b. 天冷了。妈妈给我买了＿＿＿件毛衣。

c. 买旅游用品您得去＿＿＿楼。

d. 我们的飞机晚了。导游在机场等了＿＿＿个小时。

e. 他们十二月＿＿＿号飞往美国。

Grammar focus 7.5   p.131

最好: had better, it is used to make a suggestion.

★ subject + 最好 + action

你累了。你最好去睡一觉。

Read each scenario below and write a sentence of advice using the phrase 最好.

a. 你的朋友要去美国。你觉得美国航空公司的飞机最舒服。你会给他/她什么建议？

b. 天气寒冷。你又生病了。妈妈可能会说什么？

c. 你要去北京旅游。朋友觉得北京秋天天气最好。朋友可能会给你什么建议？

d. 朋友圣诞节去德国。德国的冬天特别冷。你想朋友多带几件暖和的衣服。你会说什么？

Grammar focus 7.6   p.133

着: often used after a verb to describe an action is in progress

★ verb + 着

我们现在在机场，正等着办票呢。

Reorder the words to make sentences.

a. 看着 / 远去 / 慢慢地 / 她 / 火车 / 。

b. 都 / 安静地 / 孩子们 / 听着 / 。

c. 一边 / 一边 / 吃着 / 聊着 / 他们 / 。

d. 最近 / 去澳大利亚 / 留学 / 准备 / 忙着 / 小美 / 。

Grammar focus 7.7   p.134

更喜欢 means liking something or to like doing something even more

★ subject + 喜欢 + action 1, 但是 + 更喜欢 + action 2 (+ reason)

我喜欢参观历史文化古迹，但是更喜欢看美丽的天然风景，因为我喜欢大自然。

Translate these sentences into English.

a. 我喜欢坐飞机去西班牙，但是更喜欢坐船去，因为我可以在船里四处走动。

b. 我喜欢秋天的五颜六色，但是更喜欢冬天的冰天雪地，因为我喜欢滑雪。

c. 我喜欢古老的城镇，但是更喜欢美丽安静的乡村，因为我喜欢人少的地方。

Grammar focus 7.8　　p.137

忙不忙: busy or not busy

★ stative verb + 不 + stative verb?

你今晚累不累?
骑自行车安不安全?

Choose the most suitable phrase from the list to complete each sentence.

方不方便　　快不快　　多不多
舒不舒服　　满不满意

a. 你哥哥跑步_____?　我跑得很慢!
b. 你这星期功课_____?　我的功课不少。
c. 你对这次考试成绩_____?
d. 你上次住的酒店_____?　能告诉我它的名字吗?
e. 伦敦的公共交通_____?

Grammar focus 7.9　　p.138

被: translated as 'by', it is used to describe how a particular object is dealt with by somebody or something

★ object + 被 + subject + verb action
最后一条围巾被人买了。

Following the grammatical structure above, rewrite these sentences in the passive voice.

a. 妈妈拿走了我的书。
b. 机场工作人员找到了小美的护照。
c. 她吃完了巧克力。

Unit 8

Grammar focus 8.2　　p.145

1. 试一试: give it a try

★ subject + (verb) + verb + 一 + verb.
我想看一看世界有名的兵马俑。

Choose the correct phrase from the list below to complete each sentence.

尝一尝　　听一听　　用一用　　聊一聊

a. 我没有听过首歌,我想_____。
b. 我想_____北京烤鸭。
c. 让我们_____下周去做义工的事吧。
d. 我们可以_____这儿的电脑吗?

Grammar focus 8.2　　p.145

2. 学……学了: have learned ... for

★ subject + verb + object + verb + 了 + duration.
我唱民歌唱了两年。

Following the grammatical structure above, make full sentences using the information below.

a. 做义工 (三年)
b. 上网 (一个上午)
c. 听音乐 (一小时)

Grammar focus 8.3　　p.147

1. 坐…… 去: take (a vehicle) ... to

★ subject + 坐 + object + 去 + location
我坐飞机去泰国。

Answer these questions following the grammatical structure above and using the clues in brackets.

a. 你怎么去日本?　　　　　　　　(飞机)
b. 你怎么去学校?　　　　　　　　(走路)
c. 你怎么去植物园?　　　　　　　(骑自行车)
d. 你怎么去马来西亚?　　　　　　(船)

Grammar focus 8.3　　p.147

2. 住在: live in (verb followed by post verb)

★ subject + 住 + 在 + place
在北京那几天我住在酒店里。

Reorder these words to form proper sentences.

a. 大学宿舍 / 心美 / 在 / 住 / 。

b. 上海的 / 在 / 住 / 我 / 市区 / 。

c. 小华 / 一起 / 和父母 / 广州的 / 住在 / 郊区 / 。

Grammar focus 8.4   p.149

几 : how

★ subject + verb + 几 + measure word + noun + (action)

你们有几个人(参加明天晚上的聚会)?

Following the grammatical structure above, write out the questions according to the responses.

a. 问: _____?
答: 我学中文学了三年了。

b. 问: _____?
答: 我家有五个人。

c. 问: _____?
答: 我参加过四次。

Grammar focus 8.5   p.151

1. 不……吗? : Don't you...?

★ subject + 不 + verb phrase + 吗?

毕业后你不想在大城市工作吗?

暑假里你不做义工吗?

Reorder the words to make proper sentences.

a. 你 / 不 / 做义工 / 打算 / 在暑假里 / 吗 /?

b. 你 / 吗 / 想 / 不 / 读医科 /?

c. 你 / 喜欢 / 外出 / 不 / 吗 / 吃饭 /?

Grammar focus 8.5   p.151

2. 为什么…? : Why?

★ subject + 为什么 + predicate?

有的中学生为什么在假期做义工?

安迪为什么申请去那所大学?

Write down the questions according to the responses.

a. 问: _____?
答: 因为我觉得中文特别有意思，还非常有用。

b. 问: _____?
答: 因为中学生做兼职工作可以赚零花钱。

c. 问: _____?
答: 因为那所大学有最好的中文专业。

Grammar focus 8.6   p.153

1. 如果……就……: if... then...

★ 如果 + statement + (subject) 就 + result

如果现在学习不努力，你考试就很难考出好的成绩。

Following the grammatical structure above, make full sentences using the information below.

a. 今天天气好 → 我们踢足球

b. 有地图 → 你不会谜路

c. 下雨 → 不外出

d. 妈妈没有煮饭 → 我们去外面吃饭吧

Grammar focus 8.6   p.153

2. 只要……, 就……: as long as ...

★ 只要 + condition + (subject) 就 + result

只要努力学习，认真上课，就有可能考出好的成绩。

Following the grammatical structure above, make full sentences using the information below.

a. 努力读书 → 你得到好成绩

b. 认真准备 → 你顺利通过面试

c. 肯努力 → 我能成功

d. 经常练习 → 你的汉语会进步

Grammar focus 8.7   p.155

1. 要是…… 就……: If ... then...
- ★ 要是 + situation + (subject) 就 + result

    要是你不准备面试，就不能顺利进入大学。

Following the grammatical structure above, make full sentences using the information below.

a. 今天下雨 ➜ 带雨伞

b. 带了雨伞 ➜ 不会被淋湿

c. 在家不能上网 ➜ 做一些户外活动

Grammar focus 8.7   p.155

2. 或者: or
- ★ possibility A + 或者 + possibility B

    现在人们可以用电脑或手机上网。

Following the grammatical structure above, make full sentences using the phrases below.

a. 周末 / 哥哥 / 读书 / 画画

b. 我们家 / 晚饭 / 意大利菜 / 中国菜

c. 明年 / 我 / 会去 / 台湾 / 北京 / 旅行

Grammar focus 8.8   p.157

1. 第一、二、三: ordinal numbers in list-making
- ★ 第 + number

    我喜欢跑步有三个原因：第一，可以锻炼身体。第二，可以随时随地进行。第三，心情会好起来。

Following the grammatical structure above, write out the answers to these questions in full by listing the reasons in order.

a. 高铁有哪些好处?
1. 比飞机便宜
2. 很快
3. 座位很舒服

b. 打游戏有哪些坏处?
1. 影响学习
2. 对眼睛不好
3. 影响你和家人的关系

c. 你有哪些优点?
1. 聪明
2. 热爱生活
3. 心地善良

Grammar focus 8.8   p.157

2. 只: only
- ★ subject + 只 + auxiliary verb + complete sentence

    我只会说中文。

Reorder these words to form complete sentences.

a. 妹妹 / 我 / 三岁 / 只 / 有 / 。

b. 一个 / 只 / 有 / 我 / 弟弟 / 。

c. 跳舞 / 我 / 只 / 唱歌 / , / 会 / 不会 / 。

Grammar focus 8.9   p.159

1. 为了……而……: to do something for something's sake
- ★ subject + 为了 + effect + 而 + cause

    苏菲为了赚零花钱而去快餐店做兼职。

Decide whether or not the structure 为了……而 is used accurately in the sentences below, and write the incorrect sentences out correctly.

a. 我考第一名为了努力读书。

b. 妈妈为了照顾家人而不做全职工作了。

c. 他为了每天学40个汉字而提高汉语水平 。

d. 爸爸为了给家人好的生活而努力工作。

Grammar focus 8.9　　p.159

2. 一边……一边……: one thing is done while doing something else

★ subject + 一边 + action A + 一边 + action B

她喜欢一边跑步，一边听音乐。

Choose the most suitable phrase to complete each sentence.

驾驶　　做功课　　吃东西

a. 吃饭时不要一边_____，一边说话。

b. 老师告诉我们不要一边_____，一边看电视。

c. 交通警察告诉我们不要一边_____，一边看手机。

Unit 9

Grammar focus 9.3　　p.167

很，比较，十分: very, relatively, extremely

★ intensifier + adjectival verb or stative verb

很便宜，比较难，十分快乐

Choose the most suitable phrase to complete each sentence.

十分有礼貌　　十分流利　　很吸引人
比较无聊　　很快乐

a. 海南岛有蓝蓝的大海，美丽的海滩，是一个_____的旅游胜地。

b. 他觉得办公室的工作有时候会_____。

c. 大家都觉得新来的同事_____。

d. 能做自己喜欢的工作是一件_____的事情。

e. 实习生迪伦的汉语说得_____。

Grammar focus 9.4　　p.169

过: used after a verb to indicate completion of a task or process

★ subject + verb + 过 + task or process

她给中国学生上过英文课。

Choose the correct words to fill in the gaps to complete the passage below.

做过　　学过　　吃过　　爬过
参观过　　坐过　　来过

丽亚是一个英国大学生，是我的网友。她对中国文化感兴趣。她不仅_____汉语，还_____中国旅游。她_____万里长城，_____北京的故宫，还_____"全聚德"北京烤鸭。她还_____中国高铁。我的这个英国网友_____很多有意思的事情。

Grammar focus 9.6　　p.174

是: used for linking two noun phrases

★ noun phrase A + 是 + noun phrase B

父母是我们最亲的家人，在很多时候也是我们的老师和朋友。

Following the grammatical structure above, translate these sentences into Chinese.

a. Taking a gap year is a good experience for many young people.

b. Travelling during your gap year is a good way to learn about different cultures.

c. Volunteering in the community is a good way to gain work experience.

Grammar focus 9.7　　p.178

刚刚: just

★ subject + 刚刚 + action.

他刚刚结束在银行的实习。

Following the grammatical structure above, translate these sentences into Chinese.

a. She has just completed her work experience.

b. Dad has just arrived at the supermarket.

c. The aeroplane has just taken off.

Grammar focus 9.8   pp.179–180

1. 得: a structure particle that provides additional meaning to an associated verb phrase
   ★ verb + 得 + stative verb or verb phrase
   我做饭做得比妈妈好!

Following the grammatical structure above, make full sentences with these words.

a. 马可: 学汉语 ➞ 很快
b. 飞机: 飞 ➞ 越来越高
c. 心美: 说英语 ➞ 比我流利

Grammar focus 9.8   pp.179–180

2. 趟: a measure word for a trip, a journey, or an action
   ★ subject + verb phrase + number + 趟
   今年爸爸因为工作去中国去了三趟。

Following the grammatical structure above, reorder these phrases to make proper sentences.

a. 需要 / 这一趟 / 两个星期 / 中国之旅 / 。
b. 一趟 / 每十分钟 / 地铁 / 开出 / 。
c. 睡前 / 晚上 / 他 / 喝了 / 上了 / 很多水 / 所以 / 三趟 / 卫生间 / 。

Grammar focus 9.9   p.182

还是: or
   ★ subject + option A + 还是 + option B?
   你想继续读书还是出来找工作?

Following the grammatical structure above, write out the questions according to the responses.
Example: 问: 我们开车还是坐公共汽车去市区?
        答: 我们坐公共汽车去市区。

a. 问: _____?
   答: 我晚上想吃法国菜。

b. 问: _____?
   答: 我想读历史专业。

c. 问: _____?
   答: 我要买来回票。

Unit 10

Grammar focus 10.2   p.187

1. 差不多: almost the same
   ★ noun A + 和 + noun B + (situation) + 差不多
   暑假里去美国的机票和去英国的机票价格差不多。

Following the grammatical structure above, make full sentences using these words.

a. 陈明 + 志军 + 身高
b. 中国 + 印度 + 人口
c. 日本 + 英国 + 气候

Grammar focus 10.2   p.187

2. 比 …… 一点儿: by a little bit
   ★ noun A + 比 + noun B + stative verb + 一点儿。
   亚洲比非洲大一点儿。
   我觉得夏天西安比上海凉快一点儿。

Following the grammatical structure above, make full sentences using these words.

a. 他 / 我 / 高
b. 中文语法 / 写汉字 / 难
c. 去广州 / 坐飞机 / 坐高铁 / 去 / 快

Grammar focus 10.3   p.190

1. Omitting 的: the possessive 的 can be omitted when a pronoun is followed by another noun that describes a relationship
   我哥哥今晚要去上班。

Following the grammatical structure above, reorder these words to form sentences.

a. 房间 / 我 / 一张 / 书桌 / 有 / 。

b. 爸爸 / 医生 / 是 / 我 / 。

c. 姐姐 / 国庆节时 / 去了 / 她 / 新加坡 / 度假 / 。

Grammar focus 10.3 p.190

2. 别: don't

★ 别 + verb + 了 + follow-up phrase

别买了，你已经有很多衣服了!

Following the grammatical structure above, translate these sentences into Chinese.

a. Don't say anymore, I know what to do!
b. Don't rush – the train has already departed.
c. Don't eat now, we will have a big meal later.

Grammar focus 10.4 p.193

一些: some; a few

★ 一些 + noun

一些好玩的地方

Translate these sentences into Chinese. Remember to include 一些 in each one.

a. He bought some sweets as souvenirs for friends.
b. You had better bring some food and water with you when you go hiking.
c. I spent some of my pocket money when I went shopping last week.

Grammar focus 10.5 p.196

1. 左右: around, approximately

★ number + measure word + 左右

参加比赛的人数有五十个左右。

Following the grammatical structure above, make full sentences using the information below.

a. 到最近的地铁站往前走： 大约三百米
b. 这次到欧洲跟团旅游： 人数八十人
c. 明天去郊游： 大约十点出发

Grammar focus 10.5 p.196

2. 不 + stative verb

★ noun + 不 + stative verb

这个公园里的树木不太老。

Following the grammatical structure above, rewrite these sentences (while keeping their meanings) by replacing the underlined stative verbs with new ones of your own.

a. 美美说普通话说得<u>很好</u>。

b. 在商场里购物的人<u>非常多</u>。

c. 我觉得这次考试的问题<u>很容易</u>。

Grammar focus 10.6 p.198

1. 谁: who

★ subject + verb + 谁?

你想找谁?

Based on each response below, write out an appropriate question.

a. 问:……?
答:我要找老师。

b. 问:……?
答:他是我好朋友。

c. 问:……?
答: 我想邀请米娜参加生日聚会。

Grammar focus 10.6 p.198

2. 哎呀: an interjection expressing frustration

★ 哎呀 + statement

哎呀，我要迟到了!

Using the expression above, write down a sentence of your own in response to each of these scenarios.

a. 去机场的路上交通很拥挤，你的飞机一个小时后就要起飞了。你说……。

b. 你到了露营的营地，可是发现包里没有毛巾和牙膏，你说……。

c. 今天是你在澳大利亚旅游的最后一天。你需要买礼物，可是找不到你的钱包了。你说……。

Grammar focus 10.7   p.202

1. Using 不 and 没(有)

★ 不 negates present or future actions; used with verbs, stative verbs, and adjectives

他不喜欢坐公车，因为觉得比较拥挤。

★ 没 negates past actions; negates the verb 有; used for making comparisons

这个城市没有便利的交通。

Choose the correct term to complete each sentence.

不   没有

1. 跟团游_____用自己花时间计划行程。
2. 跟团游_____自由行自由、好玩。
3. 在国内旅游，你_____需要带护照。
4. 回国时我_____给家人买礼物。

Grammar focus 10.7   p.202

2. 到底: after all

★ 到底 + question phrase

网络到底给人们带来了哪些好处与坏处？

Reorder these words to make proper sentences.

a. 去逛街呢 / 我们 / 到底 / 去看电影 / 还是？
b. 怎么样 / 想 / 到底 / 你 / ？
c. 去上海 / 到底 / 还是 / 是 / 坐飞机 / 坐高铁 / 我们？

Grammar focus 10.8   p.204

米，吨： metre, ton (units of measurement)

★ number + measure word + stative verb

我有1.6米高。
这辆车有一吨重。

Decide whether or not 米／吨／层 are used correctly in each of these sentences, and rewrite the ones that are incorrect.

a. 这座教学楼有六层楼，总共有十八米高。
b. 这个建筑有差不多三百吨高。
c. 在今天的体育课上他跑了五千层。
d. 非洲大象是陆地上最大的动物，体重可以有五吨重。

Grammar focus 10.9   p.207

1. 到: arrive/to go to

★ subject + 到 + place

我到北京参观故宫、爬长城。

Following the grammatical structure above, reorder these words to form proper sentences.

a. 到 / 五点半 / 我 / 家。
b. 找 / 体育馆 / 李老师 / 请到 / 报名。
c. 要到 / 种树 / 今天 / 山上 / 我们 / 郊外的 / 。

Grammar focus 10.9   p.207

2. ……既……也: it is … but also …

★ subject + 既 + A + 也 + B

吃素对于我来说既是保持健康的方式，也是对环保做的一点努力。

Following the grammatical structure above, make full sentences using the information below.

a. 我们去过：日本 ＋ 美国
b. 小明爱看：中文书 ＋ 英文书
c. 中国的四川省：许许多多的历史古迹 ＋ 众多的奇特的自然风景

Unit 11

Grammar focus 11.3　p.217

又……又……: describes two features of one thing, often used with stative verbs and verbs.

★ 又 + description A + 又 + description B

他们的大学校园又安静又漂亮。

Match each item on the left to the most suitable description on the right.

a. 这个橙子　　　　　　　i. 又流利又准确

b. 这些花　　　　　　　　ii. 又高又帅

c. 今年中秋节的月亮　　　iii. 又甜又多汁

d. 这个年轻人长得　　　　iv. 又圆又亮

e. 她的汉语说得　　　　　v. 又香又漂亮

Grammar focus 11.6　p.225

知道 and 明白: 知道 can be used to describe when a person knows/acknowledges something; 明白 means to understand something

★ subject + 知道 /明白 + description / situation

我知道中国新年时人们都会包饺子和吃饺子，但我不明白为什么他们这样做。

Following the grammatical structure above, translate these sentences into English.

a. 我知道排灯节是印度最重要的传统节日之一。

b. 他明白了金钱不是人生中最重要的东西。

c. 心美知道下个月爸爸要去德国。

d. 在朋友的帮助下我明白怎么做这道数学题了。

Grammar focus 11.7　p.227

上 (up), 下 (down), 进 (in), 出 (out), 来 (to come), 去 (to go) are used after verbs to show the direction of an action.

★ verb + directional complement

拍下，卖出，送去

Choose the most appropriate directional word to complete each sentence.

上　　下　　进　　出　　来　　去

a. 你能写＿＿你的答案吗？

b. 这是女儿给我们带＿＿的礼物。

c. 火车向西边开＿＿。

d. 天很冷，你把毛衣穿＿＿吧。

Grammar focus 11.8　p.229

不要: don't; used to command someone not to do something

★ 不要 + action

乘坐火车时不要在车厢内吃东西。

Complete these sentences with the most appropriate phrases.

不要看手机　　不要大声说话
不要浪费食物

a. 在图书馆请……。

b. 学校餐厅墙上的海报上写着……。

c. 开车的时候请……。

Acknowledgements (continued from page ii)

p123: Chantal de Bruijne/Shutterstock; p124: Ababsolutum/Getty Images; p126(a): Graphi-Ogre; p126(b): Ocean; p126(c): Graphi-Ogre; p126(d): Graphi-Ogre; p126(e): Bodrumsurf/Shutterstock; p126(f): Paul Stringer/ Shutterstock; p126(g): Ricky Edwards/Shutterstock; p126(h): Graphi-Ogre; p127: ImageBroker/Alamy Stock Photo; p128(a): S.Borisov/Shutterstock; p128(b): Beboy/Shutterstock; p128(c): Photodisc; p128(d): Cris Haigh/Getty Images; p128(e): Hung Chung Chih/Shutterstock; p128(f): Matej Hudovernik/ Shutterstock; p129: ESB Professional/Shutterstock; p131: Frank Bach/ Shutterstock; p132(a): Aha-Soft/Shutterstock; p132(b): Aha-Soft/Shutterstock; p132(c): Aha-Soft/Shutterstock; p132(d): Aha-Soft/Shutterstock; p132(e): Aha-Soft/Shutterstock; p132(f): Aha-Soft/Shutterstock; p132(g): Vectorchef/ Shutterstock; p134(a): Igorstevanovic/Shutterstock; p134(b): Marco Govel/ Shutterstock; p134(c): Michaelpuche/Shutterstock; p134(d): Claudio Divizia/ Shutterstock; p134(e): Lornet/Shutterstock; p134(f): NAN728/Shutterstock; p137(T): Igor Plotnikov/Shutterstock; p137(B): TonyV3112/Shutterstock; p138(a): Planner/Shutterstock; p138(b): Quetton/Shutterstock; p138(c): Kocetoiliev/Shutterstock; p138(d): Quetton/Shutterstock; p138(e): Liubomir/ Shutterstock; p140(T): Photodisc; p140(C): Cris Haigh/Getty Images; p140(a): Lornet/Shutterstock; p140(b): Kitigan; p140(c): Igorstevanovic/Shutterstock; p140(d): Marco Govel/Shutterstock; p140(e): NAN728/Shutterstock; p141(T): S.Borisov/Shutterstock; p141(B): ESB Professional/Shutterstock; p142: Monkey Business Images/Shutterstock; p143: Sergey Novikov/Shutterstock; p144(L): SpeedKingz/Shutterstock; p144(CL): Janine Wiedel Photolibrary/Alamy Stock Photo; p144(CR): Monkey Business Images/Shutterstock; p144(R): Asia Images/Shutterstock; p147(a): Lukasz Stefanski/Shutterstock; p147(b): Graphi-Ogre; p147(c): Arteki/Shutterstock; p147(d): Ken Hawkins/Alamy Stock Photo; p147(e): Ivylingpy/Shutterstock; p147(f): Gang/Fotolia; p149(L): Billion Photos/Shutterstock; p149(C): SpeedKingz/Shutterstock; p149(R): Asia Images/Shutterstock; p150(b): 32 pixels/Shutterstock; p150(c): Ganibal/ Shutterstock; p150(d): VectorA/Shutterstock; p153: Bjdlzx/iStockphoto; p154: Arek_malang/Shutterstock; p155: Skynesher/Getty Images; p156: Lou Linwei/Rex Shutterstock; p157: Monkey Business Images/Shutterstock; p158(a): Victor/iStockphoto; p158(c): Appleuzr/iStockphoto; p158(d): Panda Vector/Shutterstock; p159: Monkey Business Images/Shutterstock; p160(a): SpeedKingz/Shutterstock; p160(b): Asia Images/Shutterstock; p160(c): Janine Wiedel Photolibrary/Alamy Stock Photo; p160(d): Monkey Business Images/ Shutterstock; p170: ESB Professional/Shutterstock; p171(TL): Kagai19927/ Shutterstock; p171(TR): Have a nice day Photo/Shutterstock; p171(CL): PeopleImages/Getty Images; p171(CR): ChrisVanLennepPhoto/Shutterstock; p171(B): Rawpixel.com/Shutterstock; p173: Drumcheg/Shutterstock; p175: EpicStockMedia/Shutterstock; p176: RelaxFoto.de/iStockphoto; p179: Monkey Business Images/Shutterstock; p181: Vadim Georgiev/Shutterstock; p183: Vadim Georgiev/Shutterstock; p185: Testing/Shutterstock; p187: Lisa Kolbasa/ Shutterstock; p190: STR/AFP/GettyImages; p192(T): Hemis/Alamy Stock Photo; p192(B): Maridav/Shutterstock; p193: Africa Studio/Shutterstock; p194(TL): Ke Wang/Shutterstock; p194(TC): Sunxuejun/Shutterstock; p194(TR): TonyV3112/Shutterstock; p194(BL): Jojo Pensica/Getty Images; p194(BC):

Wnights/iStockphoto ; p194(BR): Mikhail Nekrasov/Shutterstock; p195: Jojo Pensica/Getty Images; p196(a): Konstantin Faraktinov/Shutterstock; p196(b): BeeBright/Shutterstock; p196(c): Milos Luzanin/Shutterstock; p196(d): Nikolasm/Shutterstock; p196(e): Voronin76/Shutterstock; p196(f): Nils Z/ Shutterstock; p196(g): Alex Khripunov/Shutterstock; p196(h): Sumroeng Chinnapan/Shutterstock; p196(i): Chas Spradbery; p198: Jenn Huls/ Shutterstock; p199: Bikeriderlondon/Shutterstock; p201: ChameleonsEye/ Shutterstock; p202(a): Matej Hudovernik/Shutterstock; p202(b): WDG Photo; p202(c): Jan Tadeusz; p202(d): Richard Whitcombe/Shutterstock; p202(e): Images & Stories; p204: Daniel Fung/Shutterstock; p206: ESB Professional/ Shutterstock; p207(a): Ke Wang/Shutterstock; p207(b): Jan Tadeusz; p207(c): Mikhail Nekrasov/Shutterstock; p207(d): WDG Photo; p207(e): Matej Hudovernik/Shutterstock; p208: OUP; p211: Sihasakprachum/iStockphoto; p212: Neil Mitchell/Shutterstock; p213: Luciano Mortula/Shutterstock; p214: Matej Kastelic/Shutterstock; p215: In Pictures Ltd./Corbis/Getty Images; p216: Windmoon/Shutterstock; p217: Enmyo/Shutterstock; p218(L): Mark Ralston/ AFP/Getty Images; p218(CL): Margaret Tong/Shutterstock; p218(CR): Peiling Lee/Shutterstock; p218(R): Szefei/Shutterstock; p220(TL): ImageMore Co. Ltd/Getty Images; p220(TR): Lcc54613/iStockphoto; p220(BL): ImageMore Co. Ltd/Alamy Stock Photo; p220(BR): Kletr/Shutterstock; p221: Shi Yali/ Shutterstock; p222: ImageMore Co. Ltd/Getty Images; p224: Daniel Jedzura/ Shutterstock; p225(TL): Phive/Shutterstock; p225(TR): Lakov Filimonov/ Shutterstock; p225(B): Rodho/Shutterstock; p227: Phatymak's Studio/ Shutterstock; p229: Alex Mares-Manton/Getty Images; p230: Joesayhello/ Shutterstock; p231(TL): Rocketclips, Inc/Shutterstock; p231(TR): Kpatyhka/ Shutterstock; p231(BL): Gil C/Shutterstock; p231(BR): ESB Professional/ Shutterstock; p232: Gst/Shutterstock; p236(L): 54613/Shutterstock; p236(C): Robyn Mackenzie/Shutterstock; p236(R): Warongdech/Shutterstock; p237(L): Valery121283/Shutterstock; p237(C): Tavizta/Shutterstock; p237(R): Andrey Armyagov/Shutterstock; p244: Jacek Chabraszewski/Shutterstock; p245: MistikaS/Getty Images; p249: Monkey Business Images/Shutterstock; p251: Antonio Guillem/Shutterstock; p252(L): Monkey Business Images/ Shutterstock; p252(CL): Ingram; p252(CR): Aerostato/Shutterstock; p252(R): Marco Mayer/Shutterstock; p254(a): Mark Mason/OUP; p254(b): 5 second Studio/Shutterstock; p254(c): DenisMArt/Shutterstock; p254(d): Christopher Gardiner/Shutterstock; p254(e): Photodisc; p254(f): Tacar/Shutterstock; p254(g): Jazz3311/Shutterstock; p256: Monika Wisniewska/Shutterstock. Artwork by Toppan Leefung Best Set and OUP.

Although we have made every effort to trace and contact all copyright holders before publication this has not been possible in all cases. If notified, the publisher will rectify any errors or omissions at the earliest opportunity.

Links to third party websites are provided by Oxford in good faith and for information only. Oxford disclaims any responsibility for the materials contained in any third party website referenced in this work.

IGCSE® is the registered trademark of Cambridge International Examinations.